**Deep Learning Approaches for Security
Threats in IoT Environments**

Deep Learning Approaches for Security Threats in IoT Environments

Mohamed Abdel-Basset
Zagazig University
Egypt

Nour Moustafa
UNSW Canberra at the Australian Defence Force Academy
Australia

Hossam Hawash
Zagazig University
Egypt

IEEE PRESS

WILEY

Published by John Wiley & Sons, Inc., Hoboken, New Jersey.
Published simultaneously in Canada.

For general information on our other products and services or for technical support, please contact our Customer Care Department within the United States at (800) 762-2974, outside the United States at (317) 572-3993 or fax (317) 572-4002.

Wiley also publishes its books in a variety of electronic formats. Some content that appears in print may not be available in electronic formats. For more information about Wiley products, visit our web site at www.wiley.com.

Library of Congress Cataloging-in-Publication Data
Names: Abdel-Basset, Mohamed, 1985- author. | Moustafa, Nour, author. | Hawash, Hossam, author.
Title: Deep learning approaches for security threats in IoT environments / Mohamed Abdel-Basset, Zagazig University, Egypt, Nour Moustafa, UNSW Canberra at the Australian Defence Force Academy, Australia, Hossam Hawash, Zagazig University, Egypt.
Description: First edition. | Hoboken, New Jersey : John Wiley & Sons, Inc., [2023] | Includes bibliographical references and index.
Identifiers: LCCN 2022035671 (print) | LCCN 2022035672 (ebook) | ISBN 9781119884149 (hardback) | ISBN 9781119884156 (adobe pdf) | ISBN 9781119884163 (epub)
Subjects: LCSH: Internet of things–Security measures–Data processing. | Deep learning (Machine learning)
Classification: LCC TK5105.8857 .A255 2023 (print) | LCC TK5105.8857 (ebook) | DDC 004.67/8–dc23/eng/20220923
LC record available at https://lccn.loc.gov/2022035671
LC ebook record available at https://lccn.loc.gov/2022035672

Cover Design: Wiley
Cover Image: ©metamorworks/Shutterstock

Set in 9.5/12.5pt STIXTwoText by Straive, Pondicherry, India

Contents

About the Authors

Mohamed Abdel-Basset
He received the B.Sc. and M.Sc. degrees from the Faculty of Computers and Informatics, Zagazig University, Egypt, and the Ph.D. degree from the Faculty of Computers and Informatics, Menoufia University, Egypt. He is currently an Associate Professor with the Faculty of Computers and Informatics, Zagazig University. His current research interests include data mining, computational intelligence, applied statistics, deep learning, security intelligence, and IoT. He holds the program chair in many conferences in the fields of AI optimization, complexity, and editorial collaboration in some reputable journals. He is also an editor or a reviewer in different international journals and conferences.

Nour Moustafa

He is Postgraduate Discipline Coordinator (Cyber) and Senior Lecturer in Cybersecurity at the School of Engineering and Information Technology (SEIT), University of New South Wales (UNSW) Canberra, Australia. His areas of interest include Cyber Security including Network Security, intrusion detection systems, statistics, and machine learning techniques. He is interested in designing and developing threat detection and forensic mechanisms for identifying malicious activities from cloud/fog computing, IoT, and industrial control systems over cyber-physical systems. He is also an ACM Distinguished Speaker and IEEE Senior member. He has published more than 75 research outputs in top-tier computing and security journals and conferences.

Hossam Hawash

Hossam Hawash received the B.Sc. and M.Sc. degrees from the Department of Computer Science, Faculty of Computers and Informatics, Zagazig University, Egypt. He is currently an Assistant Lecturer with the Department of Computer Science, Zagazig University. His research interests include machine learning, deep learning, the Internet of Things (IoT), cyber security, fuzzy learning, and explainable artificial intelligence.

1

Introducing Deep Learning for IoT Security

1.1 Introduction

Internet of Things (IoT) applications and relevant technologies are presently proliferating in all sectors of daily life, including intelligent transportation, smart buildings, smart healthcare, smart manufacturing, smart farming, irrigations, etc. Many security concerns surround the massive amounts of data being sent and received by and from smart devices as they become more widely adopted. Since many IoT applications need safety and defense, authentication and classification systems, as well as sufficient technologies to ensure integrity and confidentiality, are becoming increasingly important. An additional danger posed by a criminal IoT device use is the potential impact on internet security and robustness across the board. Mirai, an IoT-targeted malware, has demonstrated the disruptive power of malevolent operations and the need to implement proper defenses.

1.2 Internet of Things (IoT) Architecture

The purpose of this part is to emphasize the attributes of typical IoT systems and to present the most significant security risks that such systems may be subjected to in their operation. The most

Deep Learning Approaches for Security Threats in IoT Environments,
First Edition. Mohamed Abdel-Basset, Nour Moustafa, and Hossam Hawash.
© 2023 The Institute of Electrical and Electronics Engineers, Inc.
Published 2023 by John Wiley & Sons, Inc.

significant breakthrough that the IoT has brought to our world is the conversion of standard physical things into digital things that interconnect with each other through the internet using a variety of networking protocols and communication technologies such as 5G and 6G communications [1].

While it may appear to be a straightforward concept, IoT systems involve a lot of dynamic components that should operate jointly to enable them to achieve their tasks appropriately and efficiently. It is crucial for all these various cogs in the machinery or system to run collectively when the IoT solution is functioning as required. In this regard, IoT architecture could be defined as a framework that characterizes the physical elements, the operational structure, network configurations, patterns of data, as well as operational procedures to be applied. However, since IoT spans a wide range of technologies, there is no standard reference architecture. This implies that there is no unified and easy-to-follow template for all viable applications [2].

When it comes to the implementation of the IoT, there is a wide range of architectures and protocols that could be used to support many network applications. The architecture of the IoT system might vary greatly according to its implementation; thereby, it must be flexible or standardized enough to allow the development of a diversity of smart applications.

Despite the fact that there is no standard IoT architecture that is globally approved, a three-layer design seems to be the most common and broadly accepted architecture for both research and industrial communities. Then, the research efforts continue trying to improve over this architecture to cope with recent developments. The three-layer architecture of the IoT system can be displayed in Figure 1.1. As illustrated, the IoT ecosystem could be decomposed into three primary operational layers, namely the physical layer, the network layer, and the application layer. Each of these layers could be further partitioned into additional fundamental sublayers. Each level is briefly summarized in the following subsections, with special emphasis placed on the specific sublayers that can be found inside each level [3].

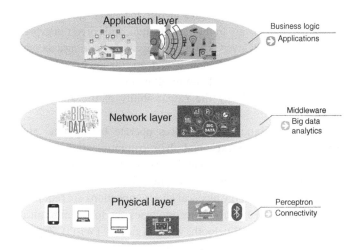

Figure 1.1 Illustration of the three-layered architecture of the IoT ecosystem. *Source:* Geralt/Pixabay.

1.2.1 Physical Layer

The physical layer is sometimes called the perception layer and includes both perceptive activities and fundamental networking resources provided by physical IoT devices, which are all included in this layer.

For perceptive functionality, it involves the primary activities of physical things such as detecting, accumulating, and handling the data perceived from the real world to the extent that it can be done efficiently. Thus, the perception layer incorporates various sensors, such as gas sensors, proximity sensors, infrared sensors, and motion sensors, in addition to actuators, which are used to perform various activities on real-world objects. For setup purposes, a plug-and-play method is typically applied at this layer to deal with the variability of sensors and actuators. Because of their limited battery capacity and compute performance, IoT devices are demonstrated as resource-constrained devices in many ways. A significant portion of the big data volumes that are currently overflowing the cyber-physical systems originates at this IoT layer; nevertheless, these volumes of data are in their raw format, and correct interpretation of them, at this layer, is a critical stage in developing a secure, efficient, and scalable IoT system. In fact, an efficient knowledge of big data pertaining to the IoT can result in a variety of advantages. However, this is typically the responsibility of the application layer [4, 5].

On the other hand, smart devices operate in resource- and power-constrained contexts, and their communication features must be able to cope with lossy and noisy communication environments. Consequently, in order to communicate the data obtained by the sensors, low-energy physical layer connections are required.

Among the most important technologies for IoT communications at this layer are Bluetooth, wireless fidelity (Wi-Fi), Zigbee, ultra-wideband (UWB), radio frequency identification devices (RFID), low-power wide-area network (LPWAN), and near-field communication (NFC), all of which are confronting the aforementioned issues.

1.2.2 Network Layer

It includes communication facilities as well as middleware functions, which are both important for the sustainability of IoT systems. In the case of communication facilities, the resource restriction of IoT devices must however be delicately examined before implementation. One of the most difficult tasks at this layer is providing a distinctive internet protocol (IP) address to the millions of interconnected IoT devices that are internet-connected. By taking advantage of the IPv6 addressing protocol, we may gradually reduce the severity of this problem. Another communication issue in this layer is the volume of the transmitted packets, which will be addressed by the adoption of appropriate protocols, such as IPv6 over low-power wireless personal area network (6LoWPAN), that are capable of providing timely compression capabilities. A third problem pertains to transmission utilities, as transmission protocols should take into consideration the restricted resources in the physical layer, as well as the mobility and plasticity of the internet-connected things, among other things. As a remedy, a routing protocol for low-power and lossy (RPL) networks has been developed as a wireless vector-dependent transmission protocol that works on IEEE 802.15.4 channels, supporting and characterized by its power efficiency. Two modes of communications are supported by this protocol, namely one-to-one communication as well as multi-hop many-to-one communications.

On the other hand, middleware functions often relate to a software layer that sits between the application and network layers, and that is capable of addressing communication and computation concerns in a cooperative manner with the application and the network. Middleware could work as an intermediary between smart things, enabling communication among devices that could otherwise be inaccessible. As "software glue," middleware makes things simpler for developers and engineers to establish input/output operations and communications in such a way that allows them to concentrate on the specific aim of their application rather than becoming bogged down in the technical details.

A variety of useful operations are conceivable in an IoT environment using middleware functions – first, the collaboration and interoperability between diverse IoT devices. So, the varying smart objects could communicate with others seamlessly; second, the scalability to control numerous smart things at the same time; third, device and content look-ups; fourth, sustainability and responsiveness of IoT components; and fifth, IoT devices deeply integrated into our daily lives in the form of smart pillows, smartwatches, smart doors, and smart TVs, which raise the user's concerns about security and privacy of their stored or routed data. The middleware could empower the IoT with some security mechanisms such as identity management and authentication. Finally, when it comes to IoT and the cloud, a flawless and robust connection between these two realms is essential.

1.2.3 Application Layer

Big data analysis, business intelligence, as well as software applications logic are typically found in the uppermost layer. The physical layer of the IoT ecosystem collects a massive amount of valuable data, which is then analyzed using big data analytics. There is a huge amount of data, it is generated quickly, and there is a wide variety of styles. It is necessary to incorporate big data analytical methodologies into the overall IoT architecture, where ML algorithms can contribute significantly to extracting value from the abovementioned huge data and converting them into valuable information. Tasks devoted to delivering services for a particular IoT community based on predefined business objectives also fall under the purview of business intelligence, which falls under the application layer as well. Business intelligence usually meets data analytics, and both are often used together in this portion of the process in order to uncover aspects and make predictions or suggestions for how to improve the end result or generate the best possible tactical business strategies. The application layer also includes the software that facilitates communication between the whole IoT infrastructure and the end users, whether they are regular residents or city managers or factory managers. The IoT architecture's software components are customized to meet the specific requirements of each application. As an example, we can think of "smart cities," "smart healthcare," "smart transportation," "smart agriculture," and so forth.

1.3 Internet of Things' Vulnerabilities and Attacks

A lot of research efforts have been devoted to studying and categorizing IoT vulnerabilities and attacks. Given the attacker's activity as a categorization criterion, IoT attacks can be broadly classified as passive and active attacks. However, this is coarse-grained taxonomy. So, the two classes of attacks can be further categorized according to the definition of layers in a conventional IoT infrastructure that was provided in the previous section.

1.3.1 Passive Attacks

All communications are observed and copied by the attacker in passive attacks. They are primarily concerned with keeping tabs on the transmissions and accumulating the necessary data.

Adversary makes no attempt to alter the material they have obtained. Despite the fact that these assaults pose no threat to the system, they might put a severe threat to the privacy of users' data. As opposed to active attacks, which alter data or information, passive attacks are more difficult to detect. As a result, the victim is unaware of the attack. Despite the fact that some encryption techniques can be used to avoid it. As a result, the communication is rendered unintelligible by hackers at any point during transmission. To put it another way, this is why prevention is more important than detection. As shown in Table 1.1, IoT system is prone to different passive attacks including eavesdropping, node outage, node tampering, node malfunctioning, as well as traffic analysis. In multiple studies, node tampering, outage, or malfunctioning are regarded as active attacks. However, they actually belong to passive ones because they do not pose a significant risk to the network in comparison to the active ones. That is because they do not create a single point of failure in the IoT system, which could remain functioning without the participation of dying nodes.

1.3.2 Active Attacks

The illegal activities performed during active attacks include attacks on privacy as well as the integrity of data. Additionally, active attacks can target unauthorized access and consumption of resources as well as the disruption of an adversary's communication channels. During an active attack, the attacker emits a radio signal or performs an action that can be detected by the IoT components. A denial-of-service (DoS) assault on the network or physical layers, for instance, could reason network nodes to lose data packets as a result of the attack.

Generally speaking, a DoS is a popular attack on the accessibility of networking facilities. In general, DoS is defined as a kind of circumstance that expends the network resources and reduces the networking capability, distracting the network's attention away from carrying out its functions appropriately or in a reasonable timeframe. In other words, the DoS can be considered an attempt to inhibit authorized users from gaining access to some facilities.

Table 1.1 A summary of common passive IoT attacks.

Attack	Description
Eavesdropping	Communication lines can be tapped to gather sensitive information. As a result, eavesdropping is easier on wireless networks. Compared to long-range wireless technologies, short-range connections require an adversary to be in the near vicinity to acquire valuable information. So, IoT devices are less vulnerable to eavesdropping. The actual location of individual nodes may be revealed by intercepting IoT messages.
Node outage	When a node fails to perform as expected, this attack is launched. Network protocols must be robust as much as necessary to eliminate the undesirable consequences of node failures such as cluster head failures by selecting new cluster heads and/or offering alternative paths for network paths.
Node tampering	A node can be physically destroyed, using a physical force, electrical surge, or bullets, such that it is no longer operational.
Node malfunctioning	A variety of causes, such as overloaded sensors, other denial-of-service (DoS) attacks, sensory defects, or energy shortages, might result in such attacks.
Traffic analysis	An adversary extracts insightful information from traffic patterns that are as important as the network packets. To learn more about the network's structure, traffic patterns might be studied. This kind of vital information can be gleaned from traffic analysis. Other sensitive information such as behaviors and intents might also be revealed through traffic patterns. When it comes to strategic communications, silence can signify either an attack, a tactical decision, or an operative's infiltration. This can also be seen in a rapid surge in traffic, which could be an indication of an attack or raid.

Traditional methods of accomplishing this include flooding packets to any centralized network resource like an access point, that is, the resources become not accessible to the other nodes of that network, and as a result, the network ceases to function as expected.

This could fail to provide promised services to end users as a result of this. A serious variant of DoS is known as distributed DoS (DDoS) attack, which occurs when adversaries fool or take the control of a big number of IoT devices and turn them into zombies for the purpose of creating a botnet [1].

For active attacks, hackers essentially impact the functions of the underlying IoT system, which could be the goal of the attack and thereby could be discovered and defended. In the case of communication networks, for instance, these assaults may cause them to be downgraded or even be canceled. Occasionally, the adversary struggles to continue hidden, seeking to acquire the illegal right to use the system resources or intimidating the privacy and/or integrity of the packets of the network [6]. A common set of active IoT attacks is categorized into three major groups according to three layers of IoT architectures, as presented in Table 1.2.

Table 1.2 A summary of common active IoT attacks.

Layer	Attack	Description
Physical	Node tampering	An attacker controls a sensory node by physically attaching it to alter its content and functioning.
	Jamming DoS	By using the same frequency, a rogue device can block a signal from being sent. Signal-to-noise ratios are reduced underneath the level required by the nodes using that channel because of the jamming signal's contribution to noise. A zone can be continually jammed, preventing all the nodes in that zone from communicating with each other. It is also possible to momentarily disrupt communications by jamming for short periods of time at random intervals.

(Continued)

Table 1.2 (Continued)

Layer	Attack	Description
Network	Collision	An attacker broadcast the same channel once a legal node of the network begins transmission. Hence, the two broadcasts collide, and the receiving node becomes unable to understand the arriving data and therefore calls for retransmitting the same packet again.
	Denial of sleep	This attack is performed by executing repetitive handshaking and collision attacks to thwart the node moving into the sleep phase. This could lead to energy depletion in battery-based IoT devices.
	De-synchronization	An adversary communicates information in the timeslots devoted to another client leading the packets to be lost or collide.
	Exhaustion	An attack that is executed by continuing the collision attack till the energy of aimed node is depleted.
	Unfairness	Irregular use of fatigue attacks or misuse of collaborative MAC protocols leading to network unfairness.
	Spoofing	A malevolent node parodies the MAC address of a target node and then makes different legal personalities outside of the victim node and utilizes these personalities somewhere else in the network.
	6LoWPAN Exploit	An adversary injects their own fragments into the fragmentation chain.
	Flooding	An adversary transmits advert information to the entire network and persuades the neighboring nodes.

Table 1.2 (Continued)

Layer	Attack	Description
	Clone	An adversary deliberately poses duplications of a negotiated node in a lot of sites in the network to result in irregularity.
Application	Path-based DoS	An adversary overloads the remote nodes by overflowing an end-to-end communication route using fake or replayed packets.
	False data injection	An adversary injects false data into the measurement of mode to change its total outcome or reading intentionally.
	Software attacks	A software attack is considered as the cornerstone of malicious software, such as Trojan horses, worms, or viruses, which is introduced into an infected computer system and then proceeds to do harm, such as draining resources, destroying data, money theft, or clogging up networks.
	Privacy leakage	Private user data that is stored or sent by IoT smart objects is at risk of being leaked. An assault on a wearable device can yield a wealth of personal information, including heart rate, GPS location, phone calls and messages received and sent, and so on.

1.4 Artificial Intelligence

To answer the issue "could computers think?," artificial intelligence (AI) was originally proposed in 1950. This led to a definition of AI in the field of computer science as a branch of computer science that focuses on addressing issues that are difficult for humans to understand but are easy for computers to understand. An authoritative, mathematical, scientific set of rules can be used to designate problems. Intrinsically, AI is a very wide-ranging field that includes both learning-based and non-learning-based techniques. Some time ago, computer science experts assumed that human-level AI could be achieved simply by defining a considerable set of explicit directions for handling and fusing knowledge such that the scholars and specialists believed that achieving human-level AI can be skilled just by specifying a large number of specific guidelines and regulations for handling and processing information.

Synonymous with "symbolic AI," this paradigm dominated the AI society between 1950 and 1980. By 1980, symbolic AI had reached its zenith of fame, thanks to the success of expert systems. In spite of the fact that symbolic AI proved to be a good fit for solving logical, formally specified challenges (such as playing chess), it was not able to discover explicit rules for more complex and ambiguous situations.

Providing answers to the problems that could be solved quickly by a human but is hard to articulate in a formalized setting, such as speech analysis and fraud detection, is the real challenge for the AI system. IoT security vulnerabilities can be evaluated and formulated as an issue necessitating a smart approach to safeguard and secure IoT systems against possible attacks.

The large volumes of IoT data generated from the daily interactions among different IoT entities (i.e. human, software, and hardware) devices can be explored and learned using AI algorithms. IoT risks or malicious behaviors can be detected early on in the IoT system's lifecycle by aggregating and analyzing data provided by various IoT sectors, which can then be studied by one or some AI approaches to distinguish regular behaviors from malicious behaviors. AI can also be critical in predicting new IoT risks, which are almost always variations of previous threats because it can intelligently anticipate potential unknown attacks according to the knowledge learned from the existing IoT data. It is also possible that AI might help the IoT system automatically identify the most suited defense mechanism or solutions for diverse threats. There should be a switch in IoT-based systems to security-based intelligence rather than just secure communication across IoT parities.

Machine learning (ML) is regarded as a widely applied AI paradigm, and it has achieved notable achievement across a broad range of application domains, including intrusion detection, attack defense mechanisms, authentication, etc. ML is an AI subarea that was proposed as a computer system (playing checkers) that can learn from a significant quantity of historical data by utilizing self-adapting computing methods. In reality, the complexity of computational algorithms prevents them from adapting to constantly changing system conditions and dynamically changing requirements. Rather than being fully preprogrammed, ML algorithms learn from past experiences, allowing them to assist in prediction as well as decision-making operations and that may be completed by creating a data-driven self-adjusting system [7].

ML is a subfield of AI that emphasizes the programming of computational machines in such a way that they could *learn from data*. ML has a slightly more general definition as follows:

> Machine learning is the field of study that gives computers the ability to learn without being explicitly programmed.
>
> *–Arthur Samuel, 1959*

ML has a more industrial-tailored meaning as follows:

> A computer program is said to learn from experience E with respect to some task T and some performance measure P, if its performance on T, as measured by P, improves with experience E.
>
> *–Tom Mitchell, 1997*

Why use ML for IoT security?

Think about developing intrusion detection using conventional programming language:

- First, you need to know how intrusion is performed and how the attack seems. You might notice that attackers generally look for vulnerabilities to get access without being identified. This can be performed by performing some actions that follow some pattern.
- Next, you implement the detection program to identify these malicious patterns and warn you if something is detected.
- Then, you test your program by repeating the previous steps many times till it becomes good enough.

Given the complexity of the problem, you can expect your program to become a long list of complicated rules that will be extremely time-consuming to maintain. On the other hand, ML algorithms can enable the development of a solution to automatically learn the normal patterns of system behavior and so can learn patterns related to intrusions. The program is to the point, simpler to sustain, and relatively more precise than the previous version.

1.5 Deep Learning

Deep learning (DL) is an ML technology that creates deeper versions of neural networks (NNs) that imitate the composition and functionality of the human brain. Hierarchical learning and deep structured learning are alternative names to DL, which implies stacking a big number of hidden layers that nonlinearly process the data by transforming it into various stages of abstraction aiming to extract the important features and representations [8]. In other words, DL offers a mathematical model that learns to map a set of input data into a particular output by learning the relationship between them.

Although ML and DL share many similarities, they are not mutually exclusive. When the dataset is small and well-curated, for example, ML could be beneficial because the data has been meticulously prepared. Data preparation necessitates the involvement of a human, which means that ML algorithms will not be able to extract information from huge and complicated datasets and would underfit. ML is sometimes referred to as "shallow learning" due to its ability to learn from minimal datasets. DL shows robust performance even when the dataset size is huge. DL is capable of deducing precise conclusions on its own from any set of data, no matter how complicated the pattern is. Also, it is so powerful that it can handle unstructured data that is not sufficiently coordinated.

1.6 Taxonomy of Deep Learning Models

DL solutions can be classified into so many different categories according to multiple categorization criteria:

- Supervision criterion: It specifies the need for human supervision during the training (supervised, unsupervised, semi-supervised, and reinforcement learning).
- Incrementality criterion: It specifies whether the learning is performed incrementally or on the fly (online versus offline).
- Centralization criterion: It specifies whether the learning is centralized or distributed in nature.
- Base criterion: It specifies whether the learning is performed in a model-based or instance-based strategy.

You can use any of these criteria exclusively or by combining some of them. For example, an intrusion detection system might learn a deep network in a distributed way using normal and attack traffic data instances. This makes it a distributed, supervised, and model-based system.

1.6.1 Supervision Criterion

DL solutions could be according to the degree and the kind of supervision they use during training. This results in four major categories of methods, namely supervised learning, unsupervised learning, semi-supervised learning, and reinforcement learning. In the following section, a broad view of each of these categories will be discussed and explained.

1.6.1.1 Supervised Deep Learning

Supervised DL simulates the theory of learning in human beings, where the learner is trained and taught under the guidance of the teacher. The distinction is that the student in this case is a deep NN, while labeled training data is given to behave as a supervisor that teaches the network to correctly predict the output. Supervised DL simply receives, as input, the data samples x and the corresponding actual output *y* (sometimes called ground-truth), then, train the underlying network automatically learn a mapping function that maps the input *x* to output *y*. In other words, the network is trained to learn and discover the inherent patterns and relationships between the input samples and the ground-truth labels, facilitating it to correctly calculate the outputs of never-before-seen data. By the completion of the training procedure, the network is evaluated on an unseen subset of data (test set) by predicting the output of test samples. If the network calculates the correct output, it means that the network is efficient. Therefore, datasets comprising inputs and ground-truth labels turn out to be important because they assist the deep network to learn in an efficient way.

Many advantages could be gained by supervised learning. It does extremely well at optimizing performance in well-characterized tasks with a lot of ground-truth labels. For instance, think about a big dataset of images, where each image was labeled. When the size of the dataset is large as necessary and the training is performed using the appropriate DL models, and with robust enough computers, it would be easy to build a very good, supervised image classifier. As the supervised DL learns from labeled data, it would be possible to evaluate its performance via a loss function by the contrasting predicted label with the actual image label. The DL will clearly seek to reduce this loss function such that the error on never-before-seen images from a holdout set is as low as possible [9]. A visual illustration of supervised learning can be found in Figure 1.2.

Generally speaking, a common task for supervised DL is *classification*. Intrusion detection is an ideal instance of this: it is trained with many IoT traffic flows together with their *class* (normal or attack), and it should learn in what way to categorize IoT traffic flows. One more typical task is to forecast the numerical value of the target *variable*, such as the stock price, given a set of *features* (country, coins, brand, economy, quality, etc.) known as *predictors*. This kind of task is known as *regression*. To train a deep network, you should provide it with many historical examples together with the actual value of the *target variable* (i.e. the previous stock prices).

An attribute is an aspect of an instance (e.g. "brand"). Attributes are also known as features. In supervised learning, a class label is a

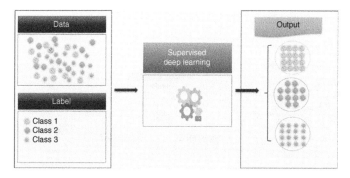

Figure 1.2 Illustration of supervised deep learning.

special attribute that defines the class to which a specific instance belongs. Features have several meanings depending on the context. Several people use the terms "feature" and "attribute" in exchange.

1.6.1.2 Unsupervised Deep Learning

As the name implies, unsupervised DL denotes the category of deep networks that are not supervised by means of labeled training data. Instead, they seek to discover the hidden patterns and discernments from the underlying unlabeled data. Unsupervised learning simulates the human learning process when the human brain learns new things. Unsupervised learning cannot be explicitly applied to a regression or classification problem since different from supervised learning, the model receives input data with no ground-truth label. The objective of unsupervised learning is to discover the inherent composition of the dataset, group that data in accordance with relationships, and characterize that dataset in a compacted layout. In other words, algorithms can operate spontaneously in order to learn more about the data and discover remarkable or unanticipated patterns those human beings were not in search of.

Categories: As with ML, two common categories of unsupervised DL exist, namely clustering and association. The former emphasizes the DL models designed to group the data instances into clusters such that instances with the greatest similarities belong to the same cluster, and ones with less or no similarities belong to different groups. The latter category emphasizes the

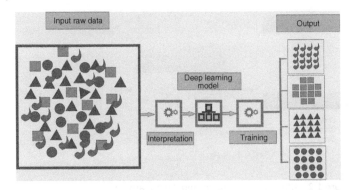

Figure 1.3 Illustration of the workflow of deep unsupervised learning.

DL models designed to discover the interactions between variables in the big dataset by determining the set of data instances that take place together in the dataset [10]. A visual illustration of unsupervised learning can be found in Figure 1.3.

1.6.1.3 Semi-Supervised Deep Learning

Semi-supervised learning is a training strategy that combines unsupervised and supervised learning by training the deep network using few amounts of labeled data samples as well as unlabeled data samples. Usually, it is tailored to solve a multitude of practical problems where data labels are hard to find since they involve immense efforts from human annotators, expensive devices, or time-consuming experiments [11]. Labels could be challenging to get due to the need for human annotators, specialized equipment, or expensive and time-consuming tests.

Step 1: Train the deep network using the labeled (or supervised) part of the data till it obtains optimal results.

Step 2: Use the supervised trained model (in the previous step) to predict the labels of unlabeled sample data. These generated labels are known as *pseudo labels*.

Step 3: Relate the pseudo labels with the supervised labels in the earlier steps and also relate the corresponding unlabeled samples to the labeled samples.

Step 4: Train the deep network using this new combination of data samples till it reaches optimal performance.

1.6.1.4 Deep Reinforcement Learning

Reinforcement learning (RL) is a branch of ML that allows for automated and goal-oriented learning through interaction with the environment where the learner (agent) learns from the consequence of its actions, rather than learning what actions to do. The agent does not have to be a software entity, such as you might see in video games, in order to function, instead it could be implanted in any IoT device to implement the concept. It is perhaps the most effective method of properly appreciating and utilizing real-world experiences because it involves actual interaction with the real world and the receipt of replies [12]. The agent occupies a physical space inside an environment. The environment represents the world in which the agent interacts and performs actions. The environment has a state that can be observed in part or its entirety by the observer. The effect of action causes the environment to change into a different state. Following the completion of an action, a proportional scalar reward is granted. By learning a policy that will determine which action to take given a particular state, the agent will be able to maximize the total amount of future reward accumulated. The psychology of RL is strikingly comparable to that of humans. Humans learn by interacting with their environment. Illegal actions result in some type of punishment and should be evaded in the future, whereas correct actions are rewarded and should be promoted in the future. It has persuaded the research community that RL can bring us toward actual AI because of its great resemblance to human psychology. RL has been around for a very long time. Beyond straightforward world models, however, RL has strived to scale up to more complex scenarios. DL was introduced to address the scalability and multidimensionality issue, paving the way for the advent of deep reinforcement learning (DRL). Accordingly, DRL turned out to be a rapidly evolving field in recent years with a wide range of applications in IoT [13, 14]. A visual illustration of the RL system can be found in Figure 1.4.

1.6.2 Incrementality Criterion

According to this criterion, the deep networks can be categorized based on whether they are performed in batch learning models or online learning from the training data.

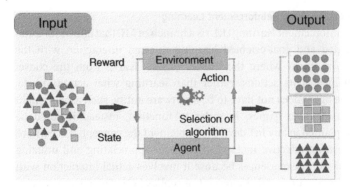

Figure 1.4 Illustration of reinforcement learning.

1.6.2.1 Batch Learning

Batch learning refers to the scenario in which the deep network is unable to be learned in an incremental way. Instead, it ought to be trained to make use of all the existing training data. Batch learning typically requires plenty of time and computational resources, thereby, it is usually performed offline. In particular, the deep network was first trained and evaluated using some representative data, and followingly moved to production to start applying its learned experiences to a real-world task. So, batch learning is sometimes known as offline learning.

Consider the scenario in which a batch learning model is deployed in an IoT system for intrusion detection. If the system encounters new data (i.e. a new class of cyber attack) that need to inform the model about it, then a new variant of the model must be trained from scratch on the complete dataset containing not only the new data but also the old data. Once the new model is trained and evaluated, it can replace the old model in production.

Luckily, the complete process of training, testing, and deploying a DL system could be programmed quite simply, so also a batch learning model could adjust to change. Merely upgrade the training dataset to retrain a new variant of a model from scratch once it requires updating its learned experiences. Despite the simplicity of this offline solution, the repetitive training using the complete dataset is a time-consuming task and also resource exhaustive.

This, in turn, may render batch learning as an improper solution in the case of a system with quickly changing data, which is a typical scenario in many IoT systems. Fortunately, a superior alternative to learning such a system is to take advantage of models that are able to learn in an incremental manner.

1.6.2.2 Online Learning

Online learning enables the deep network to be trained in an incremental way bypassing data samples to it successively, either separately or in small groups called *mini batches*. This way, the training step becomes rapid and low cost. Therefore, the new data samples could be learned once it comes. Thus, it is called learning on the fly.

The online learning model is a recommended choice for applications (e.g. IoT systems) that encounter rapidly changing data that necessitate instant response and update. It is also a decent solution for resource-limited environments. This can be attributed to the fact that as soon as an online learning model has completed training from new data samples, it can easily dispose of them (except if they are required for another purpose). This way, a large number of storage resources could be saved. For big-size datasets that cannot fit into the memory of one machine, online learning models are capable to learn by loading a small portion of the data, using it for training, and repeating this practice with different portions of data till it trains over the entire data. More details about offline and online learning can be found in later chapters.

1.6.3 Generalization Criterion

DL methods can also be classified according to the degree to which they can generalize. This means that the system must be able to generalize to instances it had never encountered, during the training process. Achieving robust performance during the training process is not enough; the actual goal is to work well on new examples. In this regard, DL can be according to generalization approaches to model-based learning and instance-based learning.

1.6.3.1 Model-Based Learning

A popular approach to making a generalization based on a group of data instances is to develop a model to learn from these instances, and then exploit that model to perform predictions. Typically, this model has a set of parameters to be optimized to better improve the learned experience from the available data instance. This is known as model-based learning.

1.6.3.2 Instance-Based Learning

It is possible that memorizing something by heart is the tiniest form of learning. Consider you build an intrusion detection system in this sense, it will only detect all IoT traffic flows that are the same ones that have already been identified by a specialist – not the most terrible solution, but definitely not the most excellent. Rather than detecting IoT flows that are identical to well-known attacks, your intrusion detector can be designed to also detect IoT traffic flows that are very similar to well-known attacks. This needs a *metric of similarity* between traffic flows. A fundamental similarity metric between two traffic flows could be to calculate the number of bytes they share. The system will identify a traffic flow as an attack if it has something in common with an identified attack. This can be referred to as *instance-based learning*: the model that learns the data instances by heart then generalizes to other instances utilizing a similarity metric. It is sometimes known as *memory-based learning*.

1.6.4 Centralization Criterion

The widespread of IoT applications and advanced communication technologies have been leading to an extraordinary expansion in the quantities of daily generated data in the cyber-physical world. According to the International Data Corporation (IDC), it is expected that billions of IoT devices will generate around 79ZB of data by 2025, forcing companies and corporations to reconsider their data retention, governance, and control policies. The storage and analysis of these large quantities of data could be easily achieved on the cloud, due to the gained benefits from cloud computing paradigms in terms of robust storage capacities, powerful processing capabilities, cost efficiency, etc. Traditionally, DL solutions are trained centrally on a central server (e.g. cloud or data center) where the model is hosted along with the corresponding training data. As a result, all of the data acquired by local IoT devices and sensors is transmitted up to the central server for training purposes; thereby, real-time learning is hindered by this round trip. However, owing to the ever-increasing concerns about network constraints, data privacy, latency issues, and fully centralized cloud-based data storage and analytics methods (i.e. ML or DL solutions) turn out to be impractical.

Many data owners are afraid to share their personal information with other parties, even if the organization is well-known or unknown to them. Regulations like the US. Consumer Privacy Bill of Rights and the General Data Protection Regulation (GDPR) of the European Commission have been designed to protect consumers' privacy in this setting. In GDPR, articles 5 and 6, for example, limit storing and aggregating the data to just that which is permitted for the user, and which is absolutely necessary for processing [15].

Shifting toward the problem of network constraints and the development of real-time IoT applications necessitating rapid decisions, the reality that the cloud servers are frequently situated in remote sites that are distant from the users results in a substantial data latency because of the very distant communications. Considering these two critical concerns, the tendency in data storage and analysis is turning from being centralized on the cloud to being distributed over IoT devices. Edge computing is a crucial enabler technology for this change, in which edge devices like sensors, smartwatches, smart cars, road-site units, and home appliances are equipped with computational resources to enable storing and analyzing the data privately with negligible latency. For ancient and long-term archiving, edge nodes transfer the analyzed data to the cloud servers occasionally [11].

Adapting the AI methods to this vision is essential to enable realizing the concept of edge intelligence in real-world IoT applications. In this regard, McMahan et al. introduced, in 2016, a decentralized learning paradigm of federated learning (FL) that collaboratively train ML models at the resource-constrained edge devices of IoT networks. Local data samples are stored locally on many edge devices or servers, known as participants, and can be used to train a single deep network locally and cooperatively without sharing raw data. Followingly, a coordinating server, known as a parameter or aggregation server, later accumulates the learning gradients of the participants to originate a global model. The participants download the updated global model to learn from the learning experience of others and to enable them to improve their learning capabilities in the next iterations [16].

IoT applications can benefit greatly from FL's unique operating paradigm, which includes the following: training at the aggregator does not require access to the raw data in FL. Because of this, the exposure of private data to the outer third party is minimized and a degree of data secrecy is raised. The privacy preservation characteristics render FL a suitable choice for designing smart and secure IoT applications. In addition, a short lag time since IoT data does not need to be sent to a server, FL can help lessen the communication delays incurred by offloading data from the cloud. Unlike centralized training, federated training can save network resources (e.g. transmission bandwidth, energy, network overhead, etc.). FL has the ability to increase the convergence performance of the total learning procedure and obtain an improved model that can scale up on a network of IoT devices, which could not be accomplished with the centralized AI methodologies given the limited data size and restrictive processing abilities [17]. A visual illustration of the FL system can be found in Figure 1.5.

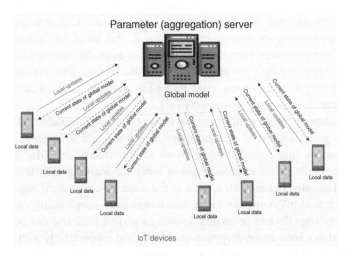

Figure 1.5 Illustration of federated deep learning over the IoT network.

1.7 Supplementary Materials

https://github.com/DEEPOLOGY-AI/DL-Book-Wiley-2022/tree/main/Ch1

References

1 Neshenko, N., Bou-Harb, E., Crichigno, J. et al. (2019). Demystifying IoT security: an exhaustive survey on IoT vulnerabilities and a first empirical look on internet-scale IoT exploitations. *IEEE Commun. Surv. Tutor.* https://doi.org/10.1109/COMST.2019.2910750.

2 Butun, I., Osterberg, P., and Song, H. (2020). Security of the internet of things: vulnerabilities, attacks, and countermeasures. *IEEE Commun. Surv. Tutor.* https://doi.org/10.1109/COMST.2019.2953364.

3 Aversano, L., Bernardi, M.L., Cimitile, M., and Pecori, R. (2021). A systematic review on deep learning approaches for IoT security. *Comput. Sci. Rev.* https://doi.org/10.1016/j.cosrev.2021.100389.

4 Rodríguez, E., Otero, B., Gutiérrez, N., and Canal, R. (2021). A survey of deep learning techniques for cybersecurity in mobile networks. *IEEE Commun. Surv. Tutor.* 23 (3): 1920–1955. https://doi.org/10.1109/COMST.2021.3086296 (thirdquarter 2021).

5 Al-Garadi, M.A., Mohamed, A., Al-Ali, A.K. et al. (2020). A survey of machine and deep learning methods for internet of things (IoT) security. *IEEE Commun. Surv. Tutor.* https://doi.org/10.1109/COMST.2020.2988293.

6 Chaabouni, N., Mosbah, M., Zemmari, A. et al. (2019). Network intrusion detection for IoT security based on learning techniques. *IEEE Commun. Surv. Tutor.* https://doi.org/10.1109/COMST.2019.2896380.

7 Olowononi, F.O., Rawat, D.B., and Liu, C. (2021). Resilient machine learning for networked cyber physical systems: a survey for machine learning security to securing machine learning for CPS. *IEEE Commun. Surv. Tutor.* https://doi.org/10.1109/COMST.2020.3036778.

8 Hussain, F., Hussain, R., Hassan, S.A., and Hossain, E. (2020). Machine learning in IoT security: current solutions and future challenges. *IEEE Commun. Surv. Tutor.* https://doi.org/10.1109/COMST.2020.2986444.

9 Ullah, K., Rashid, I., Afzal, H. et al. (2020). SS7 vulnerabilities – a survey and implementation of machine learning vs rule based filtering for detection of SS7 network attacks. *IEEE Commun. Surv. Tutor.* https://doi.org/10.1109/COMST.2020.2971757.

10 Rodriguez, E., Otero, B., Gutierrez, N., and Canal, R. (2021). A survey of deep learning techniques for cybersecurity in mobile networks. *IEEE Commun. Surv. Tutor.* https://doi.org/10.1109/COMST.2021.3086296.

11 Hu, S., Chen, X., Ni, W. et al. (2021). Distributed machine learning for wireless communication networks: techniques, architectures, and applications. *IEEE Commun. Surv. Tutor.* https://doi.org/10.1109/COMST.2021.3086014.

12 Padakandla, S. (2021). A survey of reinforcement learning algorithms for dynamically varying environments. *ACM Comput. Surv.*: https://doi.org/10.1145/3459991.

13 Luong, N.C., Hoang, D.T., Gong, S. et al. (2019). Applications of deep reinforcement learning in communications and networking: a survey. *IEEE Commun. Surv. Tutor.* https://doi.org/10.1109/COMST.2019.2916583.

14 Kiran, B.R., Sobh, I., Talpaert, V. et al. (2021). Deep reinforcement learning for autonomous driving: a survey. *IEEE Trans. Intell. Transp. Syst.* https://doi.org/10.1109/TITS.2021.3054625.

15 Wahab, O.A., Mourad, A., Otrok, H., and Taleb, T. (2021). Federated machine learning: survey, multi-level classification, desirable criteria and future directions in communication and networking systems. *IEEE Commun. Surv. Tutor.* https://doi.org/10.1109/COMST.2021.3058573.

16 Yin, X., Zhu, Y., and Hu, J. (2021). A comprehensive survey of privacy-preserving federated learning: a taxonomy, review, and future directions. *ACM Comput. Surv.* https://doi.org/10.1145/3460427.

17 Yin, X., Zhu, Y., and Hu, J. (2021). A comprehensive survey of privacy-preserving federated learning. *ACM Comput. Surv.* https://doi.org/10.1145/3460427.

2

Deep Neural Networks

2.1 Introduction

This chapter introduces the trace of the development of deep neural networks (DNNs). This is done by discussing the biological foundation of neural networks and how it motivates the scientist to introduce artificial neural networks (ANNs) in their simplest form known as multilayer perceptron (MLP). Then, we explain how the design of DNN originated from ANNs, which shape the foundation of models of deep learning (DL). A variety of activation functions have been introduced to activate the neurons in layers of DNNs, each with different mathematical formulation and characteristics. An intuitive understanding of the learning process of DNNs is essential to dive into DL. Thus, we present a thorough introduction to the concepts of forward and backward propagation to learn a simple ANN. Gradient descent is discussed, in this regard, to enable understanding the general ideology of gradient calculation to learn different variants of DNNs. When it comes to high-capacity DNNs, we need to know about the parameter initialization and objective function. Thus, this chapter offers a rigorous introduction to the parameter initialization as well as the loss functions for different learning problems. DNNs are adaptable, robust, and scalable, making them ideal for large-scale, high-complexity cyber-security tasks like the classification of billions

Deep Learning Approaches for Security Threats in IoT Environments,
First Edition. Mohamed Abdel-Basset, Nour Moustafa, and Hossam Hawash.
© 2023 The Institute of Electrical and Electronics Engineers, Inc.
Published 2023 by John Wiley & Sons, Inc.

IoT traffic flows. All over, this chapter aims to give the reader a deep understanding not just of the notions but also of the practice of applying DNN for IoT security. Therefore, by the end of this chapter, the introduced concepts are applied so far to a real case study on IoT security.

2.2 From Biological Neurons to Artificial Neurons

2.2.1 Biological Neurons

Let us take a quick look at a biological neuron before we go into artificial ones (Figure 2.1). Most often seen in animal cerebral cortexes, this peculiar cell has several branching extensions known as dendrites and an extremely long extension known as axon. The nucleus and most of the cell's complicated components are housed in the cell body. There are multiple telodendria at the axon's end, and at the tips of these branches are tiny structures known as synapses that link directly to the cell body or to the dendrites of other neurons. The synapses in biological neurons allow other neurons to send short bursts of electrical energy, which are known as signals. An individual neuron fires its own signal when it receives enough impulses from other neurons within a few milliseconds of each other. Single neuron may appear to function in a very straightforward manner, but they are actually part of a network of billions of neurons, where each one is linked to thousands of neurons. A huge network of relatively simple neurons can execute highly complicated calculations [1].

The synapse at the dendritic tip receives signals provided by the central nervous system as a stimulus. A stimulus is delivered to the neuron via synaptic receptors that modify the strength of the signal supplied to the nucleus whenever it reaches in the brain. The dendrites carry this message to the nucleus, where it is processed in conjunction with other signals from other dendrites. Therefore, in the nucleus, all of these signals are brought together. The nucleus's solitary axon will transmit an output signal when it has processed all of these input signals. The axon terminations will

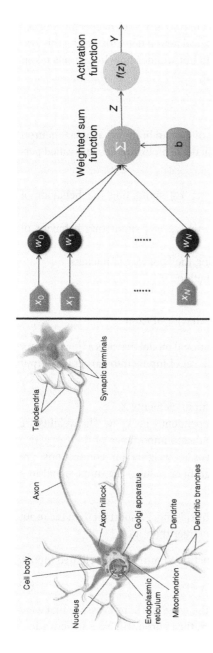

Figure 2.1 Illustration of the biological neuron (left) and artificial neuron (right).

subsequently send this signal to a number of other downstream neurons. As a result, a neuron analysis is pushed deeper and deeper into the brain, building a biological neural network. Seeing this system in action, you cannot help but wonder how long it has taken our species to get to this point.

2.2.2 Artificial Neurons

Driven by biological behavior of human brain, an artificial neuron was defined a mathematical model of biological neuron, called perceptron, and it consists of:

- Many inputs $X = \{x_1, x_2, ..., x_N\}$ simulating the behavior of dendrites.
- Interconnections $W = \{w_1, w_2, ..., w_N\}$ simulating behavior of synapse and bias.
- A calculation unit simulating the behavior of nucleus.
    - A linear combination function.
    - An activation function.

- An output simulating the behavior of axon.

The perceptron is a computational model that acts a linear binary classifier for simply mapping a set of inputs into particular output through the following steps:

Step 1: Receive one or more input elements X.

Step 2: Weight each input independently i.e. $x_i \cdot w_i$. The weights are a group of N values that indicate importance of the respective input values. In other words, weights on connections are parameters that scale (magnify or reduce) the input signal to a particular artificial neuron.

For example, When the input x_1 is more important than the input x_1, the weight w_1 ought to be larger than w_2.

Step 3: Apply combination function to sum up the weighted inputs.

$$y = x_1.w_1 + \cdots + x_N.w_N \tag{1}$$

Step 4: Add the bias value to the weighted sum to assure that even when all the inputs are zeros, the neuron will have an activation.

Keep in mind that, depending on whether it is positive or negative, bias can increase or decrease the weighted sum in the activation function.

$$y = \sum_{i=1}^{N} x_i . w_i + b \tag{2}$$

Step 5: Feed this weighted sum to an activation function to generate output. The logic of this activation function determines whether or not an artificial neuron is fired.

$$Z = f(y) \tag{3}$$

Historically, the perceptron was firstly presented by Frank Rosenblatt, in 1957, at the Cornell Aeronautical Laboratory. It used a Heaviside step function as an activation function that generates two-valued output which could be either 0 or 1 according to its input. The output perceptron is the same as this activation function and provides us a classification of the input values. The bias variable, in this regard, adjusts the decision boundary around for the model without any dependency on the input value, and it is updated through the perceptron learning algorithm. The perceptron will not learn to do successful classification if the input data is not linearly separable. A dataset is characterized to be linearly separable if and only if there exist some values of a hyperplane that could cleanly split up the data into two classes, otherwise it is called nonlinearly separable (Figure 2.2).

2.3 Artificial Neural Network

The initial incapacity to learn from nonlinear input data was demonstrated as a major limitation of such single-layer perceptron. As a remedy, the AI community addresses the shortcomings of linear models and handles a more general class of tasks by including one or more layers of artificial neurons (hidden layer). The simplest approach to do this is to stack several fully connected layers one after the other, where the output of

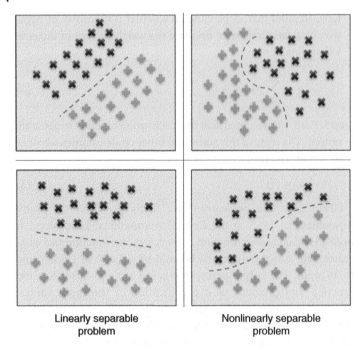

Linearly separable   Nonlinearly separable
problem   problem

Figure 2.2 Illustration of linear separable and nonlinear separable data.

each layer passed as an input to the next layer till the output is generated at the last layer. This structural design is generally known as an MLP and could indeed solve nonlinear problems. The artificial neuron in MLP is similar to its ancestor, the perceptron, however it improves plasticity in the type of activation function to be used. A typical MLP consists of input layer, hidden layer, and output layer (Figure 2.3). The neurons in one layer communicate with those in other layers. Neurons in the same layer, on the other hand, do not communicate with one another. This can be attributed to the fact that neurons in adjacent layers have connections or edges between them, however neurons in the same layer do not connect to each other. The neurons in the MLP are referred to as nodes or units [2]. A detailed comparison between the biological and artificial neural networks can is displayed in Table 2.1.

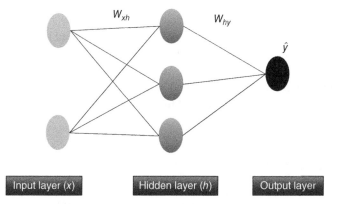

Figure 2.3 Illustration of simple multi-layer perceptron.

Table 2.1 Comparison between artificial neural network and biological neural network.

	Artificial neural network	Biological neural network
Topology	Node	Cell nucleus (Soma)
	Input	Dendrites
	Weights	Synapse
	Output	Axon
Computation	Layer-by-layer	Asynchronous
Complexity	Structured in layers	Very complex
Size	Small (thousands)	Large (billions)
Speed	Relatively small depending on computing resources	High
Fault-tolerance	No	Yes
Power	Consume more power	20 W approximately

2.3.1 Input Layer

It is the layer in which the network is provided with input information. The number of neurons in the input layer corresponds to the number of inputs to be fed to the network. Predicting the outcome is influenced by all of the inputs. There is, however, no computing in the input layer; it is just used to transfer data from the outside world into the network.

2.3.2 Hidden Layer

It refers to the intermediate layer between the input and output layers in which the taken inputs are processed. This layer is accountable for creating complicated interactions between input and output. In other words, it learns the inherent representation in input values to precisely map them into targeted output.

2.3.3 Output Layer

It refers to a layer for receiving the outcome of the hidden layers, and as the term implies, it is responsible for providing the final output of MLP. It is up to us to decide how many neurons we need in the output layer in order to accomplish our goals.

In MLP, each layer has its own weight matrix and bias vector, which are referred to as the parameters of the layer. Biases are added to the weighted input to guarantee that some units per layer are activated irrespective of input concentration. Biases enable the learning to take place by providing the network activity in the case of low-level input, thereby allow the network to learn and explore new interpretations or patterns.

When the number of hidden layers in MLP exceeds one layer, it can be called ANN. A feedforward neural network (FNN) is the most well-identified and simple form of ANN consisting of input layer, one or more hidden layers, and one output layer. Each layer contains a different number of neurons, and each layer is completely linked to the neighboring layer. The connections between neurons in two subsequent layers are one-directional and acyclic, as depicted in Figure 2.3.

2.4 Activation Functions

An activation function is a mathematical function that is attached to an ANN to control whether a neuron/node would be activated or not. When compared to biological neurons, the activation function is at the end determining what is to be fired to the following neuron. That is precisely what an activation function performed in an ANN too. It gets in the output signal from the earlier cell and transforms it into some structure that can be received as an input to the subsequent cell. In other words, the activation decision determines if the input of the neuron is important or not for the learning process of the underlying problem. This way activation function can help the ANN learn complicated relationships in a group of input values so as to derive the targeted output [3].

2.4.1 Types of Activation

Now, as the fundamental concepts of activation function are covered, let us explore the main categories of activation functions [4].

2.4.1.1 Binary Step Function

A threshold value determines whether or not a neuron is triggered in a binary step function. It is checked to see if the input received by the activation function exceeds a particular threshold, and if so, the neuron is activated; otherwise, it is deactivated, and the output it produces is not passed to the following hidden layer. The binary step function can be calculated as follows:

$$f(x) = \begin{cases} 1 & \text{for } x \geq 0 \\ 0 & \text{for } x < 0 \end{cases} \tag{4}$$

Unfortunately, the binary step function suffers from two primary limitations limiting its applicability. First, it can generate only two-value outputs, hence unable to be applied for multi-class classification problems. Second, it has a zero-gradient leading to a hindrance in the backpropagation procedure.

2.4.1.2 Linear Activation Function

An activation function, known as the identity function, is a linear activation function in which the activation is directly proportionate to the input. It can be formulated as follows:

$$f(x) = ax + c \qquad (5)$$

where a and c represent a coefficient and constant. An identity activation suffers from two main challenges. Firstly, backpropagation is not an option because the function's derivative is a constant with no connection to the input x. Secondly, if a linear activation function is applied, all levels of the FNN will collapse into one. The last layer of a neural network will always be a linear function of the first layer, regardless of the number of levels. In essence, identity activation reduces the FNN to a single layer.

2.4.1.3 Nonlinear Activation Functions

There is nothing special about the linear activation function provided here. It is not possible for the model due to its lack of processing capability to construct and learn more sophisticated input–output mappings. Nonlinear activation comes into sight to provide a solution to these issues by introducing nonlinearity into the layers of deep networks. A primary motive for nonlinear activation functions is the need to keep the output value of the neuron constrained to a particular limit. This is an important criterion because if the estimated weighted sum is not confined to a certain limit, it might become larger in value, specifically in the case of DNNs with millions of parameters. This typically results in increased computational complexity. Additionally, nonlinear activations are calculated numerous times according to the depth of DNNs. Hence, they must be computationally efficient to compute. Moreover, the output of the nonlinear activation should be symmetrical at zero to evade the gradient's shift to a certain direction. As previously stated, gradient descent algorithms are used to train ANNs. Hence, the network's layers must be differentiable or at least partially differentiable. All these characteristics must be satisfied in a function to be able to be used as a nonlinear activation function.

- Rectified linear unit (ReLU) activation function

ReLU is a popular activation that shows wide acceptance in DL. As well as being simple to compute, it avoids the vanishing gradient dilemma and does not saturate.

$$\mathrm{ReLU}(a) = \max(x, 0) \tag{6}$$

There is only one drawback with it: it is not zero-centered. It suffers from the "dying ReLU" issue in which all negative inputs are mapped to a zero output. Hence, this formula has no effect. In certain cases, it leads nodes to fully die and not learn anything at all. ReLU also has the issue of explosive activations due to its infinity-high upper limit. As a result, there are instances when nodes are rendered useless.

- Parametric ReLU (PReLU) activation function

PReLU was introduced as an extension to the ReLU function by adding a linear variable α to the definition of ReLU, such that when the input is less than zero, some information gets through:

$$\mathrm{PReLU}(x) = \max(\alpha x, x) \tag{7}$$

where α represents the slope of the negative part of ReLU in which the most appropriate value of α is learnt through backpropagation.

- LeakyReLU activation function

A variant of PReLU activation that sets the value of α to be 0.1.

$$\mathrm{LeakyReLU}(x) = \max(0.1x, x) \tag{8}$$

Both LeakyReLU and PReLU enable backpropagation even for the nonpositive value of the input.

- Exponential linear unit (ELU) activation function

A variation of ReLU that adjusts the slope of the negative portion of the function to be defined using a log curve with the main aim to evade the dead ReLU problem.

$$\mathrm{ELU}(x) = \begin{cases} x & \text{if } x \geq 0 \\ \alpha * (\exp(x) - 1), & \text{if } x \leq 0 \end{cases} \tag{9}$$

Unfortunately, the exponential operation can increase the computational time of the network.

- RELU6

Another variant of ReLU that constrains the positive part of the function can be defined as:

$$\text{RELU6}(a) = \min\left(\max\left(0,\ a\right),6\right) \tag{10}$$

- Sigmoid activation function

The sigmoid function converts its input value x into another value in range $[0, 1]$. As a result, the sigmoid is frequently referred to as a squashing function as it squashes any input in the range $(-\infty, \infty)$ to a certain value in the range $(0, 1)$

$$\text{Sigmoid}(x) = \frac{1}{1 + \exp\left(-x\right)} \tag{11}$$

- Hyperbolic tangent (Tanh) activation function

If a neuron is looking for an efficient way to squash input x into a value in range $[-1, 1]$, you will want to use the Tanh function. When compared to the sigmoid, it just addresses the issue of zero-centeredness.

$$\text{Tanh}(x) = \frac{1 - \exp\left(-2x\right)}{1 + \exp\left(-2x\right)} \tag{12}$$

- SoftMax activation function

A nonlinear activation function that is defined as a mixture of many sigmoid functions. It computes the relative probability of each output class in range $[0, 1]$.

$$\text{Softmax}(x) = \frac{\exp\left(x_i\right)}{\sum_i \exp\left(x_i\right)} \tag{13}$$

- Swish activation function

A self-gated nonlinear activation function, developed by Google's research team, that is an extension of the sigmoid function and can be defined as follows:

$$Swish = x * sigmoid(x) \tag{14}$$

In contrast to ReLU, Swish activation does not suddenly alter the direction close to $x = 0$ in the same way as ReLU does. As a result, the curve gradually shifts from 0 to values below 0 and then back up again. In the ReLU activation function, small negative values were canceled out. Those negative values, on the other hand, may still be useful for identifying patterns in the data. This is a win-win scenario as large negative values are wiped out due to their scarcity. The nonrepetitive nature of the swish function facilitates the expressiveness of input data and the weight to be learned.

- Gaussian error linear unit (GELU) activation function

A nonlinear function proposed for transformer networks, such as BERT, ROBERTa, ALBERT, etc., it is driven by merging estates from dropout, zoneout, and ReLU.

$$GELU(x) = xP(X < x) = x\phi(x)$$

$$= 0.5\left(1 + \tanh\left[\sqrt{\frac{2}{\pi}}(x + 0.044715x^3)\right]\right) \tag{15}$$

- Scaled exponential linear unit (SELU)

SELU was proposed for self-normalizing DNNs wherein each layer maintains the mean and variance from the preceding layers. Then it uses these statistics to perform internal normalization by updating the output to have a mean of zero and a standard deviation of one. To shift the mean, SELU can map the input to either positive or negative values, which is not viable for the ReLU function.

$$SELU(x) = \left\{\lambda \left\{ \begin{array}{l} \propto (\exp(x) - 1) \\ x \end{array} \right. \right. \tag{16}$$

where $\propto = 1.6732632423543772848170429916717$, and $\lambda = 1.0507009873554804934193349852946$. The normalization incurred by this function is different from external normalization performed with normalization layers.

More variants of nonlinear activation functions have been proposed to introduce nonlinearity in neural networks in different manners. The readers can refer to the further reading section to understand and know more about other activation functions [4].

2.5 The Learning Process of ANN

This section gives a detailed explanation of how ANNs learn from the input data. Typically, the input data is processed by the neurons in each layer in both forward directions from the input to the output layer. This process is called forward propagation. Then the output information is reprocessed back in the opposite direction, which is known as *backward propagation or, for convenience, backpropagation*. When it comes to the learning of ANN, one can usually discover that the majority of calculations in forward and backward propagations follow the linear algebra theories. So, to communicate some perception for both kinds of propagation and their implementations, this section discusses some fundamental linear algebra and computational graphs. To begin with, the discussion will take a two-layer ANN, with a simple example for explaining how ANNs are being learnt. As shown in Figure 2.3, the input layer is not counted when computing the number of layers in ANNs. Only the number of hidden layers as well as the number of output layers are encountered.

Given an MLP, where the number of received inputs in the input layer, x, is $n1$, the number of neurons in the hidden layer, h, is $n2 = 2$, and the output layer, Y, consisting of just one neuron. For each layer, the number of neurons as well as the corresponding activation function should be determined. Once the architecture of ANN is built successfully, the weight matrix W and bias vector b must be initialized before we can proceed. It is impossible to tell which input is more significant in order to weigh them and calculate the output in the real world. However, since it is often unknown which input is more significant than others, random values will be generated as initial weights and biases.

2.5.1 Forward Propagation

Given that each layer consists of multiple neurons, where each neuron has its own initial weight and bias value, dealing with values individually can be difficult. Thus, the weights and biases of each layer are represented using matrices to facilitate the calculation and updates. In our case, the weight and bias matrix are denoted as W_{xh} and b_h. Following the fundamental matrix multiplication regime. For multiplying matrix A with matrix B, the number of columns in A must be the same as the number of rows in B. So, the dimension of the weight matrix, W_{xh}, should be $n1 \times n2$. By weighing the input X with weight W_{xh}, the input to hidden layer h can be formulated as:

$$z_1 = XW_{xh} + b_h \tag{17}$$

The obtained vector is followingly passed to some activation function to determine the nodes to be activated. A sigmoid activation function σ is used in this example:

$$a_1 = \sigma(z_1) \tag{18}$$

By activating the nodes of the hidden layer, we need to reweight the elements of a_1 using the weight matrix of the hidden layer, and then add the bias value. The weight matrix and bias matrix between the hidden layer and the output layer could be denoted as W_{hy} and b_y, respectively. The dimension of the weight matrix, W_{hy}, will be $n2 \times n3$. So, a_1 is multiplied by W_{hy}, and the result is summed to the bias b_y to generate z_2, to the next layer, which is the output layer:

$$z_2 = a_1 W_{hy} + b_y \tag{19}$$

Again, in the output layer, the combination element in z_2 is activated using a sigmoid function to generate the network's output:

$$\hat{y} = \sigma(z_2) \tag{20}$$

Forward propagation is sometimes referred to as a forward pass and it represents the entire process of calculating and storing the intermediate parameters of each layer starting from the input layer and ending at the output layer. The final output of this propagation of inputs across the network layers is to learn to predict the output value as possible. A function of activation is applied to the resulting values after they have been multiplied by the weights assigned to each layer. To sum up, the overall steps involved in forward propagation in our ANN can be articulated as follows:

$$
\begin{aligned}
z_1 &= XW_{xh} + b_h \\
a_1 &= \sigma(z_1) \\
z_2 &= a_1 W_{hy} + b_y \\
\hat{y} &= \sigma(z_2)
\end{aligned}
\tag{21}
$$

As discussed, forward propagation seems to be straightforward. However, the output generated from forward propagation still needs to be validated as correct. To do so, a loss or cost function $L(\cdot)$ is defined at the end of the ANN to compare the generated output from ANN with the actual which provides an indicator about how well the ANN is performing. The literature is full of a variety of loss functions that vary according to the underlying task. A detailed discussion about loss functions will be discussed in later chapters. For convenience, let us consider the mean squared error (MSE) as a loss function in our ANN, which is simply characterized as the average of the squared difference between the output of ANN and actual output:

$$
L = \text{MSE} = \frac{1}{n} \sum_{i=1}^{n} (y_i - \hat{y}_i)^2
\tag{22}
$$

where n represents the number of training examples, y and $\hat{y}$ represented the actual output and the predicted output, respectively by ANN. So, this loss function can be used after forward propagation step to inform us how the ANN is able to predict the output. Till this point, if the actual learning of ANN is still not clear as the network just tried to calculate or predict the targeted output, then its prediction is passed by $L(\cdot)$.

2.5.2 Backpropagation (Gradient Descent)

Before explaining the backpropagation in depth, it is worth noting that when the estimated loss is extremely high, it implies that the ANN is not calculating the right output. This way, the main objective of ANN is to minimize the loss function with the aim of making the predictions of ANNs better and closer if not identical to the actual one. A question arises here that how could the loss function be minimized in ANN? Since the ANN learned to estimate the output in forward propagation, hence, it is possible to make some changes in the forward propagation to allow the ANN to minimize the loss value. In this regard, the randomly initialized weights and biases are the main values to be updated to achieve this purpose as they chiefly contribute to the calculation of output during the forward propagation. Now, the weight matrices (W_{xh} and W_{hy}) are updated in such a way that the ANN generates or predicts an output that is closer to the correct output. Typically, the process of updating weight matrices is usually performed using a gradient descent algorithm, which enables ANN to learn the ideal values of the weight and bias matrices initialized at random. When the optimum weights and biases are reached, the ANN can calculate the exact output and reduce the loss value.

We will now look into how the ideal values of weights are discovered through the use of gradient descent. Gradient descent is one of the most extensively applied optimization methods. Yet it is also one of the most complex. It is employed in the reduction of the cost function, which enables us to reduce the error and acquire the least potential error value by reducing the objective functions.

To understand the main idea behind gradient descent optimization, consider the following scenario: you are on top of a hill, as depicted in Figure 2.4, and we wish to get to the lowest place on the hill. There may be several places on the hill that appear to be the lowest positions, but we must move to the lowest position, which is lower than all low positions. In other words, you should not be trapped in a position that incorrectly seems like the lowest position.

Similarly, the loss function of ANN can be represented as a plot of loss value against weights. The main aim of ANN is to reduce the loss value, which corresponds to searching the global minimum at which the loss is the lowest.

The randomly initialized weights are represented by the solid green point in Figure 2.5. It is notable that the minimum loss can be reached when the solid point is shifted downward.

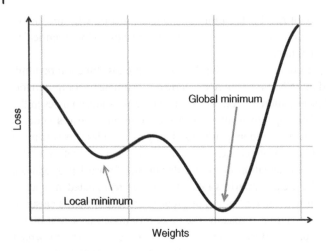

Figure 2.4 Illustration of the gradient descent.

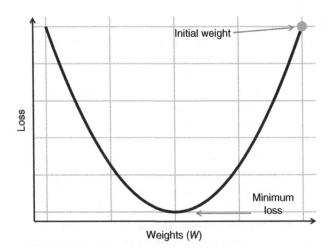

Figure 2.5 Illustration of weight initialization process.

Mathematically, the process of moving the green point (initial weight) toward the lowest point can be achieved by calculating a gradient of the loss function with respect to that point, namely $\frac{\partial L}{\partial W}$. In particular, the gradient information denotes the derivatives

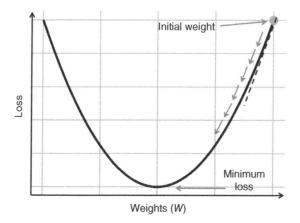

Figure 2.6 Illustration of gradient calculation as the derivative of loss function.

of the loss function that are essentially the slope of a tangent line as shown in Figure 2.6. Consequently, as the gradient is computed, the point goes downhill till it reaches the point of the global minimum. Gradient descent is a first-order optimization approach, which implies that it calculates the first derivative of the loss function when conducting the updates. Thus, with gradient descent, we move our weights to a position where the cost is minimum.

By the completion of forward propagation, the network stops at the output layer. Flowingly, ANN starts backpropagating the network from the output layer to the input layer by calculating the derivative of the loss function with respect to all the weights between the output and the input layer so as to reduce the loss. Following the calculation of the gradients, the network updates the old weights according to the weight update law:

$$W = W - \alpha \frac{\partial L}{\partial W} \tag{23}$$

where W represents the overall *Weights* of the network, while α represent the learning rate.

As illustrated in Figure 2.7, a small step downhill can be achieved by using a small learning rate, which typically implies slow

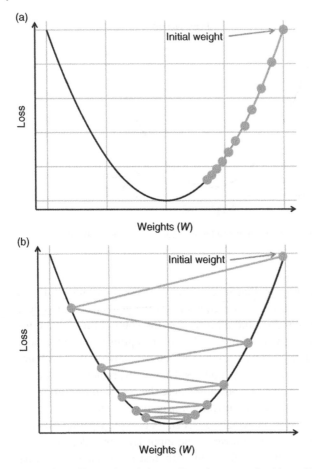

Figure 2.7 Illustration of the gradient descent under (a) small learning rate and (b) large learning rate.

gradient descent. On the other hand, fast gradient descent can be caused by a large movement step, which can be achieved using large learning rates and our gradient descent will be fast, but we might fail to reach the global minimum and become stuck at a local minimum. So, the learning rate should be chosen optimally:

This whole process of backpropagating the network from the output layer to the input layer and updating the weights of the network using gradient descent to minimize the loss is called backpropagation. Now that we have a basic understanding of backpropagation, we will strengthen our understanding by learning about this in detail, step-by-step. We are going to look at some interesting math, so put on your calculus hats and follow the steps.

Backpropagation is the term used to describe the entire process of backpropagating a network from the output layer to the input layer and upgrading the weights of the network using gradient descent to reduce the loss. Assuming that we have a fundamental grasp of backpropagation, let us further improve our comprehension by further exploring it in more detail, by discussing the corresponding mathematical calculations [5].

Given the before-mentioned weight matrices W_{xh} and W_{hy}, the ANN seeks to find the optimum values for these two matrices that can lead to the lowest possible loss. Hence, it calculates the derivative of the loss function L with respect to each of these weights.

As the network propagates in the backward direction, the derivative should be firstly calculated for loss function L with respect to W_{hy}. However, this is not possible as the loss function (Eq. (22)) does not contain the term W_{hy}. Hence, rather than direct calculation of the derivative, ANN calculates the partial derivative.

First, the partial derivative is firstly computed with respect to $\hat{y}$, and then the partial derivative is calculated for from $\hat{y}$ with respect to z_2. Followingly the partial derivative is calculated for z_2 with respect to derivative W_{hy}. Its steps are essentially known as the chain rule. So, the derivative of L with respect to W_{hy} becomes as follows:

$$\frac{\partial L}{\partial W_{hy}} = \frac{\partial L}{\partial \hat{y}} \cdot \frac{\partial \hat{y}}{\partial z_2} \cdot \frac{\partial z_2}{\partial W_{hy}} \tag{24}$$

while the derivative of L with respect to b_y becomes as follows:

$$\frac{\partial L}{\partial b_y} = \frac{\partial L}{\partial \hat{y}} \cdot \frac{\partial \hat{y}}{\partial z_2} \cdot \frac{\partial z_2}{\partial b_y} \tag{25}$$

Now, we will compute each of the terms in the preceding equations:

$$\frac{\partial L}{\partial \hat{y}} = (y - \hat{y}) \tag{26}$$

$$\frac{\partial \hat{y}}{\partial z_2} = \sigma'(z_2) \tag{27}$$

where σ' denotes the derivative of the sigmoid activation function and is calculated as

$$\sigma'(z) = \frac{e^{-z}}{(1 + e^{-z})^2} \tag{28}$$

$$\frac{\partial z_2}{\partial W_{hy}} = a_1 \tag{29}$$

$$\frac{\partial z_2}{\partial b_y} = 1 \tag{30}$$

Thus, substituting all the preceding terms in Eqs. (24) and (25), we can write:

$$\frac{\partial L}{\partial W_{hy}} = (y - \hat{y})\sigma'(z_2) \cdot a_1 \tag{31}$$

$$\frac{\partial L}{\partial b_y} = (y - \hat{y})\sigma'(z_2) \tag{32}$$

Next, the derivative of L needs to be calculated with respect to our next weight, W_{xh}. This cannot be directly calculated as the term W_{xh} is not contained in loss function L. So, the chain rule can be used. By recalling the forward propagation steps, the derivative of L with respect to W_{xh} is given as:

$$\frac{\partial L}{\partial W_{xh}} = \frac{\partial L}{\partial \hat{y}} \cdot \frac{\partial \hat{y}}{\partial z_2} \cdot \frac{\partial z_2}{\partial a_1} \cdot \frac{\partial a_1}{\partial z_1} \cdot \frac{\partial z_1}{\partial W_{xh}} \tag{33}$$

while the derivative of L with respect to W_{xh} is given as:

$$\frac{\partial L}{\partial W_{xh}} = \frac{\partial L}{\partial \hat{y}} \cdot \frac{\partial \hat{y}}{\partial z_2} \cdot \frac{\partial z_2}{\partial a_1} \cdot \frac{\partial a_1}{\partial z_1} \cdot \frac{\partial z_1}{\partial b_h} \tag{34}$$

The first two terms are previously computed in Eqs. (26) and (27), while the latter three terms are calculated as follows:

$$\frac{\partial z_2}{\partial a_1} = W_{hy} \tag{35}$$

$$\frac{\partial a_1}{\partial z_1} = \sigma'(z_1) \tag{36}$$

$$\frac{\vartheta z_1}{\vartheta W_{xh}} = X \tag{37}$$

$$\frac{\vartheta z_1}{\vartheta b_h} = 1 \tag{38}$$

Thus, substituting all the preceding terms in Eqs. (33) and (34), we can calculate the gradients as follows:

$$\frac{\vartheta L}{\vartheta W_{xh}} = (y - \hat{y}) \cdot \sigma'(z_2) \cdot W_{hy} \cdot \sigma'(z_1) \cdot X \tag{39}$$

$$\frac{\vartheta L}{\vartheta b_h} = (y - \hat{y}) \cdot \sigma'(z_2) \cdot W_{hy} \cdot \sigma'(z_1) \tag{40}$$

Once the gradients are calculated for W_{hy} and, W_{xh}, the ANN updates its weight matrices for each layer as follows:

$$W_{hy} = W_{hy} - \alpha \frac{\vartheta L}{\vartheta W_{hy}} \tag{41}$$

$$W_{xh} = W_{xh} - \alpha \frac{\vartheta L}{\vartheta W_{xh}} \tag{42}$$

2.6 Loss Functions

The loss function is indispensable for learning DNN that takes over the responsibility of defining "how good" the model is at making predictions for a given set of parameters. The loss function has its own curve and its own gradients, where the slope of this curve defines how to update network parameters to make the model more precise. Thus, deciding on the right loss function determines how well your model will be [6].

2.6.1 Regression Loss Functions

An important aspect of regression is the ability to forecast the value of a continuous variable. Regression networks can be used to forecast the device failure or rate of cyberattacks in the IoT system as the goal is to develop a model that predicts a true value.

2.6.1.1 Mean Absolute Error (MAE) Loss

MAE, sometimes known as $L1$ loss, is a common robust loss function showing wide adoption in different regression networks. In regression tasks, there exist some variables that are not rigorously Gaussian in nature because of the occurrence of outliers (data points that strictly differ from the data they belong to) in data. MAE can be a perfect choice in such circumstances for the reason that it does not take into consideration the outliers' direction whether it was highly positive or highly negative values. To calculate MAE, the absolute differences between the forecasted data points $\widetilde{Y}$ and actual data points Y are averaged. Given N as the number of data points, the calculation of MAE loss is defined as follows:

$$\text{MAE} = \frac{1}{N} \sum_{i=1}^{N} |\widetilde{Y}_i - Y_i| \tag{43}$$

2.6.1.2 Mean Squared Error (MSE) Loss

MSE, also referred to as $L2$ loss, is a popular preference for the AI community when it comes to loss functions for regression networks. This can be attributed to the fact that the majority of variables can be modeled into a Gaussian distribution. MSE is calculated as the average of the squared differences between the forecasted data points $\widetilde{Y}$ and actual data points Y, where N represents the total number of data points in the dataset.

$$\text{MSE} = \frac{1}{N} \sum_{i=1}^{N} \left(\widetilde{Y}_i - Y_i \right)^2 \tag{44}$$

2.6.1.3 Huber Loss

A contrast between $L1$ and $L2$ found the following findings. First, the $L1$ loss is more robust than $L2$. A closer examination of the formulas reveals that when the discrepancy between the expected and actual values is large, $L2$ loss increases the impact when contrasted to $L1$. $L1$ is the more robust loss function since $L2$ is susceptible to outliers. Second, the $L1$ loss is less stable than the $L2$ loss. Because $L1$ loss handles with distance differences, a little horizontal variation could cause the regression line to jump a long way. A considerable difference in the slope between iterations would result from such an impact occurring over numerous iterations. Then again, MSE guarantees the regression line turns delicately for a small adjustment in the data point. Huber loss integrates the robustness of $L1$ with the stability of $L2$, fundamentally the most excellent of $L1$ and $L2$ losses. For large errors, it is linear and for small errors and it is quadratic in nature. Huber loss is characterized by the hyper-parameter delta (δ). For each data point Y_i, the prediction $\widetilde{Y}_i$, the Huber loss is expressed as:

$$
L_\delta = \begin{cases} \dfrac{1}{2}\left(\widetilde{Y}_i - Y_i\right)^2, & \text{if } \left|\widetilde{Y}_i - Y_i\right| \leq \delta \\[2mm] \delta\left|\widetilde{Y}_i - Y_i\right| - \dfrac{1}{2}\delta^2, & \text{otherwise} \end{cases} \tag{45}
$$

where the hyper-parameter δ controls the degree to which the error can be made quadratic.

2.6.1.4 Mean Bias Error (MBE) Loss

MBE is a measure of the average bias in the DNNs, where a positive bias implies that the DNN overestimated the error and a negative bias implies that the error is underestimated. MBE is computed as the tangible difference between the forecasted value and the real value. One must be careful as the negative and positive error values can cancel each other out, which makes it one of the least loss functions.

$$
\text{MBE} = \frac{1}{N}\sum_{i=1}^{N}\widetilde{Y}_i - Y_i \tag{46}
$$

2.6.1.5 Mean Squared Logarithmic Error (MSLE)

In some cases, it might not be necessary to punish the model too much for forecasting unscaled data points right away. Soothing the penalty on massive changes could be achieved by MSLE. The calculation of MSLE is similar to those of MSE, but it is computed as the mean of the squared differences between the natural logarithm of forecasted data points $\widetilde{Y}$ and the natural logarithm actual data points Y:

$$\text{MSLE} = \frac{1}{N}\sum_{i=1}^{N} \log\left(\widetilde{Y}_i\right) - \log\left(Y_i\right) \tag{47}$$

where N represents the total number of data points in the dataset.

2.6.2 Classification Loss Functions

Classification of data, using DNNs, denotes the problem of determining the class to which a given input belongs. As the name implies, binary classification implies that data contain only two classes; on the other hand, classifying data containing three or more classes are referred to as multi-class classification.

2.6.2.1 Binary Cross Entropy (BCE) Loss

BCE, sometimes called log loss, is the most popular loss function applied for binary classification tasks. The term "entropy," apparently out of place, has a statistical interpretation. When it comes to information processing, entropy is a measure of the amount of unpredictability, while cross entropy is the difference in the amount of unpredictability between two random variables. When the difference between the forecasted data points $\widetilde{Y}$ and the natural logarithm actual data point Y increases, the cross-entropy loss increases. In the best scenario, an "ideal" model would have a log loss of zero. To make things clearer, the BCE can be computed as follows:

$$\text{BCE} = -\sum_{i=1}^{N} Y_i \cdot \log\left(\widetilde{Y}_i\right) - (1-Y_i) \cdot \log\left(\left(1-\widetilde{Y}_i\right)\right)$$

$$\tag{48}$$

2.6.2.2 Categorical Cross Entropy (CCE) Loss

CCE loss is basically the same as BCE loss, except that it is applied to multi-class classification problems. It is necessary for the labels to be one-hot encoded when the CCE loss function is applied. The output layer should be designed with n nodes, one for each class, where "SoftMax" activation is applied to calculate the probability for each node.

2.6.2.3 Hinge Loss

Hinge loss is principally proposed for a support vector machine (SVM) for computing the highest margin between the separation hyperplane and the data classes. Hinge loss set the binary values of Y_i to be -1 and 1, instead of using 0 and 1 as with BCE loss. Hinge loss not only punishes the incorrect predictions but also the correct ones that are unconfident. Hinge loss can be calculated as follows:

$$\text{Hinge loss} = \sum_{i=1}^{N} \text{Max}\left(0, 1 - Y_i * \tilde{Y}_i\right) \tag{49}$$

Hinge loss is also extended to the squared version as well as the categorical version.

2.6.2.4 Kullback–Leibler Divergence (KL) Loss

KL loss is a measure of how the distribution of the output of model $P(x)$ differs from a standard distribution $Q(x)$. If KL loss is zero, then the probability distributions are the same. In fact, the KL loss behaves as cross-entropy. It computes the amount of information lost when the forecasted probability distribution is applied to approximate the actual probability distribution. The number of information missed in the projected distribution is computed as

$$\text{KL}(P(x), Q(x)) = \begin{cases} -\sum_{x} P(x) \cdot \log \dfrac{P(x)}{Q(x)} & \text{discrete dist.} \\[2ex] -\displaystyle\int P(x) \cdot \log \dfrac{P(x)}{Q(x)} & \text{continuous dist.} \end{cases}$$

$$\tag{50}$$

2.7 Supplementary Materials

https://github.com/DEEPOLOGY-AI/DL-Book-Wiley-2022/tree/main/Ch2

References

1 Goodfellow, I., Bengio, Y. and Courville, A. (2016). *Deep Learning.* MIT Press.

2 Aggarwal, C.C. (2015). *Neural Networks and Deep Learning*, vol. 25. San Francisco: Determination Press.

3 Singh, P. and Manure, A. (2020). *Learn TensorFlow 2.0*, 1–24. Berkeley, CA: Apress.

4 Apicella, A., Donnarumma, F., Isgrò, F., and Prevete, R. (2021). A survey on modern trainable activation functions. *Neural Netw.* https://doi.org/10.1016/j.neunet.2021.01.026.

5 Lillicrap, T.P., Santoro, A., Marris, L. et al. (2020). Backpropagation and the brain. *Nat. Rev. Neurosci.* https://doi.org/10.1038/s41583-020-0277-3.

6 Wang, Q., Ma, Y., Zhao, K., and Tian, Y. (2022). A comprehensive survey of loss functions in machine learning. *Ann. Data Sci.* https://doi.org/10.1007/s40745-020-00253-5.

3

Training Deep Neural Networks

3.1 Introduction

In the previous chapter, the backpropagation method of training neural networks is briefly described. There are various ways this chapter will elaborate on the previous chapter's description. The backpropagation algorithm and its implementation are described in greater detail. In order to avoid having readers constantly look back to Chapter 2, this chapter extends our previous discussions to further explain how deep neural networks (DNNs) are trained. First, gradient descent is revisited by exploring different variants including the difference between them, and their advantages and disadvantages. Then, we take a look at the gradient-vanishing and the gradient-exploding problems, which are the major challenges facing the successful training of any deep networks. After that, we investigate the main methods (such as gradient clipping, nonlinear activations, etc.) to be adopted in order to avoid the above problems during the training.

Moreover, parameter initialization is considered essential to start the training of any deep network. Different methods have been proposed in this regard, each following a distinct way for the initialization of network parameters. This chapter provides a deep dive into the state-of-the-art parameter initialization methods.

To better train deep networks, some in-depth knowledge about advanced optimization algorithms is of great importance. On one

Deep Learning Approaches for Security Threats in IoT Environments,
First Edition. Mohamed Abdel-Basset, Nour Moustafa, and Hossam Hawash.
© 2023 The Institute of Electrical and Electronics Engineers, Inc.
Published 2023 by John Wiley & Sons, Inc.

side, the task of training a complicated deep network could require much time ranging from some to some weeks. The choice of an optimization algorithm is crucial for the efficiency of the training. This way interpreting the tenets of various optimization algorithms along with their hyperparameters is essential to fine-tune the hyperparameters in a directed way to enhance the performance of the deep network. In this chapter, we investigate the state-of-the-art optimization algorithms for deep networks along with the distinct characteristics of each of them.

Furthermore, when it comes to training high-capacity deep networks, the curses of overfitting and underfitting come into sight. Therefore, this chapter offers you a rigorous introduction to the concepts of overfitting and underfitting that one may encounter during the training of deep networks, with the main aim to provide an in-depth understanding of these concepts and their related practices.

3.2 Gradient Descent Revisited

3.2.1 Gradient Descent

Gradient descent is simple and general optimization algorithm that is able to search and find ideal solutions for a broad range of tasks. The primary concept behind gradient descent is to adjust network parameters in an iterative manner seeking to minimize the value of the loss function. Imagine someone is lost in the mountains in a dark cloud such that he/she can just feel the slope of the ground under his/her feet. A great approach to rapidly moving to the bottom of the valley lies in going downhill toward the sharpest slope. Gradient descent follows a similar ideology when it works. In particular, it estimates the local gradient of the network's loss function with respect to the weight W, and it steps toward descending gradient. As soon as the gradient becomes zero, the optimizer reached a global minimum, which means that the algorithm *converges* to a minimum.

An essential hyperparameter of the gradient descent is the step size in which it moves, which is called the learning rate. A too small learning rate implies that the algorithm has to go through lots of steps to reach a convergence state, thereby consuming a long time.

In contrast, the high value of the learning rate implies that one may jump beyond the valley and wind up on the other side, perhaps even upper than the previous location. This, in turn, could lead the algorithm to diverge. If it encounters higher and higher values, then it becomes unable to reach a good solution.

Lastly, loss functions are not always seemed good in smooth bowls. The main challenge facing the gradient descent is the possibility to stuck in a *local minimum*, while the other one is the very long time required to reach the global minimum.

Disadvantages

- The more stable error gradient might lead to premature convergence of the parameters of the deep network to a less optimum set of parameters.
- The updates at the end of the training epoch necessitate the additional complexity of accumulating prediction errors across all training examples.
- Generally, the implementation of batch gradient descent (BGD) necessitates the entire training data to reside in memory and be available to the algorithm.
- The updates of parameters of the deep network, and accordingly the training speed, might come to be very slow for big datasets.

3.2.2 Stochastic Gradient Descent

The key challenge in meeting BGD lies in the usage of the entire training set to calculate the gradients in each iteration, which leads to extremely slow training, especially in case of larger size data. In contrast, stochastic gradient descent (SGD) was proposed to simply select an arbitrary sample from the training data in each step and calculate the gradients according to this sample only. Apparently, this greatly accelerates the algorithm as it manipulates small data per iteration. This way training on big training sets becomes an easy task because only a single sample saves memory during the training.

On the other side, thanks to the stochastic nature of the SGD algorithm, it is less consistent than BGD. Rather than slightly decreasing till it converges, the loss function here jumps up and down, shrinking just on average. Doing so, it ends up closer to the global minima, but when it reaches there, it goes on to jump around, and never remains down. Thus, as soon as the algorithm converges, the final network parameters become good, but not ideal. The highly irregular loss function could essentially enable the algorithm to not be stuck at local minima, which makes SGD a superior opportunity of reaching the global minima than BGD. Therefore, arbitrariness is excellent to get away from local minima, but bad as it implies that the algorithm could never remain at the minima. As a remedy to this problem, the learning rate could be progressively reduced, that is the algorithm starts with a big step size, to enable achieving rapid progress and escaping local minima, later getting lesser and lesser, to enable the algorithm to stay at the global minima. This operation is sometimes known as *simulated annealing*, as it seems like the procedure of annealing in metallurgy where molten metal is gradually cooled down. The *learning schedule* is responsible for determining the value of the learning rate per iteration. Rapid reduction in learning rate might lead the algorithm to converge to local minima, or just freeze midway to the global one. In contrast, a slow reduction of the learning rate might lead the algorithm to jump around the minima for a long-time and turn out with a suboptimal solution especially when the training is stopped extremely early.

Advantages

- Simple to understand and implement, specifically for beginners.
- The regular updates instantly give an insight into the performance of the deep network and the ratio of improvement.
- The increased frequency of updates of parameters of a deep network can lead to faster learning on some problems.
- The noisy update process enables the deep network to evade local minima.

Disadvantages

- Updating the parameters of the deep network so repeatedly is more computationally expensive than other variants of gradient descent, requiring a considerably long time to train the deep network on big datasets.
- The repeated updates could lead to a noisy gradient signal, which might lead the parameters of a deep network and, in turn, the loss function to exhibit a higher variance through training.

- The noisy learning process down the error gradient could also make it difficult for the algorithm to stay on a global minimum for the parameters of the deep network.

3.2.3 Mini-batch Gradient Descent

Mini-batch gradient descent (MGD) is another variant of the gradient descent algorithm that divides the training set into small batches that are employed to compute loss and update model parameters. It is fairly simple to comprehend once the reader knows about BGD and SGD. Unlike earlier discussed algorithms, MGD calculates the gradients using a minor set of randomly selected samples known as mini-batches rather than calculating them according to the entire training data or single training sample in each iteration. Compared to SGD, the MGD enables performance increase from hardware optimization of matrix calculations, specifically graphical processing units are used. The movement of the algorithm across parameter space is less inconsistent than SGD, particularly in the case of huge mini-batches. So, MGD will turn out moving around a little nearer to the global minima than SGD. However, conversely, it might be more difficult for it to get away from local minima.

Advantages

- The frequency of updates of parameters of the deep network is higher than batch gradient descent which allows for a more robust convergence, avoiding local minima.
- The batched updates make it more computationally effective than SGD.
- The batching enables the efficiency of implementing the algorithm and saving a lot of memory space.

Disadvantages

- Mini-batch requires the configuration of an additional "mini-batch size" hyperparameter for the learning algorithm.
- Loss information has to be collected across mini-batches of training samples.

3.3 Gradient Vanishing and Explosion

As explained in the previous chapter, the backpropagation algorithm functions by iterating the network layers from the output layer back to the input layer, transmitting the gradient of the loss function in a single direction. Once the algorithm has computed the gradient of the loss function with respect to each neuron in the network, the calculated gradients are used to update overall network parameters via gradient descent.

Unfortunately, the value of gradients habitually becomes smaller and smaller as the gradient descent algorithm progresses to propagate to the deeper layers. Consequently, the update of parameters at the earlier layer connection is almost practically unchanged, thereby making the training of the network no way to converge to a global optimum. This problem is commonly known as *vanishing gradients*. This usually takes place as a result of squeezing a huge input space into a small one (between zero and one) as with the sigmoid activation function. There will be no noticeable difference in output from making large changes to the sigmoid function's input value. As a result, the derivative shrinks in size.

This problem seems not so bad in the case of a shallow network with just a small number of layers that use these activations. However, training may not work properly if an additional number of layers are used, as the gradients will become too small. To put it another way, backpropagation is the process of retracing the steps of a network from its end layer back to its early layers (close to the input layer). For the early layers, the derivatives are computed by multiplying the derivatives of each subsequent layer according to the chain rule, which works its way backward from the final layer to the early layer. In this way, having multiple sigmoid activations N means multiplying together N small derivatives leading the gradient to diminishes rapidly until it disappears entirely.

In some circumstances, the opposite of this behavior could take place such that the gradients turned to grow larger and larger. So, numerous layers get insanely big parameters' updates, leading the optimization algorithm to diverge. This problem is known as the *exploding gradients*. In extreme cases, weight values can overflow and lead to NaN values as a result of multiplying gradients across layers with values greater than 1.0 in an exponential fashion. The explosion is brought on by this process.

To sum up, the gradient vanishing and exploding problems are the major challenges faced in efficient training of deep networks. Thus, they need to be carefully taken into consideration in each step of developing and training your deep networks.

3.4 Gradient Clipping

Gradient clipping can be defined as a method employed to handle the scenario wherein the partial derivatives along various directions have remarkably distinct scales. The special case of gradient clipping follows a standard comparable to that used in adaptive learning rates by attempting to make the various elements of the partial derivatives more similar. Nevertheless, the clipping is performed just according to the existing values of the gradients instead of the historical ones.

In this regard, gradient clipping has two popular formats:

- Value-based clipping: A form of gradient clipping in which lower limit and upper limit thresholds are determined for the gradient magnitudes. In doing so, the overall partial derivatives whose magnitudes are smaller than the lower limit are reset to be equal to the lower limit itself. In a similar way, the overall partial derivatives whose magnitudes are higher than the upper limit are reset to be equal to upper limit itself.
- Norm-based clipping: A form of gradient clipping in which the L2 norm is applied to normalize the whole gradient vector. Notice that this form of clipping keeps the comparative magnitudes of the updates unchanged alongside various directions. Nevertheless, the impact of these two forms of clipping is almost similar for the family of DNNs that share parameters beyond various layers (such as the recurrent network). If the gradient values are clipped, the updates from one mini-batch to the next will be more or less the same. Because of this, an abnormal gradient

explosion in a single mini-batch would not have a significant impact on the solution.

When compared to other techniques, the impacts of gradient clipping are somewhat restricted. However, it is especially active in evading the exploding gradient. A derivative is calculated for each copy of a sharable parameter by having to treat it as an independent variable in recurrent networks (discussed in later chapter). The overall gradient's temporal components are represented by these derivatives, and their values are clipped before being added. The calculated derivatives are the temporal elements of the whole gradient, and the magnitudes are clipped prior to combining them to attain the whole gradient.

3.5 Parameter Initialization

The practice of initializing the parameters of a DNN is an indispensable and crucial step for improving the training performance and accelerating its convergence. With correct initialization of the learning parameters, the gradient descent can achieve the optimal value (global minima) of the objective loss function in the shortest possible value; otherwise, the convergence to the global minimum might not be possible. One of the vital points that should be borne in mind while developing any DNN is to correctly initialize your weight matrix for various connections between layers. To this end, multiple initialization methods have evolved over time, which can be deeply explored in this section.

3.5.1 Zero Initialization

It is common that bias parameters are initialized with zero. What would happen if weights were initialised with zero? Let us pretend that there is a sigmoid activation applied on the output layer to better comprehend this. In following training iterations, if all weights are initialized with zero, the derivative with respect to the loss function is the same for every weight parameter. Setting weights to zero makes the model act as a linear one because it makes hidden units symmetrical and continues for all training iterations. This is called a symmetry problem. It is also worth mentioning that the biases have no effect whatever when initialized with zero. Let us think about the two-layer neural network with ReLu activation at the hidden layers and sigmoid activation applied at the output layer. When we initialize this network with zeros, it will shape the classification in the form of circles as shown in Figure 3.1. Then, the two-layer network should be trained to separate the data elements from different classes.

3.5.2 Random Initialization

It is preferable to assign weights with random values than with a simple zero value. Two statistical distributions can be followed to perform this initialization, namely the standard normal distribution or the uniform distribution. By applying the random initialization to the herein-stated two-layer network, we could see the results are better than zero-initialization (Figure 3.2). However, a consideration to be taken into here is what occurs when weights are set too high or too low, and what constitutes an acceptable starting point for such weights. Concerning the gradient-vanishing

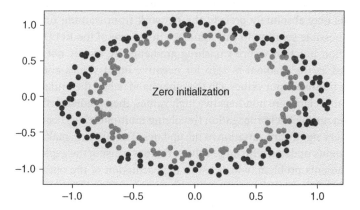

Figure 3.1 Illustration of zero-initialization of two-layer network.

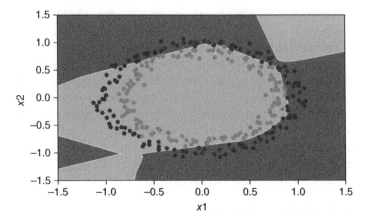

Figure 3.2   Illustration of random-initialization of two-layer network.

issue, if the initial random weight parameters are very small, then the value of activations (such as sigmoid and tanh) is significantly reduced in each layer and followingly the derivative of the loss function will become smaller and smaller as propagating backward through layers mainly in the case of deep networks. This way the weight parameters of early layers are updated slowly making the network get converged slowly, which mean slow optimization of the loss function. It could be viable in the worst case; this may absolutely prevent the network from training further. A possible solution to this issue lies in the use of the ReLU activation function where vanishing gradients are mostly not troubled as the gradient is zero for negative input values and one for positive input values. On the other hand, when the initial random weights are non-negative high values, then gradient calculation during backpropagation (involving multiplication) results in a very significant variation in the updates. This, in turn, makes the weights updated with large values, thereby causing the exploding gradients problem, which led to the oscillation of the optimizer around the global minima. Thus, the problem here is that the variance significantly varies in activation distributions of the deeper layer in the network.

3.5.3 Lecun Initialization

To address this issue, the deep network needs to retain the same variance in activation distributions as we move to the deeper layers. Thus, the Lecun initialization is introduced to normalize the variance of output of hidden units to share a constant variance. In particular, keeping the variance of outputs of each layer equal to the variance of its inputs is essential to improve the forward and backward flows of signals during training. To achieve that, Lecun initialization mathematically derived the constant variance of each neuron based on the number of input connections to a given unit called *fan-in*. Its calculation assumes that the input and weights of any neuron have zero mean. This constant variance is defined to be $\frac{1}{\text{fan-in}}$. The initial weight parameter is denoted as W_{init}, is drawn from a truncated normal distribution N with zero mean and standard deviation $= \sqrt{\left(\frac{1}{\text{fan-in}}\right)}$ such that

$$W_{\text{init}} \sim N\left(0, \sqrt{\left(\frac{1}{\text{fan-in}}\right)}\right) \tag{1}$$

3.5.4 Xavier Initialization

The Xavier initialization was proposed as an improvement of Lecun initialization and it seeks to retain the variance of output of layer in some bounds so that the network can take complete advantage of the activation functions. The idea is that the inputs of each activation function fall within the sweet range such that none of the neurons has to encounter a trapped situation. Xavier initialization introduced more complex rules for initialization considering the reality that the neurons in different layers work together to contribute to gradient calculations. Given fan-in and fan-out as the number of inputs and outputs of a particular neuron, the constant variance is derived to be variance $= \frac{2}{\text{fan-in} + \text{fan-out } n}$. Again, the calculation of variance assumes that the input and weights of any neuron have zero mean. The initial weight parameter is denoted as W_{init} can be randomly drawn from either of two statistical distributions. First, a truncated normal distribution N with zero mean and standard deviation $= \sqrt{\left(\dfrac{2}{\text{fan-in} + \text{fan-out}}\right)}$ such that

$$W_{\text{init}} \sim N\left(0, \sqrt{\left(\frac{2}{\text{fan-in} + \text{fan-out}}\right)}\right) \tag{2}$$

Second, a uniform distribution U with limit $= \sqrt{\left(\dfrac{6}{\text{fan-in} + \text{fan-out}}\right)}$ such that

$$W_{\text{init}} \sim U\left(\sqrt{\left(\frac{-6}{\text{fan-in} + \text{fan-out}}\right)}, \sqrt{\left(\frac{6}{\text{fan-in} + \text{fan-out}}\right)}\right) \tag{3}$$

Xavier initialization is sometimes called Glorot initialization [1].

3.5.5 Kaiming (He) Initialization

With the broad acceptance of ReLU, a new issue is encountered with these initialization strategies. Since ReLU is typically defined as $f(x) = \max(0, x)$, its function cannot have a zero mean. This, in turn, negates the assumption of Lecun and initialization. He initialization [2] was proposed as an initialization method for DNNs that consider the nonlinearity of activation functions, like ReLU activation and its variants. An appropriate initialization approach must evade lowering or enlarging the magnitudes of input signals with a large amount. Using a derivation, a condition found to stop this occurrence led to a variance $= \frac{2}{\text{fan-in}}$ in the case of normal distribution and variance $= \frac{6}{\text{fan-in}}$ in the case of uniform distribution. While W_{init} can be randomly drawn from uniform distribution as follows:

$$W_{\text{init}} \sim N\left(0, \sqrt{\left(\frac{2}{\text{fan-in}}\right)}\right) \tag{4}$$

While W_{init} can be randomly drawn from uniform distribution as follows:

$$W_{init} \sim U\left(\sqrt{\left(\frac{-6}{\text{fan-in}}\right)}, \sqrt{\left(\frac{6}{\text{fan-in}}\right)}\right) \qquad (5)$$

The mathematical derivation of variance in these initialization methods can be found in the supplementary material of this chapter.

3.6 Faster Optimizers

The practice of training very large DNNs is a disturbingly slow task. In this regard, a variety of design tricks are shown beneficial in accelerating the training such as proper parameter initialization, adequate activation functions, pretraining, and so on. One more massive speed increase can stem from the application of an improved optimizer faster than the conventional gradient descent optimizer. This section provides a detailed exploration of the state-of-the-art optimizers including momentum optimizers, RMSProp optimizers, AdaGrad optimizers, and Adam optimizers.

3.6.1 Momentum Optimization

Think of a tossing ball moving down a soft slope on a shiny surface: it begins moving gently, then rapidly speeds up momentum till it finally reaches the maximum speed. This is a very straightforward concept in the wake of momentum optimization presented by [3]. On the other hand, conventional gradient descent basically takes small normal steps down the slope, thereby taking lots of time to reach the bottom. Bear in mind that gradient descent merely updates the weight parameter W by immediately subtracting the derivative of loss function L with respect to learning rate α multiplied by the weight parameters such that $W = W - \alpha \frac{\partial L}{\partial W}$. This completely ignores previous gradients. Also, in the case of a small local gradient, the training process will run extremely slowly. The momentum optimizer takes into account earlier gradients such that it combines the local gradient to the momentum vector m (multiplied by α), then it updates the weight parameters by just subtracting this momentum vector as follows:

$$m = \beta m - \alpha \frac{\partial L}{\partial W} \tag{6}$$

$$W = W - m \tag{7}$$

This means instead of employing the gradient as a speed, it is employed as an acceleration. Seeking to prevent the momentum from becoming excessively high and to mimic some kind of friction method, the optimizer brings in a hyperparameter β, merely known as the momentum, whose value is between zero and one, where the former denotes high friction and the latter indicate no friction at all. The value of the momentum is typically set to 0.9. It is simple to validate that when the gradient stayed constant, the maximum speed (i.e. the extreme parameter updates) is equivalent to the multiplication of learning rate α by $\frac{1}{1-\beta}$. So, having $\beta = 0.9$, the maximum speed will be 10 times larger than the multiplication of learning rate α by gradient $\frac{\partial L}{\partial W}$. Therefore, the momentum optimizer comes to be 10 times quicker than gradient descent. This way, the momentum optimizer can better avoid hills quicker than gradient descent. It is known that if the inputs belong to various ranges, the loss function will be similar to a stretched bowl. Despite gradient descent descending quickly downhill slope, it requires a long time to descend the valley afterward. On the other hand, the momentum optimizer can spin down the rear end of the valley quicker and quicker till it reaches the global optima. In non-normalized DNN, the upper layers will often end up having inputs with very different scales. Therefore, utilizing momentum optimization enables improving the training a lot, while also aiding rolling the previous local optima. An issue worth mentioning for the momentum optimizer is that it adds an extra hyperparameter to be tuned. Nevertheless, the momentum value of 0.9 typically does well in practice and practically forever goes more rapid than gradient descent.

3.6.2 Nesterov Accelerated Gradient

In 1983, an extension of the momentum optimizer [4] was proposed to afford quicker than the vanilla momentum optimizer. The concept of Nesterov accelerated gradient (NAG) or Nesterov momentum optimization lies in measuring the gradient of the loss function not at the local point but somewhat forward in the direction of the momentum. This intuition can be briefed as "look ahead before you leap." Different from the vanilla momentum optimizer, the gradient in the NAG optimizer is calculated at $W + \beta m$ instead of θ.

$$m = \beta m - \alpha \frac{\partial L}{\partial W + \beta m} \qquad (8)$$

$$W = W - m \qquad (9)$$

This small update is beneficial for the reason that most of the time, the momentum vector m is directed toward the global minima. Hence, it could be somewhat more precise to take advantage of the gradient calculated a little farther in this direction instead of relying on the gradient at the original spot. After some time, these little advances combine, and NAG comes to an end being considerably more rapid than a regular momentum optimizer.

3.6.3 AdaGrad

Take into account the elongated bowl dilemma again: gradient descent begins by rapidly descending the sharpest hillside, then gradually descends the valley floor. As a result, if the optimizer was able to recognize the problem early on, it would be ideal. The *AdaGrad* optimizer accomplishes this by scaling down the gradient vector along the sharpest dimensions as follows:

$$g = \frac{\partial L}{\partial W}$$

$$S = S - \alpha \cdot g^2 \qquad (10)$$

$$W = W - \alpha \frac{\partial L}{\partial W} \oslash \sqrt{S + \epsilon} \qquad (11)$$

AdaGrad optimizer starts accumulating the square of the gradients into a vector S that computes the squares of the partial derivative of the loss function with regards to parameter W. The value s_i grow up in each iteration when the loss function is sharp along the i-th dimension. Following, like the gradient descent, the gradient vector is updated by scaled down by a factor of $\sqrt{S + \epsilon}$ where $\oslash$ denotes element-wise division operation, and ϵ represents a smoothing factor to evade division by zero, and usually has the value of 10^{-8}. In summary, the AdaGrad optimizer decays the learning rate. However, it acts more rapidly in sharp dimensions than in the case of gentle slopes, which is known as an *adaptive learning rate*. It facilitates pointing the resultant updates more promptly in the direction of the global minima. One additional benefit is that it requires much less tuning of the learning rate hyperparameter η.

AdaGrad often does well when dealing with simple quadratic problems, but when it comes to training DNNs, it frequently stops too early. As a result, the learning rate is reduced to the point where the algorithm stops working altogether before it has reached its global minimum.

3.6.4 RMSProp

Though AdaGrad slows down a little very quickly and terminates without converging to the global optimum, the *RMSProp* optimizer handles this issue by collecting just the gradients from the latest iterations instead of all the gradients from the start of the training. To do so, it applied exponential decay as follows:

$$S = \beta S - \alpha g^2 \tag{12}$$

$$W = W - \alpha g \oslash \sqrt{S + \epsilon} \tag{13}$$

Typically, the decay rate β is set at 0.9. This actually adds an extra new hyperparameter, but the default value often works well. So, tuning it may not be necessary at all. However, AdaGrad is almost always beaten by the RMSProp optimizer except for some cases. It also outperforms momentum optimization and NAG on a consistent basis.

3.6.5 Adam Optimizer

Adaptive moment estimation (Adam) [5] was introduced to integrate the ideology of momentum and RMSProp optimizers such that it keeps track of an exponentially decaying average of earlier gradients as with momentum optimizers and keeps track of an exponentially decaying average of historical squared gradients as with RMSProp.

$$m = \beta_1 m + (1 - \beta_1)g \tag{14}$$

$$S = \beta_2 S - (1 - \beta_2)g^2 \tag{15}$$

$$S = \frac{S}{1 - \beta_2} \tag{16}$$

$$m = \frac{m}{1 - \beta_1} \tag{17}$$

$$W = W - \alpha m \oslash \sqrt{S + \epsilon} \tag{18}$$

Taking into account Eqs. (1), (2), and (5), it could be noted that the Adam optimizer is more similar to both momentum and RMSProp optimization. The only distinction is that Eq. (1) replaces an exponentially decaying sum with an exponentially decaying average, but these are equal except for a fixed factor. The momentum decay hyperparameter β_1 and the scaling decay hyperparameter β_2 are by default set to 0.9 and 0.999, respectively. When training begins, the initial moments estimate to zero such that m and S are initialized with zeros. This way, the values of m and S will remain very small, even after several iterations, which might make them biased toward zero, especially when β_1 and β_2 are close up to one. So, to prevent this, the bias-corrected estimates of m and S calculated as in Eqs. (3) and (4) have some technical aspects.

3.7 Model Training Issues

In deep learning, it is known that it is difficult to build or obtain a perfect dataset with balanced class distributions, uniform data distribution, no noise, and outliers in the real world. That implies that deep networks have thin possibilities of becoming accurate, but we still need them to correctly define the underlying patterns. Regrettably, it is not that straightforward.

3.7.1 Bias

Bias typically means the rigidity of the deep network. Think about a dataset that has a nonlinear attribute. To learn the inherent pattern of this data, a deep network has enough flexibility to capture a non-linear feature. If a linear network is applied, then it could be said that the network has a high bias such that it is rigid to model the complicated nature of the data (Figure 3.3).

3.7.2 Variance

Variance, in contrast, is a term that is often used to describe the scenario in which a deep network, during training, seeks to model the data distribution so specifically that it learns the location of every data element. Consequently, the network becomes *too elastic* and *too complicated*. In this scenario, the deep network can be said to have high variance and low bias (Figure 3.4).

3.7.3 Overfitting Issues

Overfitting takes place when a deep network concentrates on learning the noise and other details in the training data to the degree that

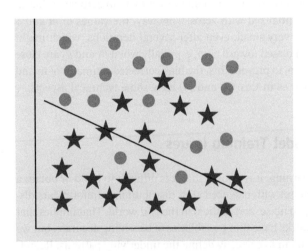

Figure 3.3 Illustration of network underfitting (high bias).

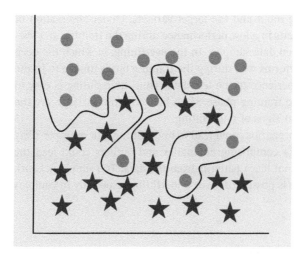

Figure 3.4   Illustration of network overfitting (high variance).

it destructively influences the performance of the network on other unseen data [6]. In this case, the noise or arbitrary oscillations in the training samples are memorized as features by the network. This destructively affects the performance of the network because these features are not available on the new datasets and multiple reasons could lead the model to overfit. For example, non-cleaned training data is containing a variety of "garbage" values that could confuse the model during the training. Small-size data could make the network memorize the data instead of learning from it. Moreover, the incorrect definition of hyperparameters is enough factor to make the network over-observe the training set and hence memorize the features.

3.7.4   Underfitting Issues

On the opposite side, *underfitting* is another popular downside in machine learning that implies the scenario in which the deep network can neither model the training data nor generalize to unseen data [7]. This is because the network is unable to find a mapping between the input and the target variable. Under-observation of features results in a low performance during the training and testing on unseen data samples. In the overfitting, in which the deep network performs well during the training but is unable to fit the learning experience to the test data. Thus, underfitting is easy to detect in the training phase. High bias and low variance are the most popular signs of underfitting.

Multiple scenarios could lead to underfitting. For example, dirty training data comprising anomalies and outliers could lead the network to not learn patterns from the data. Too simple network architecture is possible deriver underfitting, especially in complex scenarios.

3.7.5 Model Capacity

From a conceptual standpoint, the capacity of the model denotes the number of functions (linear or nonlinear) that a deep network could choose as the best possible solution [8]. The performance of the deep networks mainly relies on their capacity. A fundamental law of thumb is that the capacity of the deep network has to be proportionate to the complication of the underlying task and the structure of training data. Low-capacity deep network is more than worthless once it reaches solving complicated tasks. They have a tendency to underfitting. Similarly, deep networks with greater capacity than required are almost prone to overfitting. Fundamentally, the capacity of a deep network denotes a metric by which one could approximate whether the network is vulnerable to underfitting or overfitting. To make things simpler, Figure 3.5 provide s simple illustration of overfitting, underfitting, and model capacity according to the behaviour of loss curves.

3.8 Supplementary Materials

https://github.com/DEEPOLOGY-AI/DL-Book-Wiley-2022/tree/main/Ch3

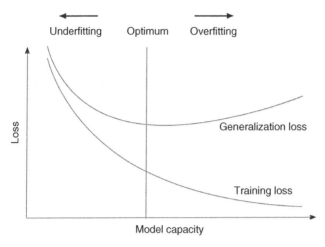

Figure 3.5 Illustration of model capacity as a measure of overfitting and underfitting.

References

1 Glorot, X. and Bengio, Y. (2010) Understanding the difficulty of training deep feedforward neural networks. *Proceedings of the Thirteenth International Conference on Artificial Intelligence and Statistics*, 249–256. JMLR Workshop and Conference Proceedings.

2 He, K., Zhang, X., Ren, S., and Sun, J. (2015). Delving deep into rectifiers: surpassing human-level performance on imagenet classification. https://doi.org/10.1109/ICCV.2015.123.

3 Polyak, B.T. (1964). Some methods of speeding up the convergence of iteration methods. *USSR Comput. Math. Math. Phys.* https://doi.org/10.1016/0041-5553(64)90137-5.

4 Nesterov, Y. (1983). A method for unconstrained convex minimization problem with the rate of convergence o(1/k^2). *Dokl. AN USSR* 269: 543–547.

5 Kingma, D. P. and Ba, J. L. (2015). Adam: A Method for Stochastic Optimization. *arXiv preprint arXiv:1412.6980*.

6 Goodfellow, I., Bengio, Y., and Courville, A. (2016). *Deep Learning*. MIT Press.

7 Aggarwal, C. C. (2018). *Neural Networks and Deep Learning*. Springer.

8 Singh, P. and Manure, A. (2020). Introduction to tensorflow 2.0. In: Learn TensorFlow 2.0, 1–24. Berkeley, CA: Apress.

4

Evaluating Deep Neural Networks

4.1 Introduction

Deep neural networks (DNNs) are strong learners capable of understanding complicated tasks in a wide range of areas. However, deep learning models' greatest strength is also their main drawback; if precautions are not taken to build the learning process appropriately, deep networks might merely overfit the training data. To put it another way, an overfitting neural network will perform better on training data than on unseen test cases. This is referred to as overfitting. Due to the learning process' tendency to recall training data artifacts that do not translate well to real-world situations, this happens. Memorization is an extreme kind of overfitting. If you think of a child who can solve all analytical issues for which he or she has seen the solutions, but cannot come up with a fresh solution, you will get a better picture of the difficulty.

Generalization is a term that typically means the ability of machine learning models to perform well on the new unseen data. After being trained on a training set, a model could receive new data and perform accurate predictions according to its learned experiences. The main success of the model is the ability of the model to generalize well. If the model has been trained too well on the training data, it will be difficult for the model to generalize. Generalization is greatly associated with the idea of overfitting. If the model is overfitted, then it will not generalize well. It will make

Deep Learning Approaches for Security Threats in IoT Environments,
First Edition. Mohamed Abdel-Basset, Nour Moustafa, and Hossam Hawash.
© 2023 The Institute of Electrical and Electronics Engineers, Inc.
Published 2023 by John Wiley & Sons, Inc.

incorrect predictions when new data is given, which makes the model useless even though it is able to make correct predictions for the training data [1].

This chapter explores the concepts of generalization and the methods and strategies that can empower the deep networks to generalize on previously unencountered data. This typically includes the method for solving the problems of overfitting and underfitting. In this spectrum, the concept of validation data is investigated to empower the generalization of a deep network. Besides, a variety of regularization techniques are covered in this chapter along with their role in eliminating the overfitting issues. Moreover, the chapter provides a full overview of the cross-validation strategies that can be adopted to train and evaluate deep networks. By the end of this chapter, the performance metrics that are necessary to indicate the performance of the model during the validation and evaluation process.

4.2 Validation Dataset

A deep network can use the validation dataset for a more objective assessment once it has been trained on the training dataset. It aids in the design step of the model or in refining the hyperparameters of the model. Pre-deployment and testing data performance are both improved as a result of this practice. It is important to remember that training and validation data are utilized during the training process to ensure that the model does not overfit or underfit. The test set is the one employed to validate the model's generalization ability. As shown in Figure 4.1, a nice procedure is to build two

Figure 4.1 Illustration for data split for training, validation, and test subsets.

subsets of data one to train the model and the other to test or evaluate it, then divide the training set into two other subsets, one for training and the other for validation.

4.3 Regularization Methods

Regularization methods perform a significant role in developing deep learning solutions, specifically complicated models that are susceptible to overfitting issues. Packed up, the term "regularize" indicates the action of getting something regular [2]. Deep networks can be made regular by including information that prevents them from being overfitted. In particular, the thing to be made regular is the loss function that the model seeks to optimize during the training. To make it simpler, regularization adds some bias to the loss function of the deep network to prevent it from overfitting our training data. This way, the network ends up with robust training performance and robust generalization ability for data instances unseen during training.

4.3.1 Early Stopping

The early stopping is a straightforward approach to regularizing iterative optimization to break off the training process once the validation loss reaches a minimum. Figure 4.2 illustrates the concept of early stopping based on generalization loss. With the increase of the number of epochs, the algorithm learns and its loss on the training data instinctively decreases, and so carries out its validation loss on the validation data. Nevertheless, a short time later, the validation loss does not decrease and, in fact, begins to move up. This implies that the network began to overfit the training samples. In short, the early stopping allows regularization of the training of the deep network in a simple and efficient way that terminates the training when there are no improvements in validation performance [3]. It is known as a "beautiful free lunch". Though early stopping functions very well in practice, the network could typically achieve higher performance if regularized by another regularization mechanism.

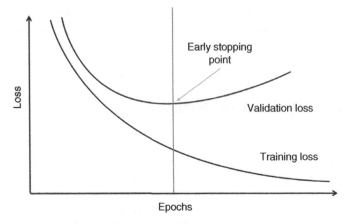

Figure 4.2 Early stopping regularization.

4.3.2 *L*1 and *L*2 Regularization

*L*1 regularization, sometimes known as *L*1 norm or Lasso in the context of regression task, is a method for combating overfitting by decreasing the parameters to approximate zero. This turns a few features outmoded.

Sometimes it can be considered as a kind of feature selection for the reason that it gives a zero weight for a certain feature, hence multiplying the feature values by zero, eliminating the importance of that feature. *L*1 norm could be sparse if the weight parameters of input features are approximating zero. This way, the weights of a subset of the input features will be zero, while the remainder will be non-zero. Mathematically speaking, by applying the *L*1 regularization, the loss function extends to be:

$$L = \frac{1}{n}\sum_{i=1}^{n}(y_i - \hat{y}_i)^2 + \lambda \sum_{i=1}^{n} \mid w_i \mid \tag{1}$$

Fundamentally, the usage of *L*1 regularization means penalizing the absolute value of the weight parameters.

On the other hand, *L*2 regularization, sometimes called *L*2 norm, or Ridge in the context of regression tasks is another method for combating overfitting issues by pushing weight parameters to have small values, without getting them exactly zero. So, the less important features can still contribute to the calculation of the loss function. By applying *L2* regularization, the loss function will be:

$$L = \frac{1}{n}\sum_{i=1}^{n}(y_i - \hat{y}_i)^2 + \lambda\sum_{i=1}^{n}(w_i)^2 \qquad (2)$$

This way, *L2* regularization provides a non-sparse solution because the weight parameters are non-zero. A point to take into consideration is that *L2* regularization is not strong for outliers as the squared parameters fill out the discrepancies in the error of the outliers [4]. The regularization would then attempt to fix this by penalizing the weights.

To sum up, the *L1* norm penalizes the sum of absolute values of the weight parameters, while the *L2* norm penalizes the sum of squares of the weights. Moreover, the former norm is sparse while the latter is non-sparse. The *L1* norm performs feature selection, while *L2* regularization has built-in feature selection. Finally, the *L1* norm is vigorous to outliers, while the *L2* norm is not.

4.3.3 Dropout

Dropout is a common regularization method designed specifically for deep networks and it has been achieving great success in a wide variety of learning tasks [1]. Dropout is a simple mechanism by which the hidden or output neurons have the chance to be momentarily "dropped out," which means it would be totally disregarded in this iteration. However, it might be activated in a later iteration (Figure 4.3). This method introduces a new hyperparameter *p* denoting the *dropout rate*, which usually has a value of 50%. Once the training gets completed, neurons are not dropped anymore. Neurons that have been trained using dropout are unable to co-adapt with their neighbors; instead, they must be as valuable on their own. They also cannot depend only on some input neurons; they have to give importance to each of their input neurons individually. They become less receptive to even little variations in the inputs. In the end, you will have a more resilient network that is more generalizable.

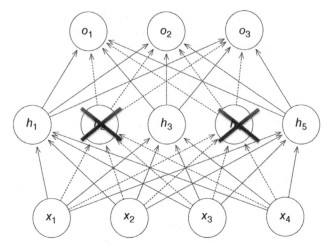

Figure 4.3 Illustration of dropout regularization.

4.3.4 Max-Norm Regularization

Max-norm regularization is a regularization method that is pretty common for training deep networks by constraining the weight parameter w of each neuron, such that $\|w\|_2 \leq r$, where $\|\cdot\|_2$ denotes the $L2$ norm and r represents the max-norm hyperparameter. This condition is performed by calculating $\|w\|_2$ after each training iteration and trimming w if necessary, $w = w \frac{r}{\|w\|_2}$. The reduction of the value of r amplifies the degree of regularization and enables avoiding overfitting issues [5].

4.3.5 Data Augmentation

Increasing the size of training data provides the model with more critical features to be extracted so that it can learn the interrelationship between these input features as well as the output variable. The only hypothesis in increasing the size of training data is that these data must be clean; otherwise, the overfitting issue would be worsened.

Apart from other regularization methods, data augmentation can regularize the network training by exploiting the available training samples to generate new artificial samples that can amplify the size of the training set. The generated data samples look somewhat changed every time the model processes it. The method has been demonstrated efficient for reducing overfitting in different learning tasks [6]. The idea is to create realistic training examples in an ideal way such that no one would be able to distinguish which ones were generated and which ones were not. Furthermore, merely adding white noise will not help; the changes you make should be learnable (white noise is not).

4.4 Cross-Validation

An algorithm's capacity to work well with a variety of data is known as a generalization in deep learning. New inputs from the same distribution as the training data do not affect the model's performance. Generalization is an inherent part of human life. We are able to categorize on the spot. Even if we had never seen a dog of that particular species previously, we could instantly identify it. An ML model, on the other hand, might have a difficult time with this task. As a result, ensuring that the method is able to generalize is a critical part of the model-building process, which also means that the model is not overfitting. To address that, cross-validation is performed.

The performance of the deep learning model can be evaluated and tested using the cross-validation technique in different learning tasks (regression, classification, etc.). Predictive modeling can be improved by comparing and selecting a suitable model. A major advantage of cross-validation, that is worth to be mentioned, is that it is less prone to bias than other techniques of calculating a model's efficiency scores. Also, it is simple and easy to implement. Hence, cross-validation is a great tool for finding the optimal model for a certain task. Moreover, through the use of several validation datasets, cross-validation helps us prevent overfitting our ML models. To cross-validate a model, a variety of methods are available. However, they all share some basic steps.

1. Split up the data into two subsets, one for training and the other for testing.

2. Use the training set to train the model.
3. The trained model is validated on the test set.
4. Repeat the steps from 1 to 3 a predefined number of times.

In this context, there are lots of cross-validation methods. Some of them are frequently applied, while others can be just studied theoretically.

4.4.1 Hold-Out Cross-Validation

The hold-out method is the easiest and most popular cross-validation that broadly used in machine learning communities (Figure 4.4). It works by executing the following steps:

1. Split the data into two subsets one for training and the other for testing.
2. The model is trained on a training set using some optimization algorithm.
3. The trained model validates its performance on the test set.
4. Report the validation results.

Even yet, a holdout suffers from a serious drawback. As an illustration, consider a dataset in which the distribution is not uniform. If this is the case, the divide could leave us in a difficult position. There is a difference between the training set and the test set, for example. It is possible that the training and test sets be vastly different, with one being significantly simpler or more difficult than the other. Even more problematic is the fact that we only test the model once, i.e. test one problem. The result hold-out method may

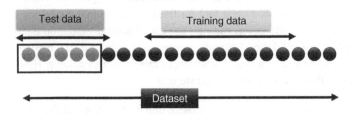

Figure 4.4 Illustration of the holdout cross-validation.

be deemed erroneous, in some cases, because of the reasons already indicated.

4.4.2 *k*-Folds Cross-Validation

k-Fold is a popular cross-validation that is primarily introduced to address the limitations of the hold-out validation. *k*-Fold presents a novel approach for separating the dataset in such a way that helps resolve the "test once problem" existing in the hold-out method (Figure 4.5). The following steps are followed to perform *k*-fold cross-validation:

1. Initialize a variable k with some integer value. The value of k must be less than the size of the dataset. Commonly, the value of k is initialized to be 5 or 10.
2. Divide the dataset into k equivalent (if viable) pieces of data known as data folds.
3. Select a single fold as the test set and use the leftover folds will be collectively used as the training set.
4. Use the training set to train the model using a particular optimization algorithm.
5. The trained model validates its performance on the test set.
6. Report the validation results.
7. Repeat steps 3 to 6 for k times. In each iteration, a distinct data fold is selected as the test set, and the other folds are used for

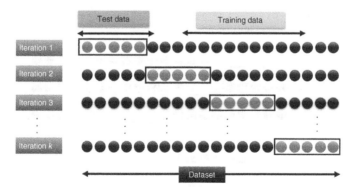

Figure 4.5 Illustration of the *k*-fold cross-validation.

training. In each iteration, each model must be trained separately from the model trained in the earlier iterations.

8. Finally, the final validation results are calculated by averaging the results reported for all test folds.

The *k*-fold approach is always preferable to hold out. Due to the fact that *k*-fold uses distinct regions of the dataset for training and testing, it consistently outperforms other methods in head-to-head comparisons. With the increase in the number of data folds, the results of the deep learning model can be further improved. However, there is a drawback to the *k*-fold approach. As *k* increases, more models must be trained, which can be costly and time-consuming. This may make it an improper choice for resource-constrained IoT environments.

4.4.3 Stratified *k*-Folds' Cross-Validation

Occasionally, a huge class imbalance could be encountered in some datasets. For instance, in the case of IoT security datasets, normal classes often contain a large number of samples, while some attack classes may contain a very small number of samples because of their scarcity in IoT environments (Figure 4.6).

The stratified *k*-fold method is a version of the *k*-fold CV technique that is designed to be useful in situations where the class imbalance is high. It goes like this: It is possible to divide a dataset into many folds, each of which has an equivalent (if feasible)

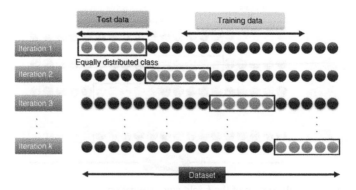

Figure 4.6 Illustration of the stratified *k*-fold cross-validation.

number of samples from each target class. In regression, stratified *k*-fold guarantees that the mean target value is roughly equivalent in all folds.

1. Initialize a variable *k* with some integer value.
2. Divide the dataset into *k* equivalent data folds, where each fold should comprise nearly the same proportion of examples from every target class.
3. Select onefold as a test set, and the remaining folds are used as a training set.
4. Use the training set to train the model.
5. The trained model validates its performance on the test set.
6. Report the validation results.
7. Repeat steps from 3 to 6 for *k* times in the same way as with the *k*-fold method.
8. Lastly, the final results are computed by averaging the results reported in step 6.

4.4.4 Repeated *k*-Folds' Cross-Validation

The repeated *k*-fold method, also referred to as repeated random sub-sampling, is another extension to the *k*-fold method in which the *k* is not denoting the number of folds. However, *k* denotes the number of times the model would be trained. The broad notion is that the model will arbitrarily choose a group of samples to act as a test set in each iteration (Figure 4.7). For instance, given that the size of the test set is decided to be 20% of data, then 20% of data instances will be arbitrarily chosen and the rest 80% will be used for training. The repeated *k*-fold method operates as follows:

1. Define *k* as the number of times for which the training will be repeated.
2. Select a random group of samples as the test. Then, set the remaining samples as a training set.
3. Use the training set to train the model.
4. The trained model validates its performance on the test set.
5. Report the validation results.
6. Repeat steps from 3 to 6 for *k* times.
7. Lastly, the results are computed by averaging the results reported in step 6.

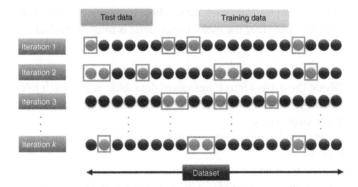

Figure 4.7 Illustration of the repeated *k*-fold cross-validation.

In comparison to the regular *k*-fold method, repeated *k*-fold offers clear advantages in terms of performance. In the first place, the percentage of train/test split is not dependent on the number of iterations. It is also possible to create a custom set of proportions for each iteration. Repeated *k*-robustness folds to selection bias is further enhanced by the random selection of samples from the dataset.

In spite of this, there are certain drawbacks. While Repeated *k*-fold relies on randomness, *k*-fold CV assures that the model will be tested on all samples, which means that certain samples may never be included in the test set at all. At the same time, it is possible that some samples will be chosen more than once. Because of this, it is a poor choice for datasets that are skewed.

4.4.5 Leave-One-Out Cross-Validation

Leave-one-out cross-validation method is an acute instance of the *k*-fold method, where the value of *k* is equivalent to the number of data instances in the dataset, *N* (Figure 4.8). In other words, the leave-one-out method is *N*-fold cross-validation. The next steps represent the workflow of leave-one-out:

1. Select a single instance as the test set.
2. Use the leftover instances to train the model using a particular optimization algorithm.
3. The trained model validates its performance on the test set.

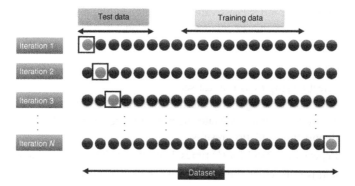

Figure 4.8 Illustration of the stratified leave-one-out cross-validation.

4. Report the validation results.
5. Repeat steps 1 to 4 N times. In each iteration, a distinct data sample is selected as the test set, and the others are used for training. In each iteration, each model must be trained separately from the model trained in the earlier iterations.
6. After all, the final validation results are computed by averaging the results reported for all N test samples.

The leave-one-out method has the greatest advantage of not wasting a lot of data as it considers a single sample of data as the test set. However, when compared to the k-fold method, the leave-one-out method requires N models instead of k models, which is significantly larger. This implies that leave-one-out is computationally intensive than k-fold, and, hence, it consumes a longer time to execute. Even the theoretical interpretation of the leave-one-out method seems simple. However, it is impractical from a technical standpoint especially when the size of the dataset is large which is a common case in IoT security datasets.

4.4.6   Leave-p-Out Cross-Validation

The leave-p-out cross-validation method is an extension of the leave-one-out cross-validation method. It built the test set using p instances. All stated about the leave-one-out method is also applied to the leave-p-out method. However, it is stated that being different from other cross-validation methods, the test sets could overlap if the value of p is greater than one. The main steps of leave-p-out are pointed out as follows:

1. Initialize a variable p by some integer value between one and N.
2. Select p samples as the test set.
3. Use the remaining samples as the training set to train the model.
4. The trained model validates its performance on the test set.
5. Report the validation results.
6. Repeat steps 2 to 5 for C_p^N times. In each iteration, a distinct data fold is selected as the test set, and the other folds are used for training. In each iteration, each model must be trained separately from the model trained in the earlier iterations.
7. Again, the final validation results are computed by averaging the results reported for all C_p^N test samples.

4.4.7 Time Series Cross-Validation

This type of cross-validation is ineffective for time-series data since it is impossible to select arbitrary data instances and allocate them to either the test or train sets because it is not possible to predict the past values based on future values. In general, cross-validation for time series could be done in one of the two ways.

4.4.8 Rolling Cross-Validation

The rolling method acts as an iterative process of forecasting future values and verifying the accuracy of those predictions, which begin with a small subset of data for training purposes. The working flow can be illustrated in Figure 4.9.

4.4.9 Block Cross-Validation

The model could be compromised by leakage of future data in case the rolling method is used [7]. The model will monitor future patterns in order to predict them and attempt to store them in its memory. To address these limitations, blocked cross-validation was proposed. Blocked cross-validation functions by adding margins

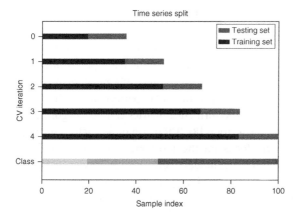

Figure 4.9 Illustration of the rolling cross-validation.

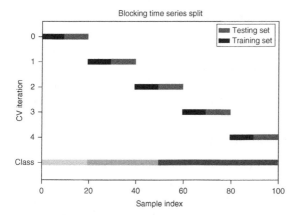

Figure 4.10 Illustration of the blocking cross-validation.

in two places. The former is situated between the folds of training and validation to avoid the model from seeing lag values that are employed two times: one for the regressor and one as a reaction. The second margin is situated between the folds of different iterations to stop the model from memorizing patterns (Figure 4.10).

4.5   Performance Metrics

As a matter of fact, every deep learning model has its own performance indicators that tell the degree to which it is performing well in a numerical value. All categories and subcategories of DNNs necessitate some way to measure their performance. Similar to deep learning models, performance metrics can be categorized as a regression or classification [8]. There are other metrics for both tasks, but we will focus on the most prominent ones and the insights they offer into the model's performance. Having an understanding of how your model views your data seems to be essential!

Performance metrics, also referred to as evaluation metrics, are not the same as the loss functions. The training performance of the network can be evaluated via loss functions. Hence, loss functions are used to train deep networks utilizing a particular optimization algorithm, such as gradient descent, and they are differentiated with respect to parameters. On the other hand, to track and evaluate the performance of the network in both the training and testing phases, metrics do not have to be differentiable; they are employed instead. Some learning tasks may necessitate the usage of differentiable performance metrics, like MAE, which can be utilized as loss functions probably by applying some regularizations.

4.5.1   Regression Metrics

Unlike other types of models, the output of a regression model is continuous in nature. As a result, it is required to have a metric that measures the difference between what is projected and what really happens. Here are the metrics we will use to evaluate regression models.

4.5.1.1   Mean Absolute Error (MAE)

MAE is the mean of the differences between the forecasted values $\widetilde{Y}_i$ and the actual labels Y_i. It can be computed as

$$\text{MAE} = \frac{1}{N} \sum_{i=1}^{N} |\widetilde{Y}_i - Y_i| \tag{3}$$

where N represents the number of examples in the test data.

4.5.1.2 Root Mean Squared Error (RMSE)

RMSE represents the square root of the mean of the squared differences between the forecasted values $\widetilde{Y}_i$ and the actual labels Y_i. Essentially, RMSE can be mathematically given by

$$\text{RMSE} = \sqrt{\frac{1}{N}\sum_{i=1}^{N}\left(\widetilde{Y}_i - Y_i\right)^2} \tag{4}$$

There is no loss of differentiability of MSE. Square rooting is used to deal with the penalization of lesser errors. Because the scale has become the same as the random variable, it is easier to interpret errors. It is less likely to suffer from outliers because scale factors are practically normalized.

4.5.1.3 Coefficient of Determination (R^2)

R^2 essentially functions as a post training metric that can be computed utilizing multiple performance metrics. The idea of regular estimation of this coefficient is to give a response to the question "What is the percentage of the overall disparity in Y_i described by the change in $\widetilde{Y}_i$?" This is computed utilizing the summation of squared errors and it can be formulated in terms of the overall variation in Y as follows:

$$\text{SE(regression)} = \sum_{i=1}^{N}\left(\widetilde{Y}_i - Y_i\right)^2 \tag{5}$$

$$\text{SE(mean)} = \sum_{i=1}^{N}\left(Y_i - \text{mean}(Y)\right)^2 \tag{6}$$

$$R^2 = 1 - \frac{\text{SE(regression)}}{\text{SE(mean)}} \tag{7}$$

If the regression line's total squared error is low, then R^2 will be near to one (ideal), indicating that the regression was capable of capturing all of the variances of the targeted variable. R^2 will be near zero if the regression line's total squared error is large, indicating that the regression failed to catch any variance in the targeted variable.

4.5.1.4 Adjusted R^2

Vanilla R^2 has a few flaws, such as the tendency to lead researchers astray by making them believe that the model is enhancing as the score rises, when, in fact, no learning is taking place. When a model overfits the data, this can occur, resulting in a variance explanation of 100%, but no actual learning has taken place. As a solution, the number of independent variables is truncated to R^2. To account for the growing predictors, adjusted R^2 is always lower than R^2, and it only shows improvement when there is one.

$$R_a^2 = 1 - \frac{(n-1)}{(n-k-1)}\left(1 - R^2\right) \tag{8}$$

where n is the number of data samples, and k is the number of independent variables.

4.5.2 Classification Metrics

Research into classification issues is one of the most prevalent forms of scientific inquiry. IoT and cybersecurity are common applications for that, which may be found in nearly any situation. Intrusion detection, cybercrime detection, malware classification – the list is endless.

If we want a measure that can compare discrete classes, we require one from classification models. Classification metrics assess the performance of a deep network and provide feedback on how well or poorly it classifies data, but they do so in a variety of ways.

4.5.2.1 Confusion Matrix

The confusion matrix provides a tabular illustration for comparing actual class labels with model predictions. For each row in the confusion matrix, instances of actual classes are represented, whereas occurrences in a predicted class are represented in each column. In a sense, the confusion matrix is more of a foundation for other performance metrics than it is a performance indicator in and of itself.

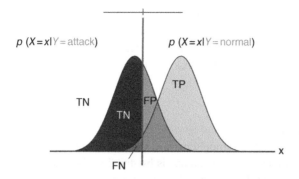

Figure 4.11 Illustration of the confusion matrix.

A null hypothesis must be assumed in order to understand the confusion matrix [9]. Given that the model is trained to classify IoT data as a normal or attacked, our null hypothesis H^0 can be "the data normal" (Figure 4.11).

An evaluation factor is represented by each cell in the confusion matrix. Take a closer look at each of the following factors:

- The count of positive class examples that the model has properly predicted is called the true positive (TP).
- The count of negative class examples that the model has properly predicted is called the true negative (TN).
- The count of negative class examples that the model has erroneously predicted is known as false positive (FP). In statistical terminology, this is a type-I mistake. Choosing the null hypothesis affects this error's location in the confusion matrix.

- The count of positive class examples that the model estimated inaccurately is referred to as false negative (FN). A type-II error in statistical nomenclature is represented by this component. The choice of the null hypothesis affects where the errors appear in the confusion matrix.

4.5.2.2 Accuracy

Accuracy is defined as a straightforward statistic and an easy way to measure classification performance is by dividing the number of correctly predicted data samples by the total number of test samples. Typically, the higher the accuracy is, the better the performance is [10]. Accuracy is a useful metric but only for datasets with a nearly equal proportion of true positives and false negatives. The accuracy metric can be mathematically defined as:

$$\text{Accuracy } (A) = \frac{\text{TP} + \text{TN}}{\text{TP} + \text{TN} + \text{FP} + \text{FN}} \tag{9}$$

4.5.2.3 Precision

The precision of a model is defined as a metric for calculating the proportion of true positives to the total number of predicted positives.

$$\text{Precision } (P) = \frac{\text{TP}}{\text{TP} + \text{FP}} \tag{10}$$

Type-I errors are the focus of the precision metric. When we reject a valid null hypothesis (H^0), we commit a type-I error. In this scenario, the type-I error is incorrectly diagnosing normal IoT data cancer as an attack. A precision score close to one indicates that your model is able to distinguish between right and wrong attack labeling and that it did not miss any true positives [11]. On the other hand, false negatives, or situations in which an attack data is mistakenly labeled as normal, are not detectable since they fall under Type-II error. Class imbalance or incorrect model hyper-parameters might lead to poor precision scores (<0.5), which indicates a significant number of FPs.

4.5.2.4 Recall

The recall, sometimes referred to as sensitivity, true positive rate (TPR), or hit rate, of a model is defined as a metric for calculating the proportion of true positives to the total number of actual positives.

$$\text{Recall}\ (R) = \frac{\text{TP}}{\text{TP} + \text{FN}} \tag{11}$$

The recall score approximating one indicates that the deep network did not miss any true positives and is capable of distinguishing well between normal data samples and malicious ones. Class imbalance or incorrect model hyperparameters might lead to a poor sensitivity score (<0.5).

4.5.2.5 Precision–Recall Curve

An illustration of precision and recall can be seen in the dual-axis graphic [12]. Precision and recall are calculated for each threshold and the results are plotted. The better your model performs, the higher your *y*-axis curve is.

When faced with the traditional precision/recall problem, you may utilize this plot to make an informed decision. Precision decreases with increasing recall. If you know how quickly your precision begins to decline, you will be able to select a more accurate threshold and produce a better model.

4.5.2.6 *F*1-Score

The *F*1-score measure incorporates both precisions and recalls into its calculation. The *F*1 score, in fact, is the harmonic mean of the two. It is calculated with this simple formula:

$$F1 - \text{score} = 2 \times \frac{P \times R}{P + R} = \frac{2\text{TP}}{2\text{TP} + \text{FP} + \text{FN}} \tag{12}$$

This way a high *F*1 score now signifies a high level of precision and recall as well. In problems of imbalanced categorization, unlike accuracy, it performs well due to its strong precision-to-recall ratio.

There is nothing to be gained from a low $F1$ score – it merely tells you about your performance at a specific point in time. Having a low recall indicates that we did not give it our all on the complete test set. In other words, only a small percentage of the positive cases were correctly recognized due to the low precision of our analysis.

Even yet, low $F1$ does not indicate which circumstances. A high $F1$ indicates that a major component of the choice is likely to have good precision and recall (which is informative). We do not know if the model has type-I or type-II errors when $F1$ is low (poor precision or low recall).

Is Formula One a fad? It is commonly used and considered a good statistic for making a decision, although it is not without certain modifications. Type-I errors can be curbed by using false-positive rates (FPRs) in conjunction with $F1$, and you will learn who is to blame for your poor $F1$ score.

4.5.2.7 Beta F1 Score

Beyond, some situations ask for a ratio to be assigned more importance to recall or precision. This necessitates a small modification to the above formula in order to accommodate the inclusion of a variable parameter beta. The beta version of the $F1$ score, $F1-$score$_\beta$ can be used to generalize this $F1$ score to a wide range of classification problems:

$$F1-\text{score}_\beta = \left(1-\beta^2\right) \times \frac{P \times R}{\left(\beta^2 \times P\right) + R} \tag{13}$$

where the value of β allows the important tradeoff between recall and precision to be controlled. Precision gets more attention when $\beta < 1$, whereas recall gets more attention when $\beta > 1$.

4.5.2.8 False Positive Rate (FPR)

The fraction of negative data items that are incorrectly interpreted as positive, when compared to all negative data points, is what we

call the false positive rate (FPR) [13]. More negative data items are
likely to be misclassified if our FPR is higher.

$$FPR = \frac{FP}{TN + FP} \qquad (14)$$

4.5.2.9 Specificity

Specificity refers to how many items are correctly classified as
belonging to a different class as compared to the total number
of samples in that class [14, 15]. As a result, it is linked to FPR
as follows:

$$Specificity = 1 - FPR = \frac{TN}{TN + FP} \qquad (15)$$

4.5.2.10 Receiving Operating Characteristics (ROC) Curve

For a single measure, we initially calculate the FPR and the TPR
using a variety threshold and then plot them together on a single
graph. With the ROC curve as our starting point, we can then calculate the area under the curve (AUC) metric.

If a classifier has no skill, it will always predict the same class,
whether it is a random class or a static class. According to the distribution of the positive to negative classes, the no-skill line shifts.
The proportion of positive examples in the dataset is shown by a
horizontal line. It is 0.5 in a balanced dataset. The probability that
an instance randomly picked is better than another example randomly selected is represented by the area, which is equal to the
probability that one example is better than the other in terms of
being positive [16–18].

The higher the ROC, the more likely it is that a positive example
will be selected at random. ROC means your system ranks test data
well, with most negative cases at one end and positive cases at the
other. When dealing with a situation characterized by a significant
class imbalance, ROC curves are a poor choice. Aside from aca-
demic study and comparisons of different classifiers, the AUC metric has no other application (Figure 4.12).

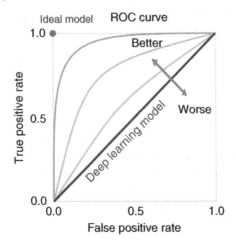

Figure 4.12 Illustration of receiving operating characteristics (ROC) curve.

4.6 Supplementary Materials

https://github.com/DEEPOLOGY-AI/DL-Book-Wiley-2022/tree/main/Ch4

References

1 Srivastava, N., Hinton, G., Krizhevsky, A. et al. (2014). Dropout: a simple way to prevent neural networks from overfitting. *J. Mach. Learn. Res.* 15: 1929–1958.

2 Goodfellow, I., Bengio, Y., and Courville, A. (2016). *Deep Learning.* MIT Press.

3 Aggarwal, C.C. (2018). *Neural Networks and Deep Learning*, vol. 10, 978–973. Springer.

4 Singh, P. and Manure, A. (2020). Introduction to tensorflow 2.0. In: *Learn TensorFlow 2.0*, 1–24. Berkeley, CA: Apress.

5 Apicella, A., Donnarumma, F., Isgrò, F., and Prevete, R. (2021). A survey on modern trainable activation functions. *Neural Netw.* https://doi.org/10.1016/j.neunet.2021.01.026.

6 Lillicrap, T.P., Santoro, A., Marris, L. et al. (2020). Backpropagation and the brain. *Nat. Rev. Neurosci.* https://doi.org/10.1038/s41583-020-0277-3.

7 Wang, Q., Ma, Y., Zhao, K., and Tian, Y. (2022). A comprehensive survey of loss functions in machine learning. *Ann. Data Sci.* https://doi.org/10.1007/s40745-020-00253-5.

8 Al-Garadi, M.A., Mohamed, A., Al-Ali, A.K. et al. (2020). A survey of machine and deep learning methods for internet of things (IoT) security. *IEEE Commun. Surv. Tutor.* https://doi.org/10.1109/COMST.2020.2988293.

9 Chaabouni, N., Mosbah, M., Zemmari, A. et al. (2019). Network intrusion detection for IoT security based on learning techniques. *IEEE Commun. Surv. Tutor.* https://doi.org/10.1109/COMST.2019.2896380.

10 Olowononi, F.O., Rawat, D.B., and Liu, C. (2021). Resilient machine learning for networked cyber physical systems: a survey for machine learning security to securing machine learning for CPS. *IEEE Commun. Surv. Tutor.* https://doi.org/10.1109/COMST.2020.3036778.

11 Hussain, F., Hussain, R., Hassan, S.A., and Hossain, E. (2020). Machine learning in IoT security: current solutions and future challenges. *IEEE Commun. Surv. Tutor.* https://doi.org/10.1109/COMST.2020.2986444.

12 Ullah, K., Rashid, I., Afzal, H. et al. (2020). SS7 vulnerabilities – a survey and implementation of machine learning vs rule based filtering for detection of SS7 network attacks. *IEEE Commun. Surv. Tutor.* https://doi.org/10.1109/COMST.2020.2971757.

13 Rodriguez, E., Otero, B., Gutierrez, N., and Canal, R. (2021). A survey of deep learning techniques for cybersecurity in mobile networks. *IEEE Commun. Surv. Tutor.* https://doi.org/10.1109/COMST.2021.3086296.

14 Hu, S., Chen, X., Ni, W. et al. (2021). Distributed machine learning for wireless communication networks: techniques, architectures, and applications. *IEEE Commun. Surv. Tutor.* https://doi.org/10.1109/COMST.2021.3086014.

15 Padakandla, S. (2021). A survey of reinforcement learning algorithms for dynamically varying environments. *ACM Comput. Surv.* https://doi.org/10.1145/3459991.

16 Luong, N.C., Hoang, D.T., Gong, S. et al. (2019). Applications of deep reinforcement learning in communications and networking: a survey. *IEEE Commun. Surv. Tutor.* https://doi.org/10.1109/COMST.2019.2916583.

17 Kiran, B.R., Sobh, I., Talpaert, V. et al. (2021). Deep reinforcement learning for autonomous driving: a survey. *IEEE Trans. Intell. Transp. Syst.* https://doi.org/10.1109/TITS.2021.3054625.

18 Wahab, O.A., Mourad, A., Otrok, H., and Taleb, T. (2021). Federated machine learning: survey, multi-level classification, desirable criteria and future directions in communication and networking systems. *IEEE Commun. Surv. Tutor.*

5

Convolutional Neural Networks

5.1 Introduction

Among different types of data, we saw two-dimensional grids of pixels in the form of image data. It is possible to assign one or more numerical values to each pixel location in black-and-white and color images, based on the nature of the image. The method we have been coping with this complex framework up until now has been terribly lacking in satisfaction. Flattening each image into one-dimensional vectors, we fed them to the deep neural network (DNN), erasing their spatial structure. According to these networks, it does not matter if we maintain an order that corresponds to how the pixels appear spatially or whether we shift our design matrix's columns prior to fitting the parameters of DNN. In order to construct effective models for learning from picture data, we would like to make use of our prior understanding that close pixels are frequently connected to one another.

This chapter presents a compelling family of deep learning models, known as convolutional neural networks (CNNs), which are specifically designed for the image recognition task. The design of the CNNs was inspired by the study of the visual cortex of the human brain, and they have been used in image recognition since the 1980s. With the recent improvements in deep learning, CNNs have succeeded to achieve formidable performance on some complicated visual tasks. Thus, they show wide acceptance in a broad

Deep Learning Approaches for Security Threats in IoT Environments,
First Edition. Mohamed Abdel-Basset, Nour Moustafa, and Hossam Hawash.
© 2023 The Institute of Electrical and Electronics Engineers, Inc.
Published 2023 by John Wiley & Sons, Inc.

range of applications in self-driving cars, robotics, smart homes, authentication, and medical image analysis and it is currently used almost exclusively in commercial software development and competitions. This chapter will cover the main concepts related to the fundamental design of baseline convolutional networks. It explains the convolutional layers and related attributes such as padding and stride, pooling layers, normalization layers, etc.

5.2 Shift from Full Connected to Convolutional

When it comes to dealing with tabular data, the models discussed in earlier chapters may persist as a suitable choice for building a deep learning solution. To remember, tabular data is a popular format consisting of rows representing samples and columns denoting the relevant features of these samples. Dealing with tabular data usually implies that the patterns the model seeks may contain interactions among the different features, but there are no assumptions to make about the structure of the interactions between the features a priori. Sometimes we simply lack the necessary information to guide the creation of more intricate structures. In these situations, an multi-layer perceptron (MLP) may be the greatest option available to us. Such structure-less networks, on the other hand, might become cultivated unwieldy when dealing with high-dimensional data.

For instance, let us consider building a regular deep network (stacking many full connected layers) to classify an image as belonging to a cat's or a dog's class. Assume the shape of the input image is $32 \times 32 \times 3$ (i.e. width, height, and the number of channels), then, according to the parameterization cost of fully connected layers, the first hidden layer would have a total of $32 \times 32 \times 3 = 3072$ parameters. This quantity still looks wieldy, but obviously, this fully connected layer does not scale to images with larger dimensions. Further, consider the case in which the image has a moderate resolution, e.g. $512 \times 512 \times 3$. This would enlarge the number of parameters of the earliest layer to be

$512 \times 512 \times 3 = 786\ 432$. Definitely, the model structure contains many such layers. So, the parameters would increase rapidly! Obviously, this complete connectivity is inefficient, and a large number of parameters would speedily lead to the network overfit. Even though we have many graphical processing units, a capacity for decentralized learning, and an astonishing quantity of perseverance, training large-sized models may become infeasible. Additionally, training a model to fit a large number of parameters might necessitate having a large-enough training dataset. In fact, classifying images of cats from dogs seems an easy task for both humans and computers, apparently denying the above intuitions due to the fact that images show rich structures that could be exploited by humans and deep learning in the same way. In this regard, CNNs evolved as the inventive approach that has been embraced by deep learning to leverage some of the acknowledged structures in natural images, and they constrain the architecture in a more sensible way. Specifically, different from a regular deep network, the layers of a CNN contain neurons organized in three dimensions: width, height, and depth. The term *depth* here denotes the third dimension of an activation volume instead of the number of layers in a network. For example, when the input is of shape $32 \times 32 \times 3$, the activation volume will have dimensions $32 \times 32 \times 3$. As shown in Figure 5.1, the neurons per layer are just connected to a small area of the previous layer, instead of all of the neurons in a regular deep network.

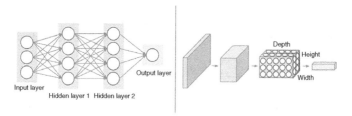

Figure 5.1 Illustration of a regular neural network compared to a convolutional network that organizes its neurons in three dimensions (width, height, and depth).

5.3 Basic Architecture

We are ready to explore how convolutional layers operate in practice now that we have figured out how they work in theory. CNNs are efficient structures for analyzing structure in picture data, which is why we chose them as motivators.

5.3.1 The Cross-Correlation Operation

As the name implies, correlation is the act of moving a filter mask, also known as a kernel, over a picture in order to calculate each location's total of the individual products. When a filter is displaced, the result is a change in correlation. Since the filter's displacement is inversely related to correlation values, each correlation value equates to one unit of displacement in the filter.

In mathematical terms, for continuous complex-valued functions, the cross-correlation operation between one-dimensional input I and a filter F can be defined as:

$$(F * I)(i) = \int F(a)\, g(i + a)da \tag{1}$$

Likewise, for discrete input sequences, cross-correlation operation between one-dimensional input I and a filter F can be defined as:

$$(F * I)(i) = \sum_a F(a)\, g(i + a) \tag{2}$$

In a similar way, when it comes to two-dimensional input, the main concept is the same, and only the dimensionality of the image and the filter has changed. Thus, the cross-correlation operation between one-dimensional input I and a filter F can be defined as:

$$(F * I)(x, y) = \sum_a \sum_b F(a, b)\, I(i + a, i + b) \tag{3}$$

In two-dimensional space, the cross-correlation operation is simple. It just sets a filter of a particular size over a specific area of the input (i.e. image) that matches the filter's dimensions. As it proceeds with this operation, the identical filter is applied to every element in the input (i.e. pixel of the image). As a result, cross-validation can obtain two extremely desirable qualities. First, the ability of a model or a system to be able to recognize the same object, no matter where it appears in an image, which is known as translational invariance. Second, the ability of a model or a system to concentrate just on the local regions of the input image, ignoring the rest of the image. When it comes to a discrete unit impulse (i.e. two-dimensional matrix of all zeros and just one), the cross-correlation function has a limitation or distinctive attribute that returns an output that is a replica of the filter but rotated by 180°.

5.3.2 Convolution Operation

Convolution operations exhibit high similarity with cross-correlation. They share the same concept, but the former rotates the filter *f* by 180° before being applied to the input *I*. This way, the essential estate of convolution operation lies in the ability to convolve kernel with a discrete unit impulse to generate a duplicate of the kernel at the site of the impulse. In the cross-correlation section, we learned that a correlation operation produces a replica of the impulse rotated by 180°. As a result, it should be easy to find the right outcome if the filter is pre-rotated and then continue doing the same sliding sum of product operation (Figure 5.2).

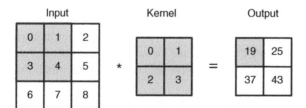

Figure 5.2 Convolution operation applied on grid input. The colored cell in the output is computed by applying the kernel to the colored cells in the input tensor.

Mathematically speaking, for continuous complex-valued functions, the convolution operation between one-dimensional input I and a filter F can be defined as

$$(F * I)(i) = \int F(a) \, g(i - a) da \tag{4}$$

Likewise, for discrete input sequences, the convolution operation between one-dimensional input I and a filter F can be defined as

$$(F * I)(i) = \sum_a F(a) \, g(i - a) \tag{5}$$

In a similar way, when it comes to two-dimensional input, the main concept is the same, but only the dimensionality of the image and the filter has changed. Thus, the convolution operation between one-dimensional input I and a filter F can be defined as

$$(F * I)(i, j) = \sum_a \sum_b F(a, b) \, I(i - a, j - b) \tag{6}$$

However, almost all machine learning and deep learning libraries use the simplified cross-correlation function and call it convolution – this book follows this naming terminology.

5.3.3 Receptive Field

As stated before, the production of a convolutional layer, simply known as the *feature map*, can be considered as the extracted features and/or learned representations from the spatial space by the sequence of a layer. In convolutional networks, for every instance x of some layer, its *receptive field of* any element x of a particular layer means all elements in the preceding layers that might contribute to the computation of x throughout the forward flow of gradients. Following this definition, the receptive field could be bigger than the concrete dimension of the input.

Recall the operation in Figure 5.2 to further interpret the receptive field. Given the convolutional layer with a 2×2 kernel, the shaded output element has a receptive field four corresponding to the shaded input elements. Moreover, let us extend the network with one convolutional layer with a 2×2 kernel that takes the previous output as input. This kernel generates a single output element whose receptive field contains all the four inputs, whereas the corresponding receptive field contains all the nine input elements. Consequently, a deeper network can be constructed when every part of the feature map requires a bigger receptive field to capture input patterns over a greater area.

5.3.4 Padding and Stride

In earlier discussions, it is agreed that the input of the convolution layer has two dimensions – width n_w and height n_h, and similarly, the kernel has both width and height. Given these dimensions, the output of the convolutional layer can have a width of $(n_w - k_w + 1)$ as well as height of $(n_h - k_h + 1)$. In some circumstances, the convolutional network may include padding and strided convolutional layer, which certainly impacts the shape of the output. As an incentive, consider a typical scenario where the dimensions of kernels are larger than one, then, stacking multiple convolutional layers makes the model tend to end with outputs that are noticeably smaller than its input. For example, consider having a 240×240 image as an input, with 10 convolutional layers of 5×5, the size of the image will be reduced to 200×200, cutting off 30% of the input which implies destroying any important information near the image boundaries. Padded convolutions offer an adequate solution to this problem. On the other hand, some tasks require the convolutional network to drastically decrease the dimensionality, especially when the original input dimensions are large. Strided convolutions provide an ideal solution to deal with these scenarios.

5.3.4.1 Padding
As stated before, one challenge faced at the time of using convolutional layers is the tendency to miss the boundary information, i.e. pixels close to the image perimeter. One may think that only a few pixels are lost when small kernels are used. However, this can grow up as the convolutional network contain numerous successive layers. A simple solution to this challenge is to add additional zero-valued elements of filling around the border of the original input, therefore enlarging the active dimension of input, as

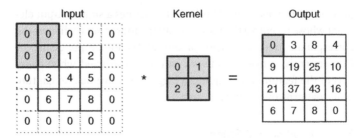

Figure 5.3 Example of convolution layer with padding.

illustrated in Figure 5.3. It is noted that 3×3 is padded to increase its size to 5×5, and accordingly, the size of its output is increased to 4×4. This way, to calculate the first output element, the colored input cells are cross-correlated with kernel matrix as follows:

$$0 \times 0 + 0 \times 1 + 0 \times 2 + 0 \times 3 = 0.$$

Generally, given p_w as the total number of added columns of padding ($\frac{p_w}{2}$ on left-side and $\frac{p_w}{2}$ on right-side) and p_h as the total number of rows of padding (unevenly $\frac{p_h}{2}$ on the upper side and $\frac{p_h}{2}$ on the lower side), then output dimension would be

$$(n_w - k_w + p_w + 1) \times (n_h - k_h + p_h + 1) \tag{7}$$

This implies that the width and height of the output expanded p_w and p_h, correspondingly. In the general scenario, one could set $p_w = k_w - 1$ and $p_h = k_h - 1$ to enable the output to have the same dimensions as the input. This way, it would be easy to estimate the output dimensions of each layer in a convolutional network. If the value of k_w is odd, then the input of the convolution layer will be padded with $\frac{p_w}{2}$ columns on both sides of the width. If k_w is even, then the input of the convolution layer will be padded with $\left\lceil \frac{p_w}{2} \right\rceil$ columns on the left side and will be padded with $\left\lfloor \frac{p_w}{2} \right\rfloor$ columns on the right side. In a similar way, the two edges of the input height will be padded. Convolutional networks usually use convolution kernels whose size is an odd value, such as one, three, five, or seven.

Setting up non-even sizes of the kernel could enable the network to reserve the spatial dimensionality while attaining an even value of padding, thereby allowing adding an identical number of columns on the right hand as well as the left hand, and an identical number of rows on top and bottom. This ability to maintain dimensionality provides a clerical advantage. For the two-dimensional input X, the odd kernel size enables attaining the output Y with the same size, in which computing the element $Y[i, j]$ is based on the convolution between the kernel centered on $X[i, j]$ and the input map.

5.3.4.2 Stride

As a matter of fact, the cross-correlation is performed by horizontally sliding a convolution kernel from the left side toward the right side of the rows of input. This process is repeated for all rows in the input. The earlier discussion assumes that the default sliding step for the convolution kernel is one element per time. Nevertheless, some tasks require downsampling the input or reducing computation, which, in turn, necessitate slipping the kernel with step size of two or more elements per time, skipping the midway elements. The term stride defines the number of rows and columns navigated per single slide. To this point, the convolutional layers are assumed to have a stride of one, for both width and height, but it can be changed according to the model you need to build. Figure 5.4 illustrates the convolution procedure with a horizontal stride of two and a vertical stride of three. To calculate the shaded output element, the

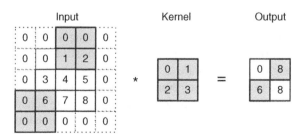

Figure 5.4 Example of convolution layer with strides of size 3 × 2.

shaded input cells are cross-correlated with the kernel matrix as follows:

$$0 \times 0 + 0 \times 1 + 1 \times 2 + 2 \times 3 = 8, 0 \times 0 + 6 \times 1 + 0 \times 2 + 0 \times 3 = 6.$$

It could be noted that once the first element in the first output row is calculated, the kernel glides by two columns toward the right. On the other hand, once the corresponding output is computed, the kernel slips down in three steps. One may ask why the kernel does not continue sliding two columns to the right. The answer is there is only a single column remaining to the right, and this way, the input elements could not match the kernel (except another column is added with padding). Generally speaking, assuming the stride of the width is s_w and the stride of the height is s_h, then the shape of the output would be

$$\left\lfloor \frac{(n_w - k_w + p_w + s_w)}{s_w} \right\rfloor \times \left\lfloor \frac{(n_h - k_h + p_h + s_h)}{s_h} \right\rfloor \tag{8}$$

If we set $p_w = k_w - 1$ and $p_h = k_h - 1$, then the shape of output would be shortened to

$$\left\lfloor \frac{(n_w + s_w - 1)}{s_w} \right\rfloor \times \left\lfloor \frac{(n_h + s_h - 1)}{s_h} \right\rfloor \tag{9}$$

In addition, if the input dimensions are divisible by the strides, the output dimension will be equal to

$$\frac{(n_w)}{s_w} \times \frac{(n_h)}{s_h} \tag{10}$$

For convenience, if the padding value on the width and height dimensions are p_w and p_h correspondingly, the padding is referred to as $P = (p_w, p_h)$ even when $p_w = p_h$. Similarly, if the stride on the width and height dimensions are s_w and s_h correspondingly, the stride is referred to as $S = (s_w, s_h)$ even when $s_w = s_h$. As an initial value, the convolution has zero padding and unit stride. In actual fact, it is rare to use heterogeneous padding or strides in practical case studies, i.e. case $p_w = p_h$ and $s_w = s_h$.

5.4 Multiple Channels

To this point, the discussion assumes the convolutional input, convolutional output, and kernels, each is structured in the form of two-dimensional tensors. However, this assumption has some limitations and cannot be generalized. So far, this assumption ignored that RGB images are made up of three channels specifying the value of red, green, and blue colors, i.e. $512 \times 512 \times 3$. In fact, the shape of images is determined with three dimensions rather than two as someone might think. These dimensions are width, height, and the number of channels. Whereas the former two dimensions encode spatial relations of image content, the latter can be considered allocating a multidimensional representation to each pixel value. Besides, just as the input of the convolutional network is shaped as a three-dimensional tensor, hidden representations, in this case, are similarly formulated as a three-dimensional map. So, the network now has a vector of features conforming to each spatial position, rather than just a single feature. To make things clearer, one can imagine the output of convolutions as a stack of feature maps, which can also be known as the *output channels or filters* of this layer. Instinctively, one could envisage that at earlier layers next to the input layer, some channels might become dedicated to features of the edges while others might be dedicated to features, textures, and so on. By taking into account the number of channels in the convolutional network, the input and/or output of the layer has a three-dimensional shape.

5.4.1 Multi-Channel Inputs

For multi-channel input data, it is necessary to build a convolutional kernel with an identical number of input channels, so as to enable the execution of convolution with the input data. Given the number of input channels c_i, the convolutional kernel must have a number of input channels that equals c_i. when the spatial dimension of convolution kernel size is $k_w \times k_h$, then having $c_i = 1$ means that the kernel has a two-dimensional tensor of shape $k_w \times k_h$. Nevertheless, if $c_i > 1$, then, for each input channel, the kernel needs to encompass a tensor of shape $k_w \times k_h$. The concatenation of c_i

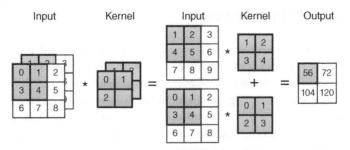

Figure 5.5 Example of two-dimensional convolution with two input channels.

tensors lead to a convolutional kernel with a shape $k_w \times k_h \times c_i$. In this way, cross-correlation can be carried out between the two-dimensional kernel and two-dimensional input at each channel. Then, the c_i results are added up together (over the channel dimension) to produce a two-dimensional tensor as the output of convolution between the kernel and input sharing the same number of channels. The convolution operation using multi-channel input is illustrated in Figure 5.5. The shaded output element can be computed based on cross-correlation between the shaded input cells and kernel tensor as follows:

$$(1 \times 1 + 2 \times 2 + 4 \times 3 + 5 \times 4) + (0 \times 0 + 1 \times 1 + 3 \times 2 + 4 \times 3) = 56$$

where the first term represents the output of cross-correlation on the first channel, while the second one represents the output of cross-correlation on the second channel.

5.4.2 Multi-Channel Output

In previous sections, convolution operation has single output irrespective of how many input channels it has. Nevertheless, as stated earlier, it comes to be absolutely necessary for convolution operation to include multiple channels. Commonly, the channel dimension gets increased by the increase of the depth of the convolutional network, where the spatial resolution is typically sacrificed in order to achieve higher channel dimensions.

Instinctively, one can imagine each channel as countering a distinct group of a learnt feature representation. Realism is a little more sophisticated than this simplistic interpretation since representations are not learned independently, but instead are designed to be beneficial when used in conjunction with other representations. As a result, it is possible that a single channel does not learn a specific set of features (edge features or texture features), but instead that these set of features occupy a certain area of channel space. To get a multi-channel output, given the c_o and c_i as number of input and output channels, respectively, and k_w and k_h as the height and width of the kernel. Then, a kernel tensor of shape $k_w \times k_h \times c_i$ must be created for *every* output channel. These tensors need to be concatenated over the channel dimension so as to get a convolution kernel of the shape $k_w \times k_h \times c_i \times c_o$. Each output channel is computed from the cross-correlation between the corresponding convolution kernel and all channels in the input tensor.

5.4.3 Convolutional Kernel 1 × 1

As the name implies, a 1×1 convolutional kernel has $k_w = k_h = 1$, which seems to make no sense. Commonly, the role of the convolutional kernel is to slide over input to correlate neighboring input elements in the spatial space. However, this does not apply to the convolution (1×1) layer. Even so, it provides common functionality that can be exploited to develop a complex and elegant convolutional network. Since the smallest kernel size is applied, the convolution (1×1) is unable to learn or extract interaction patterns among neighboring elements in spatial space. So, the calculation in the convolution (1×1) just takes place at the channel space. Figure 5.6 illustrates an example of the convolution process between the 1×1 kernel having three input channels and two output channels. Notice that the output has the same dimensions as the input, which means that every output element is computed by linearly combining the elements in *the same position* in input channels. This way the convolution (1×1) can be elegantly applied to adjust the number of channels in convolutional networks and hence enable controlling model complexity. It is commonly believed that the convolution (1×1) function as a linear/dense layer used to convert

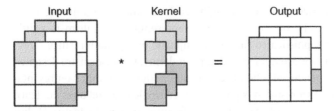

Figure 5.6 Example of two-dimensional convolution (1 × 1) with three input channels and two output channels.

c_i values of each input element to the corresponding c_o output values. Since it is still considered a convolution, the parameters are bound to the input map. Hence, the number of parameters of 1×1 kernel are computed as $c_i \times c_o$ plus the bias value.

5.5 Pooling Layers

When convolutional network processes images, the network needs to progressively decrease the spatial resolution of the learnt feature maps by aggregating the features so that the deeper the network, the greater is the receptive field of each hidden node in any deep layer.

Recall the example of classifying the image as containing a cat or a dog. It is notable that nodes need to be sensitive to the whole input (global representation). By progressively aggregating the hidden features and generating rougher maps, the objective of eventually learning a global representation can be accomplished while benefiting from the abilities of intermediary convolutions to efficiently learn valuable hidden representations. Furthermore, translation invariance is an important consideration when the convolution is looking for lower-level features, such as edges. In this regard, *pooling layers* are discussed in this section to act as a key enabler for two main objectives:

- Enable the convolution network to downsample the learnt representation across spatial dimensions.
- Enable alleviating the sensitivity of convolution network to locality.

5.5.1 Max Pooling

As with the convolutional layer, the pooling layer functions by applying a window (with fixed dimensions) to scan all input elements in accordance with a predefined stride, calculating one output for each navigated position. Nevertheless, different from kernelized convolution operation, the pooling operation does not contain any kernel. So, it does not have parameters to learn. Rather, a pooling operation is calculated with determinism, such that it calculates a particular value based on the input elements covered by the pooling window. When the pooling layer calculates the maximum input value under the pooling window as its output, it is called max-pool as an acronym for maximum pooling. As with the convolutional layer, the pooling window start sliding the input feature map from the top left corner scanning the input tensor in a row-by-row manner. By each sliding step, the max-pool layer returns the maximum value in the current input subtensor covered by the pooling window. Figure 5.7 illustrates an example of a max-pool operation on one channel input, whereas four output elements are derived from each pooling window as follows:

$$
\begin{aligned}
\max{(0; 1; 3; 4)} &= 4, \\
\max{(1; 2; 4; 5)} &= 5, \\
\max{(3; 4; 6; 7)} &= 7, \\
\max{(4; 5; 7; 8)} &= 8,
\end{aligned}
\tag{11}
$$

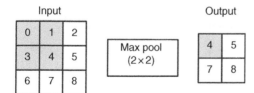

Figure 5.7 Maximum pool layer with a pooling window of shape 2 × 2.

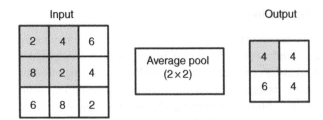

Figure 5.8 Average pool layer with a dimension of 2 × 2.

5.5.2 Average Pooling

Average pooling is a variant of the pooling layer that calculate the average of values in the input subtensor covered by the pooling window as its output.

Similar to convolutional layers, pooling layers could control and adjust the shape of output using padding and stride hyper-parameters. This way, the preferred output shape can be obtained by padding the input and/or changing the stride size. In the case of multi-channel, the pooling operation is applied on each input channel independently, instead of adding outputs up over channel dimension as stated with the convolutional kernel. This, in turn, implies that the pooling layer has no effect on the number of channels as the number of channels are always the same for both input and output. Figure 5.8 illustrates an example of an average pooling operation on multi-channel input, whereas four output elements are derived from each pooling window as follows:

$$
\text{average}(2; 4; 8; 2) = 4,
$$
$$
\text{average}(4; 6; 2; 4) = 4,
$$
$$
\text{average}(8; 2; 6; 8) = 6,
$$
$$
\text{average}(2; 4; 8; 2) = 4,
$$

$$(12)$$

5.6 Normalization Layers

Normalization is a technique typically applied to prepare data before training the model. The primary objective of normalization is to offer a uniform scale for numerical values. If the dataset includes numerical data fluctuating in a big range, it will skew the learning process, leading to inconsistent training of the model. One possible reason for this dilemma is the distribution of the inputs to layers could differ after the update of mini-batch parameters. This could lead the learning algorithm to continually follow a moving target and hence hamper the convergence of the network. This variation in the distribution of layers' inputs in the network is known as "internal covariate shift." In this regard, normalization has always been an active research point in deep learning because of its potential to reduce training time by a huge factor for several reasons. First, it can make the network unbiased to high-valued features by normalizing each feature so that they maintain the contribution of every feature, as some feature has higher numerical value than others. This way, it eliminates the Internal Covariate Shift. Second, it can smooth the loss surface Third, it can increase the convergence as it does not allow weights to explode all over the place and constrains them to a specific range. Forth, an unintentional gain of normalization is that it can help regularize the deep networks (just to some extent, not substantially). When it comes to optimizing neural networks, normalization has been proved to be beneficial since 1998 [1]. After the publication of batch normalization [2] in 2015, this study direction has been widely investigated by researchers. A slew variety of normalization approaches has emerged since then. In this section, we explore the state-of-the-art *normalization* layer as common and efficient techniques for consistently speeding up the convergence of deep networks.

5.6.1 Batch Normalization

As an example of the need for batch normalization, consider a few of the issues that arise during the training of deep networks.

First, data preparation options often have a significant impact on final outcomes. Standardization of input features to have a variance of one and a mean of zero was a trivial step to prepare real data for training. This standardization is demonstrated beneficial for optimizers because it sets the parameters on the same scale before the optimization process begins. Second, it is also important to note that as deep networks are being trained, the hidden layers' variables might take values with wildly changing magnitudes: across levels, or even between units in the same layer, and over time, as we adjust the model parameters. Batch normalization's creators speculated informally that the network's convergence could be hampered by this skewed distribution of such variables. As a final point, deeper networks are difficult to model and can be easily overfitted. As a result, the importance of regularization increases.

Batch normalization concentrates on standardizing the inputs such that they have approximately zero mean and unit variance (Figure 5.9). In practice, for each input to the batch normalization layer, the mean of the current batch is subtracted, and the output is divided by the standard deviation wherever both are projected according to the current mini-batch's statistics. You should be aware that attempting batch normalization with mini-batches of size one will yield no useful results because each hidden unit would have a value of zero if the means were subtracted. Batch

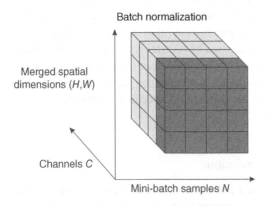

Figure 5.9 Illustration of batch normalization.

normalization may have a greater impact on batch size selection than it would otherwise have, and this is something to keep in mind.

It is possible that the model is better suited to handle inputs with a mean and variance that is not equal to zero, and one, respectively. Thus, batch normalization comes up with two trainable parameters, namely *scale parameter* γ and *shift parameter* β to avoid arbitrary selection of unit variance.

In mathematical terms, given the input x_i belonging to a mini-batch $B = \{x_1, ..., x_{|B|}\}$. The main steps to calculate the batch normalized output $y_i = BN_{\gamma,\beta}(x_i)$ is described as follows:

Step 1: Calculate the mini-batch mean

$$\mu_B \leftarrow \frac{1}{|B|} \sum_{i=1}^{m} x_i \tag{13}$$

Step 2: Calculate the mini-batch variance

$$\sigma_B^2 \leftarrow \frac{1}{|B|} \sum_{i=1}^{m} (x_i - \mu_B)^2 \tag{14}$$

Step 3: Normalize to obtain mini-batch with zero mean and unit variance.

$$\hat{x}_i \leftarrow \frac{x_i - \mu_B}{\sqrt{\sigma_B^2 + \epsilon}} \tag{15}$$

where $\epsilon > 0$ denotes a constant to be added to the variance to guarantee that there is no chance to divide by zero, even in situations wherever the practical variance value may possibly approximate to zero.

Step 4: Scale and shift

$$y_i = BN_{\gamma,\beta}(x_i) = \gamma \odot \hat{x}_i + \beta \tag{16}$$

How does batch normalization aid in the training of deep networks? Gradient descent, as explained before, enables the network to determine the gradient from the current inputs to each layer and then reduces the weights in that direction. Nevertheless, because each of the layers is built on top of the one before it, even a small change in the weights of an earlier layer can have a significant impact on how the input data is distributed, resulting in less-than-ideal signals for the network. There are several ways to update weights in a neural network; a few of them are more efficient than others; and some of them are less efficient than others. This is why batch normalization is so popular since it offers a training programme that is both consistent and efficient.

However, some drawbacks still are encountered when batch normalization is used:

- Due to the fact that why batch normalization uses the mini-batch to estimate the population mean and variance in each iteration, it requires higher batch sizes while training. Given the possibility of high input resolution, batch normalization may be a complex operation to train for applications like medical image segmentation for the reason that training with bigger batch sizes is not computationally viable.
- Recurrent networks (discussed in later chapter) are not compatible with batch normalization. As a result of this difficulty, recurrent networks would require performing normalization in each timestep, which, in turn, is more difficult to employ batch normalization in such a family of deep networks.
- Training and inference are calculated in a different way: Batch normalization layer does not compute the statistics from the mini-batch of test data; rather it uses the fixed statistics computed from the training data. Using batch normalization can be risky because it provides more complexity and demands a high degree of caution.

5.6.2 Layer Normalization

Motivated by the findings obtained by batch normalization, layer normalization [4] was proposed as a layer for normalizing the activations in which the statistics (mean and variance) are calculated *for* each individual sample *across* all channels and both spatial dimensions rather than calculated across the mini-batch *and spatial dimensions* (Figure 5.10). In other words, it normalizes input across the features rather than normalizing input features

Layer normalization

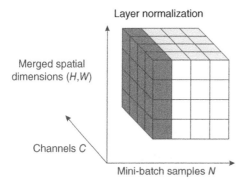

Merged spatial
dimensions (*H,W*)

Channels *C*

Mini-batch samples *N*

Figure 5.10 Illustration of batch normalization.

across the batch dimension in batch normalization. This way, layer normalization addresses the limitation of batch normalization by eliminating the reliance on batches and facilitating the normalizing of the layers of recurrent networks. Essentially, layer normalization normalizes each feature of the activations to zero mean and unit variance.

In mathematical terms, given inputs x_i belonging to a mini-batch $B = \{x_1, ..., x_{|B|}\}$, each sample x_i includes K elements, such that the length of flattened x_i is K, by normalizing the inputs using trainable scale parameter γ and shift parameter β, the outputs could be denoted $B' = \{y_1, ..., y_{|B|}\}$, where $y_i = \text{LN}_{\gamma, \beta}(x_i)$. Since layer normalization does not depend on batch statistics, it normalizes with the mean and variance of each vector as described here:

Step 1: Calculate the feature/channel mean

$$\mu_i \leftarrow \frac{1}{K} \sum_{k=1}^{K} x_{i,k} \tag{17}$$

Step 2: Calculate feature/channel variance

$$\sigma_i^2 \leftarrow \frac{1}{K} \sum_{k=1}^{K} (x_{i,k} - \mu_i)^2 \tag{18}$$

Step 3: Normalize each sample such that each feature has zero mean and unit variance. The ϵ denotes the numerical stability constant in a scenario in which the denominator turns into zero by coincidence.

$$\hat{x}_{i,k} \leftarrow \frac{x_{i,k} - \mu_i}{\sqrt{\sigma_i^2 + \epsilon}} \tag{19}$$

Step 4: Scale and shift

$$y_i = \mathrm{LN}_{\gamma,\beta}(x_i) = \gamma \odot x_{i,k} + \beta \tag{20}$$

For convolution outputs, the math has to be tweaked a bit because it does not make sense to combine all the elements from different channels together and calculate their mean and variance for all of them at once. For each of the channels, normalization was done solely for that channel, and no other channels were normalized.

Given the four-dimensional feature map $x_{n,c,h,w} \in \mathbb{R}^{[N,H,W,C]}$, where N = Batch size, C = Number of channels (filters) in that layer, H = Height of feature map, and W = Width of feature map. These calculations can generalize to these four-dimensional tensors by calculating the mean across all channels and the spatial dimension as follows:

$$\mu_n = \frac{1}{CHW} \sum_{c=1}^{C} \sum_{h=1}^{H} \sum_{w=1}^{W} x_{n,c,h,w} \tag{21}$$

$$\sigma_n^2 = \frac{1}{CHW} \sum_{c=1}^{C} \sum_{h=1}^{H} \sum_{w=1}^{W} (x_{n,c,h,w} - \mu_n)^2 \tag{22}$$

$$\hat{x}_{n,c,h,w} \leftarrow \frac{x_{n,c,h,w} - \mu_n}{\sqrt{\sigma_n^2 + \epsilon}} \tag{23}$$

$$y_{n,c,h,w} = \mathrm{LN}_{\gamma,\beta}(x_i) = \gamma \odot \hat{x}_{n,c,h,w} + \beta \tag{24}$$

5.6.3 Instance Normalization

Instance normalization [5] is another layer for normalizing the activation of layers in such a way that the mean and variance statistics are computed for each specific channel for each individual sample across both spatial dimensions (Figure 5.11). When testing, the Instance Normalization layer is used instead of Batch

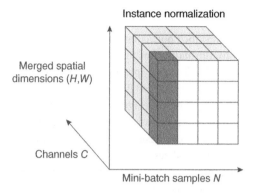

Figure 5.11 Illustration of instance normalization.

normalization because of non-dependency of mini-batch statistics. The affine parameters in Instance Normalization can have a profound effect on the final image's aesthetic. Individual samples can be normalized to the target style in instance normalization, whereas BN can only normalize the style of the entire dataset. So, it is much easier to train a model to do something in a precise way. Content manipulation and local details are more important to the rest of the network than the original global ones. To make clear how instance normalization works out, let us consider four-dimensional sample feature maps $x \in \mathbb{R}^{[N,H,W,C]}$ that establish an input tensor to the instance normalization layer. In instance normalization, a single training sample feature map (shaded in the figure) is considered to calculate the mean and variance. Thus, the instance normalization is performed for a single instance x_{nc} as follows:

$$\mu_{n,c} = \frac{1}{HW} \sum_{h=1}^{H} \sum_{w=1}^{W} x_{n,c,h,w} \tag{25}$$

$$\sigma_{n,c}^2 = \frac{1}{HW} \sum_{h=1}^{H} \sum_{w=1}^{W} \left(x_{n,c,h,w} - \mu_{n,c}\right)^2 \tag{26}$$

$$\hat{x}_{n,c,h,w} \leftarrow \frac{x_{n,c,h,w} - \mu_{n,c}}{\sqrt{\sigma_{n,c}^2 + \epsilon}} \tag{27}$$

$$y_{n,c,h,w} = \text{LN}_{\gamma,\beta}(x_i) = \gamma \odot \hat{x}_{n,c,h,w} + \beta \tag{28}$$

5.6.4 Group Normalization

Layer normalization and instance normalization are both compromises that result in group normalization [6, 7]. The main distinction between layer normalization and instance normalization is that layer normalization takes the channel dimension into account, while instance normalization does not (Figure 5.12). On the other hand, group normalization focuses on normalizing channels inside a certain group. For now, batch dimensions are not being utilized (only batch normalization normalizes over the batch dimension). Group normalization is comparable to layer normalization in that it is executed along the feature direction, but unlike LN, it separates the features into specific groups and normalizes each group separately. When used as a hyperparameter, group normalization outperforms layer normalization in most cases.

5.6.5 Weight Normalization

Unlike conventional normalization methods that concentrate on activations, weight normalization [3] was proposed as a process of reparametrizing the weight vectors in a deep network, which functions by decoupling the length of these from their direction. In other words, weight normalization can be declared as a technique for enhancing the optimizability of the weights of deep

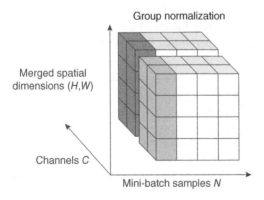

Figure 5.12 Illustration of group normalization.

networks. Weight normalization seeks to standardize the weight vectors themselves. Even more remarkably, weight normalization decouples the value and norm of the weight vectors. Therefore, rather than learning a weight vector w, the network learns a vector v representing the direction of the weight vector, as well as scalar g – the norm representing, unofficially, the intensity or significance of the weight vector.

$$w = \frac{g}{\|v\|} v \qquad (29)$$

where w are calculated normally during the forward propagation, the parameters g and v are optimized in the backward propagation step. v denotes k-dimensional vector, $\|v\|$ represents the Euclidean norm of parameter v. This decoupling has the impact of fixing the Euclidean norm of w to get $\|w\| = g$, unbiased of the parameters v. Similar to batch normalization, weight normalization accelerates the training of the deep network. However, it can be applied to recurrent networks. Weight normalization, on the other hand, is less stable than batch normalization when it comes to training deep networks, which is why it is not often employed in practice.

5.7 Convolutional Neural Networks (LeNet)

To this point, all the components necessary to build a completely functional convolutional network have been introduced throughout the previous sections. Now, let us present *LeNet* as one of the first released convolutional models that make an earlier breakthrough in computer vision tasks. The *LeNet* was proposed by Yann LeCun for learning to recognize handwritten digits in images [8].

Broadly speaking, the architecture of LeNet is composed of two main building blocks, as illustrated in Figure 5.13. First, a convolutional encoder comprising two convolutional layers. Second, the linear block constructed with three fully connected layers. In more detail, convolutional encoder stacks two convolutional layers, each followed by a sigmoid activation function, and a later average pooling layer (size $= 2 \times 2$). Bearing in mind that ReLU activation and max pooling layer provide a better performance, however, these

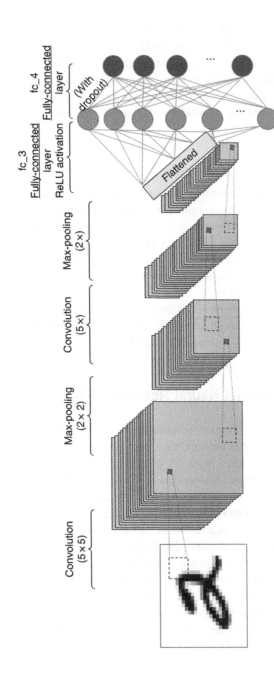

Figure 5.13 The architecture of LeNet convolutional network.

findings had not reached in the 1990s. The convolutional layers map spatially coordinated inputs to a number of two-dimensional feature maps, and normally growing up the number of channels to six output channels and 16 output channels, respectively. The feature maps of the convolutional encoder have four-dimensional shapes (i.e. batch size, number of channels, height, and width). Thus, to feed these maps into the linear block, they must be reshaped into two-order maps as projected by linear/dense layers. To remember, this new two-dimensional representation uses one dimension to index instances in the mini-batch and the other to provide the flat vector representation of each instance. The linear block in LeNet consists of three linear/dense layers, with 120, 84, and 10 nodes, correspondingly.

5.8 Case Studies

Apart from IoT security data, the convolutional networks were essentially proposed for image recognition task. Hence, the case studies presented in this chapter are related to image classification data.

5.8.1 Handwritten Digit Classification (One Channel Input)

In computer vision and deep learning, the classification of Modified National Institute of Standards and Technology (MNIST) handwritten digits issue is a popular dataset that is used to classify handwritten digits. However, despite the fact that the dataset has been successfully solved, it may be used as a starting point for learning and practicing how to create convolutional networks for image classification from scratch, including how to evaluate and use them. In this section, you will learn how to implement the concepts you learned in the previous sections of one-channel images from MNIST data.

5.8.2 Dog vs. Cat Image Classification (Multi-Channel Input)

In computer vision, the Dogs vs. Cats dataset is a popular dataset that includes two classes of photos including either a dog or a cat. Though the problem seems straightforward, it was only successfully focused on the past few years using convolutional networks. Despite the fact that this classification problem is efficiently solved, it can be utilized as the starting point to learning and practice how to develop, train, and use convolutional networks for image classification from scratch. In this section, you will learn how to implement the concepts you learned in the previous sections of one-channel images from Dogs vs. Cats dataset.

5.9 Supplementary Materials

https://github.com/DEEPOLOGY-AI/DL-Book-Wiley-2022/tree/main/Ch5

References

1 LeCun, Y.A., Bottou, L., Orr, G.B., and Müller, K.R. (2012). Efficient backprop. *Lect. Notes Comput. Sci. (including subseries Lecture Notes in Artificial Intelligence and Lecture Notes in Bioinformatics)* 7700 LECTU, Springer: 9–48.

2 Ioffe, S. and Szegedy, C. (2015). Batch normalization: accelerating deep network training by reducing internal covariate shift. In: *32nd International Conference on Machine Learning, ICML 2015*, vol. 1 (ed. F. Bach and D. Blei), 448–456.

3 Salimans, T. and Kingma, D.P. (2016). Weight normalization: a simple reparameterization to accelerate training of deep neural networks. *Adv. Neural Inf. Proces. Syst.* 29: 901–909.

4 Ba, J.L., Kiros, J.R., and Hinton, G.E. (2016). Layer normalization. *arXiv preprint arXiv: 1607.06450* [Online]. http://arxiv.org/abs/1607.06450 (accesssed 20 August 2022).

5 Ulyanov, D., Vedaldi, A., and Lempitsky, V. (2016). Instance normalization: the missing ingredient for fast stylization. *arXiv* *preprint arXiv: 1607.08022* [Online]. http://arxiv.org/abs/1607.08022 (accesssed 20 August 2022).

6 Gitman, I. and Ginsburg, B. (2017). Comparison of batch normalization and weight normalization algorithms for the large-scale image classification. *arXiv preprint arXiv: 1709.08145* [Online]. http://arxiv.org/abs/1709.08145 (accesssed 20 August 2022).

7 Wu, Y. and He, K. (2020). Group normalization. *Int. J. Comput. Vis.* 128 (3): 742–755. https://doi.org/10.1007/s11263-019-01198-w.

8 LeCun, Y., Bottou, L., Bengio, Y., and Haffner, P. (1998). β. *Proc. IEEE* 86 (11): 2278–2323. https://doi.org/10.1109/5.726791.

6

Dive Into Convolutional Neural Networks

6.1 Introduction

Having learned the fundamentals of building the convolutional network in two-dimensional space, we will now take a look at some special cases of convolutional topologies. Throughout this chapter, we will look at a variety of important convolutional layers that have served as the foundation or the backbone for building many advanced convolutional networks. A large number of achievements in convolutional layer design make this chapter not enough to cover all of them. So, we are determined to focus on the most important and common convolutional layers.

This chapter explores different variants of convolutional layers adapted for a different level of dimensionality including one-dimensional data and three-dimensional data. Then, we introduce the additional hyperparameters that might be included for three-dimensional convolutional layers and pooling layers. Next, we explore the transposed convolution layer and mathematics behind it and how it links and differs from the standard convolutions discussed in the previous chapter. A dilated convolutional layer is then explored to the main idea it covers and the possible benefits of using it to skip some of the points. The dilation hyperparameters are discussed in this regard. After that, we investigate the separable convolution as an elegant way of reducing the computation involved in the standard convolution. This argument is critically

Deep Learning Approaches for Security Threats in IoT Environments,
First Edition. Mohamed Abdel-Basset, Nour Moustafa, and Hossam Hawash.
© 2023 The Institute of Electrical and Electronics Engineers, Inc.
Published 2023 by John Wiley & Sons, Inc.

important for developing a deep learning solution for resource-constrained Internet of Things (IoT) devices.

6.2 One-Dimensional Convolutional Network

6.2.1 One-Dimensional Convolution

In the one-dimensional convolutional layer, a configurable number of filters are used, each of which has a fixed size, and a convolution operation is conducted between a vector and the filter to produce a new vector with the number of channels that correspond to the number of filters. In order to inject nonlinearity into the tensor, the activation function is applied to each value.

When working with sequence datasets, one-dimensional filters are typically utilized because they are the most simplistic (but can be used for other use-cases as well). When utilized for local one-dimensional subsequence extraction and local pattern identification within the convolution window, they can be useful. When a convolution filter is applied to a sequence, additional features can be extracted from it as seen in Figure 6.1.

Since then, convolutional networks have been used in a variety of sequence modeling applications. The term "sequential" refers to data that can be regarded as a sequence of values. One-dimensional convolutional layers are a perfect fit for jobs in this area because the sequence is used as input which contains patterns along a single spatial dimension. Thus, it can be used as a replacement for recurrent networks in some cases and it is possible to run them in parallel for extremely rapid computations.

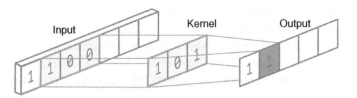

Figure 6.1 Illustration of the one-dimensional convolutional layer with a kernel size of 3.

Time series modeling is another important application area where one-dimensional convolutional layers are useful, especially in IoT environments, where sensory data mostly follow this format of data. For the same reasons as before, we are looking for patterns across time in our input data (i.e. over time dimension). In time series, the data has "temporal" dimension, which is commonly referred to as spatial.

Let us take an example. Given the input = [1, 0, 2, 3, 0, 1, 1] and kernel = [2, 1, 3], the output of one-dimensional convolutional layer can be calculated as follows:

$$
\begin{aligned}
1 \times 2 + 0 \times 1 + 2 \times 3 &= 8 \\
0 \times 2 + 2 \times 1 + 3 \times 3 &= 11 \\
2 \times 2 + 3 \times 1 + 0 \times 3 &= 7 \\
3 \times 2 + 0 \times 1 + 1 \times 3 &= 9 \\
0 \times 2 + 1 \times 1 + 1 \times 3 &= 4
\end{aligned}
\tag{1}
$$

which means that the output will be [8, 11, 7, 9, 4].

6.2.2 One-Dimensional Pooling

One-dimensional pooling layer is an extension of the pooling layers described in the previous chapter. However, it works by sliding a window with a horizontal size over the incoming vector data, calculating the max or average in each particular window. The number of steps the window takes each time is defined by the horizontal stride. These layers can be inserted following one or more one-dimensional convolutional layers to downsample the received information from the previous vector (Figure 6.2).

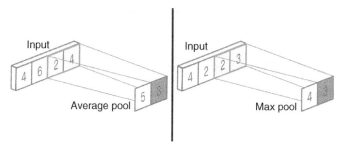

Figure 6.2 Illustration of one-dimensional pooling layers.

6.3 Three-Dimensional Convolutional Network

In the previous chapter, we demonstrated the use of a convolutional layer to process three-dimensional input such as RGB images (width, height, and depth). However, in the field of deep learning, this technique is generally referred to as two-dimensional. Such three-dimensional data is fed into two-dimensional convolution, which has a number of filters equal to the depth of its input. In two-dimensional convolution, there are just two ways in which the filter can move (height and width of the image). In this case, the result is a two-dimensional image (with one or more channels).

6.3.1 Three-Dimensional Convolution

Indeed, the three-dimensional convolutional layers were introduced as an extension to the two-dimensional convolutional layers in which the filter depth is smaller than the input layer depth. In this way, the kernel in three-dimensional convolutional layers can slide over the input column's three dimensions (height, width, and channels of the image). There is only one integer at each point, thanks to the element-by-element multiplication and addition. At each sliding step, the element-wise multiplication followed by addition results in one output value. Given that the convolutional kernel is sliding in a three-dimensional space, the output elements are also assembled in a three-dimensional space (Figure 6.3).

When it comes to learning the spatial interactions of three-dimensional data, three-dimensional convolutions work in a manner similar to two-dimensional ones. This kind of information is greatly beneficial for modeling the relationships in three-dimensional sensory data, volumetric biomedical images, etc.

6.3.2 Three-Dimensional Pooling

As the name implies, three-dimensional pooling layers are extending the pooling layers described in the previous chapter by sliding a three-dimensional window over the incoming volumetric data, calculating the max or average in each particular window. As with

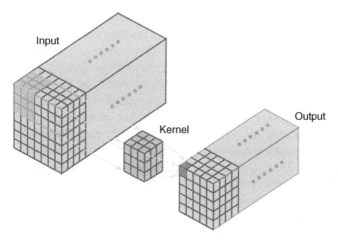

Figure 6.3 Illustration of three-dimensional convolutional operation.

three-dimensional convolutions, the three-dimensional pooling window moves over the input in three directions.

6.4 Transposed Convolution Layer

Most of the time, the opposite of convolution is what is needed in many applications and network designs; we want to do upsampling rather than downconvolution. High-resolution images can be generated by converting low-dimensional feature maps into high-dimensional ones, as in the case of an automatic encoder or a semantic segmentation algorithm, for example. By employing interpolation algorithms or manually defining rules, upsampling was formerly possible. When it comes to modern architectures like neural networks, the network is able to learn the transformation on its own, without the need for human intervention. The transposed convolution can be used to accomplish this. It is sometimes called *fractionally strided convolution*.

In literature, the deconvolution layer was incorrectly used to refer to a transposed convolution. However, the deconvolution operation is simply a reversal of the conventional convolution operation. Given the output of the convolution layer, the corresponding input can be retrieved by when that output is deconvolved. Similar to the deconvolution layer, a transposed convolution layer generates the same spatial dimension, but it only reverses the traditional convolution operation by dimensions instead of reversing it by values. The transposed convolution layer acts just like a conventional convolution but on a changed input map. Because of this, some authors object to the term "deconvolution" being used to describe the process of transposed convolution. The term "deconvolution" has stuck mostly because of its simplicity. In this section, we describe why transposed convolution is a better name for this type of operation.

In contrast, a transposed convolutional layer is typically used to perform upsampling, such that the spatial dimension of the output feature maps is larger than the counterpart in the input feature map. Padding and stride have the same definition for the transposed convolution as with the standard convolution. Generally speaking, the design of transposed convolution could be better described as a sequence of four steps:

- Step 1: Specify the padding p and stride value s.
- Step 2: Optionally insert the number of zero, say z, between each row and column of the input. This expands the input dimensions to $(2 \times i - 1) \times (2 \times i - 1)$.
- Step 3: Apply zero-padding to the input map based on hyperparameter p.
- Step 4: Perform convolution operation on the input obtained from the previous step with a stride s.

This way, standard direct convolution can be simply used to implement a transposed convolution. A typical example of that is shown in Figure 6.4, where transposed convolution (kernel size $= 3 \times 3$, padding $= 2 \times 2$) is applied on an input tensor of size 2×2 to give an upsampled output of size 4×4. In this example, step 2 is skipped.

Interestingly enough, the network could map the same 2×2 input map to an output of a different size by simply utilizing elegant padding and stride. In Figure 6.5, transposed convolution received a two-dimension input with the size of 2×2, with one zero element

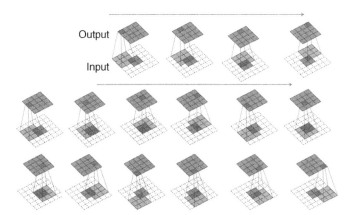

Figure 6.4 Illustration of transposed convolution.

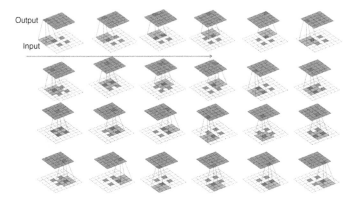

Figure 6.5 Illustration of padded transposed convolution.

between the rows and columns of the input map. With 2×2 padding to a unit stride, transposed convolution results in an output of size 5×5.

Looking at the instances of transposed convolution above can help us develop some intuitions. For a broader understanding of its application, it is helpful to consider how transposed convolution can be implemented in terms of matrix multiplication and matrix transposition concepts. This can help demonstrate that the term "transposed convolution" is a fitting name.

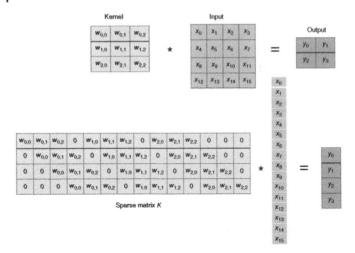

Figure 6.6 Illustration of padded transposed convolution.

Let us begin with a standard convolution scenario, in which a kernel K convolves a large-size input map, $\text{map}_{\text{large}}$ to generate a smaller output map, $\text{map}_{\text{small}}$. This is typically a downsampling operation. This can be defined in terms of matrix multiplication as $K * \text{map}_{\text{large}} = \text{map}_{\text{small}}$. In Figure 6.6, an example is given to illustrate the matrix multiplication in the context of the convolution operation. As shown, the input is reshaped into a 16×1 matrix, and similarly, the kernel is reshaped into a 4×16 sparse matrix. These two matrices are multiplied to obtain a 4×1 matrix that corresponds to the 2×2 output map.

On the other hand, the matrix multiplication of transposed convolution is illustrated in Figure 6.7. As noticed, the kernel matrix is transposed, K^T, to take a shape of 16×4 matrix. Then, it is multiplied by a small feature map, $\text{map}_{\text{small}}$, that is reshaped into a 4×1 matrix to obtain a 16×1 matrix that corresponds to larger feature maps, $\text{map}_{\text{large}}$, with a 4×4 dimension. This can be mathematically expressed as follows:

$$K^T * \text{map}_{\text{small}} = \text{map}_{\text{large}}.$$

It could be noticed that transposed convolution performs upsampling of a small input map to a large one. Hence, one could understand where the name "transposed convolution" is derived from.

$w_{0,0}$	0	0	0
$w_{0,1}$	$w_{0,0}$	0	0
$w_{0,2}$	$w_{0,1}$	$w_{0,0}$	0
0	$w_{0,2}$	$w_{0,1}$	$w_{0,0}$
$w_{1,0}$	0	$w_{0,2}$	$w_{0,1}$
$w_{1,1}$	$w_{1,0}$	0	$w_{0,2}$
$w_{1,2}$	$w_{1,1}$	$w_{1,0}$	0
0	$w_{1,2}$	$w_{1,1}$	$w_{1,0}$
$w_{2,0}$	0	$w_{1,2}$	$w_{1,1}$
$w_{2,1}$	$w_{2,0}$	0	$w_{1,2}$
$w_{2,2}$	$w_{2,1}$	$w_{2,0}$	0
0	$w_{2,2}$	$w_{2,1}$	$w_{2,0}$
0	0	$w_{2,2}$	$w_{2,1}$
0	0	0	$w_{2,2}$
0	0	0	0
0	0	0	0

$$ * \begin{bmatrix} y_0 \\ y_1 \\ y_2 \\ y_3 \end{bmatrix} = \begin{bmatrix} x_0 \\ x_1 \\ x_2 \\ x_3 \\ x_4 \\ x_5 \\ x_6 \\ x_7 \\ x_8 \\ x_9 \\ x_{10} \\ x_{11} \\ x_{12} \\ x_{13} \\ x_{14} \\ x_{15} \end{bmatrix} $$

x_0	x_1	x_2	x_3
x_4	x_5	x_6	x_7
x_8	x_9	x_{10}	x_{11}
x_{12}	x_{13}	x_{14}	x_{15}

Transposed of sparse matrix K

Figure 6.7 Unrolled transposed convolution to matrix multiplication.

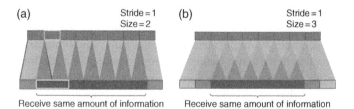

(a) Stride = 1, Size = 2

Receive same amount of information

(b) Stride = 1, Size = 3

Receive same amount of information

Figure 6.8 An illustration of transposed convolution with even overlap. (a) Deconvolution (kernel size = 2, stride = 1); (b) deconvolution (kernel size = 3, stride = 1).

Checkerboard artifacts: The so-called checkerboard artifacts appear when utilizing transposed convolution and are a common source of irritation. Convolution of transposed data produces checkerboard distortions because of "uneven overlap." As a result of this, certain areas receive a greater proportion of the metaphorical paint than others. An example of a transposed convolution output is shown in Figure 6.8, where the input map is received at the upper side and the corresponding output is the bottom side.

In Figure 6.8a, the kernel size is two and the stride is one. As noticed, the first and second output elements are derived from the first input element, as outlined on the left side. Similarly, the second and third output elements are derived from the second input element as outlined. This way, the first and second input elements are contributing to the value second to the output element. As a general rule, all pixels in the intermediate portion receive an equal quantity of input information. In this case, the transposed convolution is said to have an even overlap. Figure 6.8b shows how the center region of output reduces in size as a result of increasing the filter size to three. In any case, the overlap may not be a major concern because it is still equal, thereby the output element still accepts an even amount of input information.

In Figure 6.9a, the stride and kernel size of transposed convolution are equal to two. All output elements are driven by an equal quantity of input information. Each output corresponds to a single input with no overlap. In addition, the equally overlapped region diminishes when the filter size is increased to four, as shown in Figure 6.9b. However, one can still utilize the center of the output as an acceptable output, in which each output element gets an equal volume of input information. In Figure 6.9c and d, the kernel size of transposed convolution is changed to three and five, respectively. Accordingly, output elements receive a non-equal volume of information in these two examples. Despite looking for a continuous area, there is none to be seen. Transposed convolutions with filter sizes that are not divisible by stride have unequal overlap. The checkerboard look is created by this "uneven overlap," which places more paint in some areas than others. In reality, in two dimensions, the region with more unequal overlaps is more extreme. The unevenness is squared when two patterns are compounded together.

While using transposed convolution, there are two ways to minimize these distortions. To begin, avoid the problem of filer overlap by using a filer size split by your stride. Transposed convolution with stride = 1 can also be used to minimize checkerboard noise. However, as several recent models have shown, artifacts can still slip through.

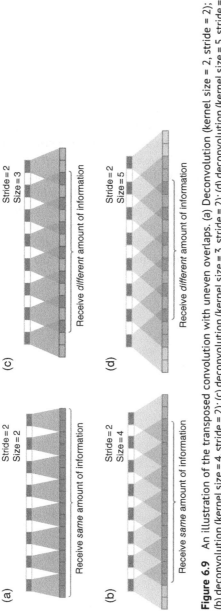

Figure 6.9 An illustration of the transposed convolution with uneven overlaps. (a) Deconvolution (kernel size = 2, stride = 2); (b) deconvolution (kernel size = 4, stride = 2); (c) deconvolution (kernel size = 3, stride = 2); (d) deconvolution (kernel size = 5, stride = 2).

6.5 Atrous/Dilated Convolution

Dilated convolution [1] was proposed as a variant of the convolutional layer in which holes are inserted between the kernel's consecutive parts in order to increase its size. To put it simply, it is the same as convolution, except that input skipping is used so that more of the input may be processed.

The input is extended by an additional parameter called dilation factor l. This means that $(l-1)$ pixels are omitted from the kernel based on the value of this parameter. A comparison of normal and dilated convolution is shown in Figure 6.10. Normal convolution is essentially a dilated convolution with $l = 1$. Convolution with normal and dilated diameters is shown in Figure 6.11. Intuitively, expanding the region of the input image covered without pooling is made possible by using dilated convolution. Every convolution process has the goal of capturing more data from the output. Using this technique allows for a more expansive vision at the same

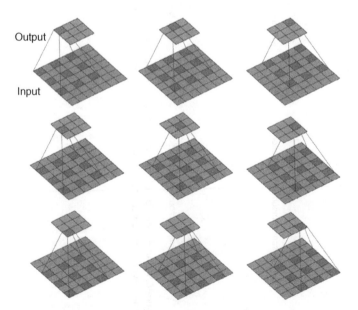

Figure 6.10 Illustration of the dilated (atrous) convolutional kernel.

(a)   (b)   (c)

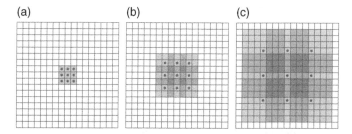

Figure 6.11 Illustration of dilated (atrous) convolutional kernel with different dilation factor: (a) one-dilated convolution, (b) two-dilated convolution, and (c) four-dilated convolution.

amount of processing effort. For example, we can get additional information without increasing the number of kernel parameters using this strategy. Dilated convolution is depicted in the right and model image in Figure 6.11. For each phase of the filtering process, $l = 2$ is kept, which means that we skip one of the input elements ($l - 1$ of pixels).

If the standard convolution is formulated as follows:

$$(F * k)(p) = \sum_{s + t = p} F(s)k(t) \tag{2}$$

then, dilated convolution is formulated as follows:

$$(F *_l k)(p) = \sum_{s + lt = p} F(s)k(t) \tag{3}$$

However, the number of parameters associated with each operation is nearly the same. No additional costs are incurred in the process of "observing" a big responsive database. Thus, dilated convolution can be used to reduce the cost of raising output units' receptive fields without expanding the size of the kernel. This is particularly true when numerous dilated convolutions are applied one after the other.

6.6 Separable Convolutions

A separable convolution refers to the operation of decomposing the standard convolution operation into many convolution operations that can calculate the same output. A single process is divided into two or more subprocesses to achieve the same effect. Primarily, there are two categories of separable convolutions including spatially separable convolution and depth-wise convolution.

6.6.1 Spatially Separable Convolutions

Spatial separable (SS) convolution is a common and simple variant of separable convolutions in which the convolution deals principally with the spatial features (i.e. width and height) of an input (image). This indicates the origin from which the name "spatial separable" comes. In this type, the convolution operation is decomposed into two convolutions that are applied separately in sequence. For instance, the 3×3 kernel given here can be decomposed into two kernels with 3×1 and 1×3 kernels.

$$\begin{vmatrix} -1 & 0 & 1 \\ -2 & 0 & 2 \\ -1 & 0 & 1 \end{vmatrix} = \begin{vmatrix} 1 \\ 2 \\ 1 \end{vmatrix} \times |-1 \ 0 \ 1| \tag{4}$$

In convolution, the input is immediately convolved using the 3×3 kernel of the convolution. In spatially separable convolutions, a kernel (3×1) convolve the input and its output is convolved directly by kernel 1×3, which lead to six learning parameters compared to 9 parameters in case 1×3. In another example, consider a convolution with 5×5 input and a 3×3 kernel (stride = 1, padding = 0). Each output element requires $3 \times 3 = 9$ element-wise multiplications leading to $9 \times 9 = 81$ multiplications to obtain the final output (Figure 6.12). Instead, for SS convolution, a 3×1

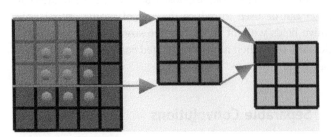

Figure 6.12 Output calculation in standard convolution with a total of 3×3 kernel.

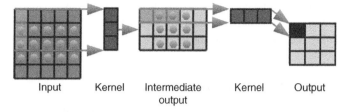

| Input | Kernel | Intermediate output | Kernel | Output |

Figure 6.13 Illustration of a simple example of SS convolution.

kernel is first applied to the 5×5 images. As expected, this kernel slides over the input by five columns in the horizontal direction and three rows in the vertical direction leading to a total of $5 \times 3 = 15$ matrix multiplications, designated as marks in Figure 6.13. At each point, three multiplications are applied leading to a total of $15 \times 3 = 45$ element-wise multiplications. As a result, a 3×5 tensor is obtained as intermediary output. Then, a 1×3 kernel is applied to convolve the intermediary output, which scans the matrix at three columns in the horizontal direction and three rows in the vertical direction. For each of these nine points, three multiplications are performed leading to a total of $9 \times 3 = 27$ element-wise multiplications. Therefore, on the whole, the SS convolution requires $27 + 45 = 72$ operations (Figure 6.13).

Here is some generalization for SS convolution. If a convolution (kernel size $= k_s \times k_s$) is applied to an $n_s \times n_s$ input map (with stride $= 1$ and padding $= 0$), then the total number of multiplications involved in standard convolution is equal to $(n_s - 2) \times (n_s - 2) \times k_s \times k_s$. On the other hand, the number of multiplications taking place spatially separable layer are $n_s \times (n_s - 2) \times k_s + (n_s - 2) \times (n_s - 2) \times k_s = (2n_s - 2) \times (n_s - 2) \times k_s$. This way, the proportion of computing burdens between the former and later layer turns to be

$$\frac{2}{m} + \frac{2}{m(N - 2)} \tag{5}$$

Despite the fact that SS convolution is computationally efficient, they are hardly applied in the early convolution networks. This can be attributed to the fact that sometimes the convolution is not decomposable into many simpler convolutions. It is impossible to search for all potential kernels during training if we use spatially separable convolutions instead of standard convolutions. The training results may not be ideal.

6.6.2 Depth-wise Separable (DS) Convolutions

Moving forward, the DS convolution is a type of separable convolution in which the decomposition of convolution operation considers the depth dimension together with the spatial dimensions. In particular, DS convolution operates by decomposing the convolution kernel into two different kernels called the depthwise kernel and the pointwise kernel.

To validate the concept of DS convolution, let us take an example of a convolution operation in which $3 \times 3 \times 3$ kernel is applied to convolve an input tensor of shape $7 \times 7 \times 3$. The output of this operation is a single channel feature map of $5 \times 5 \times 1$ as shown in Figure 6.14a. When the number of filters is 128, the shape of output turns to be $5 \times 5 \times 128$, as shown in Figure 6.14b.

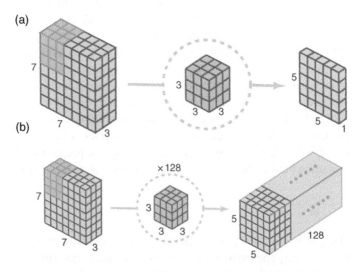

Figure 6.14 Illustration of number of multiplications in standard convolution: (a) single filter view; (b) multiple filter view.

To calculate the total number of multiplications involved in the above operation, the number of filters is firstly multiplied by the kernel size such that $128 \times 3 \times 3 \times 3 = 3456$. Then this output is multiplied by 5×5 since the filters slide over the input 5×5 times. So, the total number of multiplications is $3456 \times 5 \times 5 = 86\,400$.

To implement the above example with DS convolution, two steps are applied. First, *depth-wise* convolution where three individual kernels of size $3 \times 3 \times 1$ are applied to convolve input rather than using $3 \times 3 \times 3$ in the standard convolution (Figure 6.15a). These kernels convolve only a single channel of the input resulting in single-channel maps of size $5 \times 5 \times 1$. Therefore, by staking output maps of these kernels, the output of the *depth-wise* convolution is constituted with the shape $5 \times 5 \times 3$. By the end of this step, the spatial dimensions are shrunk while the depth stays equivalent to the input. Second, the generated feature map in the previous step is convolved with pointwise convolution with a kernel size of $1 \times 1 \times 3$ resulting in $5 \times 5 \times 1$ output for a single filter. By increasing the number of filters to 128, the output typically has a shape of $5 \times 5 \times 128$ (Figure 6.15b).

To calculate the total number of multiplications in the above two steps computation. For depth-wise convolution, the number of

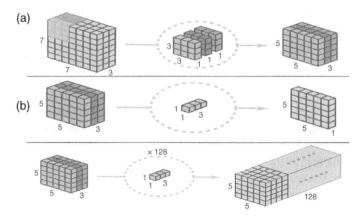

Figure 6.15 Illustration of DS convolution: (a) depth-wise convolution and (b) point-wise convolution.

filters is multiplied by the kernel size such that $3 \times 3 \times 1 \times 3 = 27$. Then this is multiplied by 5×5 since the filters slide over the input 5×5 times. So, the depth-wise convolution has a total of $27 \times 5 \times 5 = 675$ multiplications. For point-wise convolution, similar calculations are applied for 128 filters to give a total of $128 \times 1 \times 1 \times 3 \times 5 \times 5 = 9600$. Therefore, the total number of multiplications in DS convolution are $9600 + 675 = 10\,275$. Generally speaking, the fraction of computing cost between the standard and DS convolution is formulated as follows:

$$\frac{1}{F} + \frac{1}{(k_s)^2} \tag{6}$$

where F represents the number of filters and k_s denotes the kernel size (even).

6.7 Grouped Convolution

Grouped convolution (GConv) was introduced as a type of convolution that applies a group of convolution filters to process input features concurrently, aiming to enable the network to be trained on multiple low-memory graphics processing units (GPUs). A primary motivation of G-Conv is the nightmare of training deep networks due to the limitation e models of single GPU resources. Even though GPU is powerful enough to perform training, it still requires using a small batch size making the convergence complicated. To combat this, grouped convolutions offer the ability to expand the convolutional networks as wide as required by just taking a single integrated block of filter group and duplicating them. This way, each filter is dedicated to convolving just over a particular part of feature maps acquired from its group, leading to a drastic reduction in the number of calculations necessary to obtain the final feature maps.

To further interpret, the G-Conv, Figure 6.16 illustrates the operation of G-Conv and compares it with standard convolution. Our main goal here is to use a number of D_{out} filters (each has a shape of $h \times w \times D_{in}$) to convolve input feature maps with the shape of

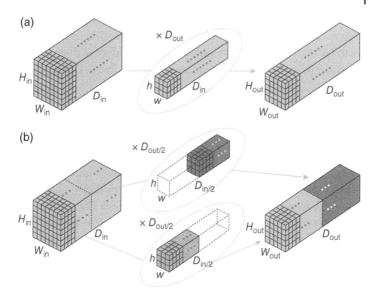

Figure 6.16 Illustration of standard vs. grouped convolutions: (a) a standard convolution in which each filter convolves overall input's channels; (b) grouped convolution in which half of the filters convolve each half of the input leading to halving the number of parameters.

($H_{in} \times W_{in} \times D_{in}$) to obtain output feature map of shape ($H_{out} \times W_{out} \times D_{out}$). In standard convolution, this task is straightforward as discussed in earlier chapters. However, in the case of grouped convolution, different sets of filters are used for convolution. Each group is in charge of a standard convolution with a specific amount of depth.

As shown in Figure 6.16, G-Conv is designed with pair of filter groups. Each of them includes $\frac{D_{out}}{2}$ as the number of filters, where the depth of each filter is just half that of a standard 2D convolutional filter $\frac{D_{in}}{2}$. In this way, the first group convolve the half part of input while the other group convolves the remaining part of the input tensor. Consequently, the number of output channels of each group is $\frac{D_{out}}{2}$ implying that both generate a total of $2 \times \frac{D_{out}}{2} = D_{out}$ channels. So, the output is the same as with standard convolutions.

G-Conv and the depth-wise convolution used in DS convolution share certain similarities and differences. A depthwise convolution can be achieved by G-Conv only when the number of filter groups is equal to the number of input layer channels, $\frac{D_{out}}{D_{in}} = 1$. Otherwise, D_{out} persists as the depth of the output layer in total. In DW convolution, the depth is unchanged in depthwise convolution, then modified with 1×1. However, the G-Conv can change the depth to be D_{out}.

Many advantages can be demonstrated for grouped convolution. First, it is possible to break the convolutions into multiple paths such that each path could be managed by various GPUs. Using this method, many GPUs can be used to train a model simultaneously. It is possible to feed a larger number of photos into the network at a time using this model parallelization over many GPUs. In comparison to data parallelism, model parallelism is seen to be superior. We then train on each batch of data that has been split apart. For tiny batches, however, stochastic than batch gradient descent is used instead. As a result, convergence would be slower and, on occasion, less accurate. Second, increasing the number of groups essentially decreases the number of trainable parameters. As illustrated here, the total number of parameters for standard convolution are equal to $h \times w \times D_{in} \times D_{out}$, while the number of parameters of the corresponding grouped convolution is equal $\left(h \times w \times \frac{D_{in}}{2} x \frac{D_{out}}{2} \right) \times 2$, which represents half of the former case.

6.8 Shuffled Grouped Convolution

One of the most computationally efficient convolution architectures for mobile devices is the ShuffleNet [2, 3]. Shuffled grouped convolution was proposed in this design. Inherent in both shuffling grouped convolution and grouped convolution are a number of related concepts. Grouped convolution and channel shuffle are both parts of the shuffled grouped convolution process.

As discussed in the previous section, G-Conv splits the filters into multiple groups that process different parts of input concurrently. The total number of operations have been greatly decreased. Three filter groups are shown in the following diagram as samples. The left-side portion of the input layer is passed via the first filter group. Additionally, the second and third filter groups are also converging with the input's green and blue colors. In each filter group, the kernel depth is only a third of the total number of channels in the input layer. When G-Conv1 has been applied, an input layer has been assigned to an intermediate feature map. A second grouped convolution, G-Conv2, is used to apply this feature map to the output layer (Figure 6.17).

Computationally, grouped convolution is the way to go. However, it still encounters a problem, which is that a fixed portion of the previous layers' information is handled by each filter group, as shown in Figure 6.17. It could be noted that the red-shaped group only processes information from the $\frac{1}{3}$ of the input features. As a result, each filter group can only learn a small number of distinct characteristics. Information cannot flow freely between channel groups because of this feature, which causes representations to

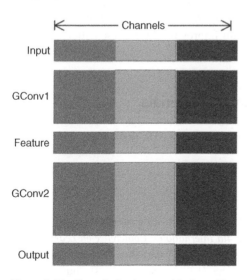

Figure 6.17 Convolution layers with three filter groups.

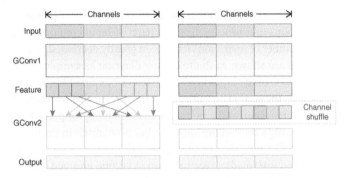

Figure 6.18 Shuffled convolution layers with three filter groups.

get weakened when being trained on new material. We use the channel shuffle to solve this issue (Figure 6.18).

Mixing up the features from various filter groups is the primary goal of channel shuffle. The feature maps shown in Figure 6.18 are obtained by running G-Conv1 with three filter groups. Then, channels in these groups are divided into subgroups that are mixed up before being fed into the second G-Conv. After this shuffle, the groups of G-Conv2 convolve over a variety of channels in the previous change, which empower the exchange of information between different group improving the representation power of the entire network.

6.9 Supplementary Materials

https://github.com/DEEPOLOGY-AI/DL-Book-Wiley-2022/tree/main/Ch6

References

1 Yu, F. and Koltun, V. (2016). Multi-scale context aggregation by dilated convolutions. *4th International Conference on Learning Representations, ICLR 2016 – Conference Track Proceedings*.

2 Ma, N., Zhang, X., Zheng, H.T., and Sun, J. (2018). Shufflenet V2: practical guidelines for efficient cnn architecture design. *Lect. Notes*

Comput. Sci. (including subseries Lecture Notes in Artificial Intelligence and Lecture Notes in Bioinformatics) 11218, LNCS: 122–138. https://doi.org/10.1007/978-3-030-01264-9_8.

3 Zhang, X., Zhou, X., Lin, M., and Sun, J. (2018). ShuffleNet: an extremely efficient convolutional neural network for mobile devices. https://doi.org/10.1109/CVPR.2018.00716.

7

Advanced Convolutional Neural Network

7.1 Introduction

In the previous two chapters of this part, we covered the foundations and essential knowledge about convolutional neural networks (CNNs), now let us talk a tour of the recent advances in CNN. This chapter explores and studies the state-of-the-art CNN that has served as the basis for many research projects and real-world applications. This includes AlexNet, block-wise CNNs that stack multiple repeating blocks, the network in network (NiN), inception networks, residual networks, dense networks, temporal convolutional network (TCN), etc. The majority of the CNNs have been proposed for computer vision tasks which could be thought of as far from the cybersecurity field. However, this chapter concentrates on the main ideology of these models and then figures out how this can be adapted and adjusted to security-related tasks.

In theory, deep neural networks are easy (just stack a bunch of neurons together), but implementations and hyperparameter choices can make a huge difference in how well they function. Intuition, a few mathematical ideas, and a lot of trial and error went into creating the neural networks presented in this chapter. Theoretically, developing CNNs seems an easy task, but it necessitates the careful choice of their hyperparameters which could result in considerable variation in the way they function. Thus, this chapter explains the main intuitions, mathematical concepts, and experimental trials involved in the creation of each CNN model.

Deep Learning Approaches for Security Threats in IoT Environments,
First Edition. Mohamed Abdel-Basset, Nour Moustafa, and Hossam Hawash.
© 2023 The Institute of Electrical and Electronics Engineers, Inc.
Published 2023 by John Wiley & Sons, Inc.

The aim of this chapter is to view these models chronologically to give you a sense of how far the field has been evolving over years and possibly even inspire you to design your own structures.

7.2 AlexNet

In 2012, AlexNet was declared the winner of the ImageNet Large Scale Visual Recognition Challenge (*ILSVRC*). AlexNet was proposed as an eight-layer convolution network, which revealed, for the first time, that the features acquired by learning could surpass physically conceived features, a breakthrough in the field of computer vision. Given a simplified illustration of AlexNet as shown in Figure 7.1, the structure of AlexNet is very similar to LeNet. AlexNet and LeNet have a lot in common, but there are also important distinctions. LeNet5 is much shallower than AlexNet. AlexNet is composed of five convolutional layers followed by three full connected hidden layers. Second, AlexNet used the *ReLU* as a replacement for the *sigmoid* as its activation function. The first layer of AlexNet has a kernel size of 11×11 to capture large size objects from the image. The kernel sizes of the second and third layers are reduced to 5×5 and 3×3, respectively. As illustrated, maximum pooling layers with a 3×3 kernel and a stride of 2 are added after convolution to reduce dimensionality.

Moreover, AlexNet used the ReLU function to perform activation instead of the sigmoid because of the simplicity of the earlier one as it did not exhibit the exponentiation calculation noticed in the later function. Instead, the ReLU activation simplifies the model training under a variety of parameter initialization techniques. This can be attributed to the fact that while the output of the sigmoid activation approximates to either zero or one, the gradient value in these areas is nearly zero. So, the backpropagation is unable to last to update some of the parameters of the network. Thus, the model could not be able to be efficiently trained with sigmoid activation if its parameters are not appropriately initialized. On the other hand, in the positive interval, the ReLU activation function's gradient is always one.

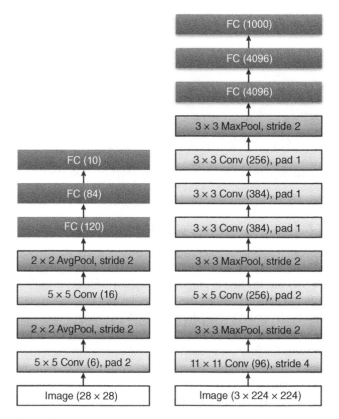

Figure 7.1 Illustration of the architecture of the AlexNet vs. LsNet.

7.3 Block-wise Convolutional Network (VGG)

Even though AlexNet provided experimental proof that deep convolutional networks could achieve robust performance, it did not provide a common outline to guide later research to build a new deep learning model. The following subsection presents a number of experiential ideas generally adopted to develop deep convolutional networks. The design of deep networks has evolved from just thinking about separate neurons to a layer neuron, and now to a

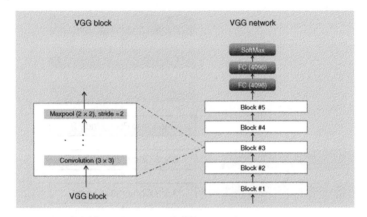

Figure 7.2 Illustration of the architecture of the VGG network.

block of stacked layers. At Oxford University, the visual geometry group (VGG) was the first to propose the notion of blocks to build a convolutional network, called the VGG network [1].

As with LeNet and AlexNet, the VGG model consists of two components: the earlier one contains convolutional bocks, while the other contains the fully connected layers, as illustrated in Figure 7.2.

As shown, the convolutional part of the network stacks multiple VGG blocks. single VGG block is composed of a stack of convolutional layers (Kernel size $= 3 \times 3$), and ends with a max-pooling layer (2×2) with stride $s = 2$. In particular, five VGG blocks constitute this part, the early two blocks contain just one convolutional layer, while the latter ones contain two convolutional layers per block. The full connected section of the network consists of two fully connected layers (4096 units) and SoftMax layer (1000 units). The network is called VGG-11 as it consists of eight convolutional layers and three linear/dense layers.

7.4 Network in Network

VGG, LeNet, and AlexNet all follow the same architectural pattern: they extract features based on spatial arrangement using a series of convolutional and pooling layers, then learn the final decision from these representations using fully connected layers. AlexNet and VGG extend LeNet to primarily make these two components broader and deeper. Alternatively, fully connected layers could be used early in the network. Nevertheless, a thoughtless usage of fully connected layers could provide the spatial composition of the pattern completely. Therefore, the *network in network* (*NiN*) module was suggested as an alternative. NiN block was developed based on a straightforward vision to apply fully connected layers on the channels for each input element, independently [2, 3].

Bear in mind that the four-dimensional shape of inputs and outputs of convolutional layers is represented by the batch size, number of channels, height, and width. Also, consider the two-dimensional shape of input and output of linear/dense layers, which are typically two-dimensional tensors corresponding to the example and feature. The concept behind the NiN network is to apply a linear/dense layer at each pixel location. If we tie the weights across each spatial location, we could contemplate this as a convolution (1×1) or as a linear/dense working separately on each pixel. It is also possible to conceive each spatial element as an instance and each channel as a feature. Figure 7.3 illustrates the structural design of the NiN model, and its constituting blocks. The structure of the NiN block three-convolutional layers, the latter two have a 1×1 kernel with ReLU function to work as per-pixel fully connected layers. These layers use the ReLU function for activation.

The design of the NiN network was greatly inspired by AlexNet. They share the same earlier convolutional layers whose kernel sizes are 11×11, 5×5, and 3×3, respectively, and even the numbers of filters are equivalent. A max-pooling layer (3×3) is added after each NiN block with a stride size of 2. Unlike AlexNet, the NiN model completely avoids fully connected layers. As an alternative, an approach is to utilize NiN blocks with output channels equal to the number of classes, then apply the global average pooling (GAP) layer to produce a logits vector. An important benefit of this building structure is that it reduces the number of model parameters required. Although this approach may appear to save time, it actually requires more time for model training.

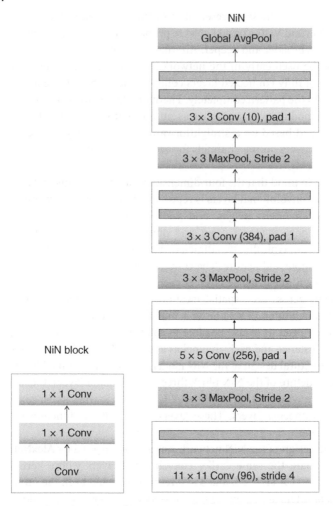

Figure 7.3 Architecture of the NiN network.

7.5 Inception Networks

The inception networks were among the most important break-throughs in the CNNs. So far, there are four editions of inception networks, which are known as inception versions 1, 2, 3, and 4. The first edition was published in 2014, and as its name "GoogleNet" implies, it was proposed by the Google research group.

Better deep learning models can be created in a simple but effective manner. You can simply increase the size of the model by increasing the number of the depth of the model. Nonetheless, this can lead to a variety of issues. First, overfitting is more likely to occur with a larger model, especially in the case of small-size data. Second, with the increase in the number of parameters, the computational burden will also increase. As a remedy, inception networks suggest moving on to sparsely connected CNNs as an alternative to fully connected CNNs. This thought can be conceptualized in Figure 7.4. This idea enables the development of deeper and wider networks while maintaining a reasonable "computational budget." Thus, this section provides a deep dive into inception networks to give the reader an intuitive understanding of the conceptual and structural design of this family of convolutional networks.

7.5.1 GoogLeNet

GoogLeNet was responsible for setting a new state of the art for classification and detection in ImageNet Challenge 2014, as a model that integrated the advantages of NiN and concepts of repetitive blocks. The main emphasis of this model was to answer the question of which sizes of convolutional kernels are most excellent. GoogLeNet tried to address the problem of the deeper network by proposing a new design idea, which presents multiple convolutional kernels with different sizes and operates at the same level. This way, the network, in fact, becomes wider instead of deeper.

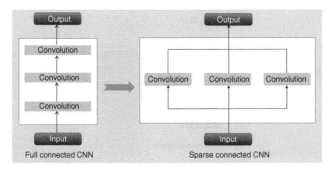

Figure 7.4 Illustration of the architecture of sparsely connected convolutional blocks.

The main finding derived from this model was that occasionally it could be valuable to engage a mixture of diversely sized convolutional kernels.

The fundamental building block in GoogLeNet is known as an *inception block*, likely inspired by the movie *Inception* ("we need to go deeper"). As shown in Figure 7.5, four parallel paths are constituting the structure of the inception block. Three paths from the left are constructed using convolutions with 5×5, 3×3, and 1×1 kernels to learn features from various spatial dimensions. The other path applied a 3×3 maximum pooling layer to reduce the dimensionality of block input, and then a convolution (1×1) is applied to reduce the number of feature maps from the input. Since deep CNNs are heavy and time-consuming to train, the GoogLeNet was designed to limit the number of input channels in the middle two paths by including an extra convolution (1×1) before the convolution (3×3) and convolution (5×5) to decrease the dimensions of the network and achieve rapid computations.

Convolutional layers in all paths apply suitable padding to generate output maps sharing the same dimensions. Finally, a concatenation of the feature maps generated for each path is applied along the channel dimension to generate the output of the inception block. The number of output channels per layer is the most commonly modified hyperparameter of the inception block.

To sum up, the structural design, as shown in Figure 7.6 of the GoogLeNet, is composed of a stack of nine inception blocks and

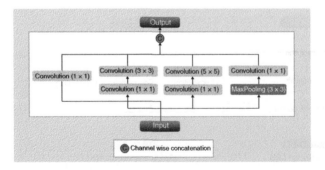

Figure 7.5 Illustration of the architecture of the inception block.

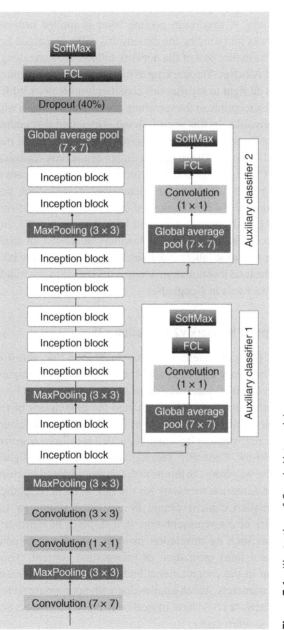

Figure 7.6 Illustration of GoogLeNet model.

GAP to produce its outcomes without the need to stack many linear/dense layers. A maximum pooling layer is applied between inception blocks for reducing the dimensions of the generated feature maps. The earlier part of the network follows the same design as LeNet and AlexNet. The stacking of inception blocks is inspired by VGG. It is all right to say that this classifier is quite deep, which makes it still susceptible to the vanishing gradient problem, as with most deep networks. In this regard, GoogLeNet found that adding two auxiliary classifiers can avoid the central portion of the network from "dying out." The structural design of auxiliary classifiers consists of (i) 5×5 average pooling layer with stride 3; (ii) a convolution (1×1) with 128 filters for dimensionality reduction and *ReLU* activation; (iii) a fully connected layer (FCL) with 1025 outputs and *ReLU* activation; (iv) dropout layer with ratio $= 0.7$; and (v) a SoftMax layer. Both auxiliary classifiers calculated an auxiliary loss over the same labels. Auxiliary loss and real loss are both included in the total loss function, whereas 0.3 is used as the weight of each auxiliary loss in GoogLeNet.

7.5.2 Inception Network v2 (Inception v2)

Inception v2 [4] is an extension to the GoogLeNet that aimed to improve the accuracy and decreased the computational complexity. The main intuition was that a convolutional network can function better when its layer did not change the dimensions of the input radically. Excessive reduction in the dimensions of feature maps could cause a loss of information, which is called a *representational bottleneck*. Generally, representation size should slightly decrease in the way from the inputs to the outputs prior to reaching the final representation necessary for the task at hand. Hypothetically, information content cannot be evaluated simply by the dimensionality of the representation as it disposes of significant considerations such as correlation patterns, and dimensionality simply offers a hard estimation of information content. Thus, any reduction in the computational budget can lead to decreased number of parameters, which implies that with appropriate factorization, the network could have more disentangled parameters and thus be able to learn faster.

Convolutional layers with large kernel sizes (e.g. 5×5 or 7×7) inherently exhibit high computational costs. For instance, the computational cost of a 5×5 convolutional layers is $\frac{25}{9} = 2.78$ times more computationally costly than a convolution (3×3) with an identical number of filters. Such large kernel sizes can capture interrelations between features in the small kernel layers. Hence, a decrease in the kernel size could come at a large quality of expressiveness. Thus, the idea is to find a subnetwork with fewer parameters that can act as an alternative to a 5×5 convolutional layer while keeping the same input size and output depth. By examining the computation graph of the 5×5 convolutional layers, it could be noted that each output acts like a tiny fully connected network sliding over a 5×5 grid of its input (Figure 7.7). By exploiting the translation invariance characteristic, the fully connected part can be replaced by two convolutional layers with kernel sizes of 3×3. Motivated by this, the design of the inception block is updated in inception v2 by factorizing the 5×5 convolutional layer into two 3×3 convolutional layers (Figure 7.7). This way, the network ends up with a 28% reduction of computation, while the same reduction is achieved in the number of parameters as each parameter is utilized just one time in the computation of each unit's activation. However, a question arises whether one could factorize convolutions with a large kernel into smaller ones, i.e. $K = 2 \times 2$

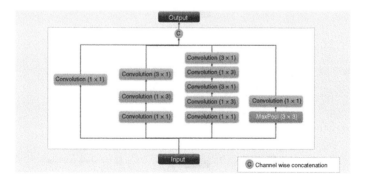

Figure 7.7 Illustration of the inception block v2.

convolutional layer. This version of inception block can be referred to as inception A block.

Inception v2 showed that the asymmetric convolutional layer $(k \times 1)$ could do even better than 2×2. In particular, applying 1×3 convolutional layer after 3×1 convolutional layer is the same as using a two-layer subnetwork sharing the same receptive field as convolution (3×3) (Figure 7.8). This factorization was reported to be 33% cheaper than convolution (3×3) given the identical number of input and output channels. This is shown better computational performance compared to the factorization of a 3×3 convolutional layer into two 2×2 convolutional layers, which achieved simply an 11% reduction of computation. Motivated by this, the design of the inception block is further updated in inception v2 by factorizing any $k \times k$ convolutional layer into $1 \times k$ layer followed by $k \times 1$ layer (Figure 7.8). This version of the inception block can be referred to as the inception B block.

Moreover, an additional improvement was made to the inception module by expanding the filter banks (widened as opposed to deepened) to eliminate the bottleneck as shown in Figure 7.9. This is because if the block becomes deeper, there would be an extreme decrease in sizes, and so a loss of information. This block can be referred to as the inception C block. This block could be used only in the case of the coarsest feature map, in which generating high-dimensional sparse representation is the most important as the

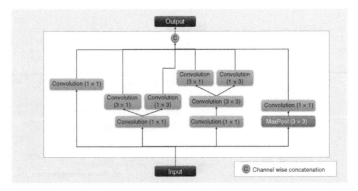

Figure 7.8 Illustration of the inception block v3.

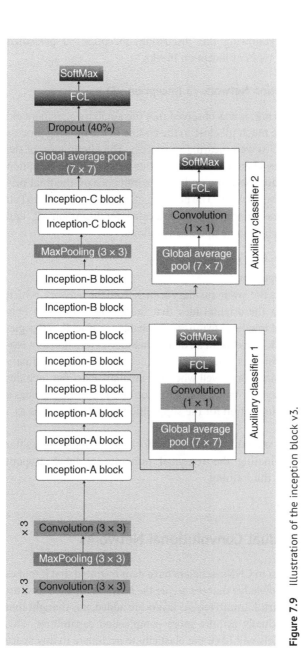

Figure 7.9 Illustration of the inception block v3.

fraction of local processing is enhanced compared to the spatial aggregation. Following this discussion, inception v2 presented three distinct types of inception blocks.

7.5.3 Inception Network v3 (Inception v3)

In the same work, it was observed that the auxiliary classifiers did not contribute much till close to the ending of the training process when accuracies were nearing saturation. The elimination of the lower auxiliary classifier in the previous version of the inception network did not show any undesirable influence on the final performance of the network. The building of inception v3 included all of the aforementioned updates indicated for inception v2, and besides, it applied some updates as follows:

- Factorized 7×7 convolutional layer.
- RMSprop optimizer.
- It eliminates the lower auxiliary branch from the network, which implies that the original idea that these classifiers could help advance the low-level features is probably misplaced in Google-Net. Instead, it injects an auxiliary classifier to function as a regularizer, which is established by the point that the primary network branch does well when the auxiliary classifier includes a dropout layer or batch normalization (BN) [7]. This provides a supportive indication for the supposition that BN performs as a regularizer.
- Add a label smoothing as a method for regularizing the classifier by approximating the relegated influence of label dropout throughout the training.

7.6 Residual Convolutional Networks

When it comes to CNNs, scholars have demonstrated that it makes sense to acknowledge that *the deeper the better* as the models must be more powerful. Intuitively, as layers are added, it is thought that they will gradually acquire more complicated capabilities. This way, the models will have the elasticity to acclimate to any space increase as they have a larger parameter space to investigate. For example, for an image recognition task, the first layer might learn the features of edges, the second layer might learn the texture features and likewise, the third layer could learn the features of objects and so on. However, it has been founded that there is an upper limit for depth, after which the performance gets worsened. This could be attributed to several factors, including the weight initialization, optimization function, network initialization, and, most crucially, the vanishing gradient and overfitting problem. This was a major limitation of VGG, which cannot go as deep as required, since it began to lose generalization capacity when it exceeds a certain depth. As a solution to the aforementioned limitations of training deep CNN, a residual network (ResNet) was introduced in 2015, and it was made up of residual blocks.

Let us examine the structure of the residual block as the fundamental building block of ResNet, as illustrated in Figure 7.10. Given the input of the block as x and the learnt feature mapping is denoted as $f(x)$, which is fed to the upper activation layer. In a regular block design, the main target is stacking some convolutional layers to explicitly learn feature mapping $f(x)$ from input x. On the other hand, the main target is to learn residual mapping $f(x) + x$, which is calculated by passing the input x to an extra operator that is a *shortcut connection known as a residual connection*. This indicates the way in which the residual block draws its name.

The design of the residual block is motivated by the fact that neural networks can act as brilliant function approximators, so they can simply solve the identity function, in which the output of a function is the same as the input itself.

$$H(x) = x \qquad (1)$$

Following the same rationality, skip connection is essentially the identity mapping where the input from the preceding layer is added directly to the output of the other layer. When the input of the block has passed to the output of the last layer of the block, the ResNet could be aware of the mapping learnt in previous blocks by exploiting the input added to it. So, the output of the residual block can be formulated as follows:

$$H(x) = f(x) + x \qquad (2)$$

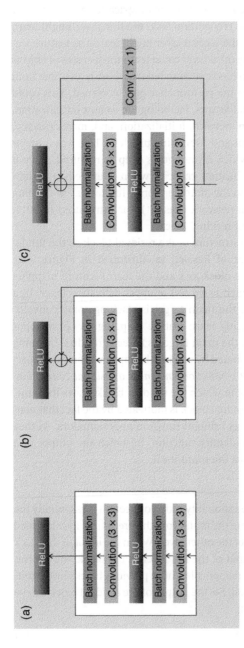

Figure 7.10 Illustration of the residual block: (a) regular convolutional block, (b) residual block without Conv(1 × 1), and (c) residual block with Conv(1 × 1).

When the identity mapping $H(x) = x$ is the main target, the residual mapping can be easy to learn by setting the weights and biases of layers, in the block, to zero. The structural design of residual blocks allows the network to forward propagate more rapidly through the residual connections between different layers. Similar to VGG, the residual block uses 3×3 convolutional layers. The convolutions in the residual block share an identical number of output channels. Batch normalization is applied after each convolutional layer and activation is performed using the *ReLU* function. Next, the skip connection is adapted to add the input of the block out of the block before the second *ReLU* activation function. When it comes to the outputs of convolutional layers, their shapes must be identical to the shape of the block's input so as to be added together.

Generally, it seems to be a trivial problem with this design once the shape of the input x differs from that of the output $f(x)$, which often takes place with convolutional and pooling layers. Two options are available to alleviate this issue. First, the skip connection can be expanded with some zero-padding entries to improve its dimensions. Second, the projection technique can be applied to match the shapes, and this is accomplished by combining convolution (1×1) with input. Unlike padding, convolution (1×1) can allow us to change the number of channels. This way, the output can be calculated as:

$$H(x) = F(x) + W_{1 \times 1} x \tag{3}$$

7.7 Dense Convolutional Networks

Densely connected convolutional networks, known as DenseNets, are another attempt to keep developing a deeper convolutional network. Again, the problem addressed by DenseNets is that when CNNs go deeper, the path for gradient information flows from the input layer to the output layer (forward and backward directions) turn out to be so long that the gradient can get vanished prior to arriving at other side. DenseNets tried to tackle this issue by simplifying the connection between convolutional layers presented in other networks to ensure the maximum gradient flow. To do so, DenseNets are designed by simply connecting every convolutional layer directly with each other.

DenseNets do not rely on the power of their architectures to drive their representational power, but rather use the network's capabilities through feature recycling. By eliminating the need to memorize repetitive feature maps, DenseNets use fewer parameters than an equivalent traditional convolutional network. In addition, several ResNets versions have shown that a large number of convolutional layers had little influence and might be removed. ResNets have so many parameters due to the fact that each convolutional layer has its own set of parameters that can be learned. Convolutions on dense networks, on the other hand, are extremely compact and only add a tiny number of new feature maps. By allowing convolutional layers to have easy accessibility to the gradient information from the loss function and the network input, DenseNets provide a flexible and responsive method for distributing gradient information.

A standard convolutional network passes the learnt representations across layers such as convolutional, pooling, normalization, and an activation layer. ResNets extended this conduct by adding the skip connection as discussed in the previous section. Here, we will look at the basic building components of a DenseNet and how they are distinctive: Dense blocks and transition layers.

A *dense block* stack is a group of convolutions that share the same number of output channels, whereas the convolutional input and convolutional output are concatenated on the channel dimension in forward propagation (Figure 7.11). The name dense block, and thereby DenseNet, is derived from the truth that the dependency graph between convolutional layers comes to be quite dense. The last convolutional layer of such a chain is densely connected to all earlier convolutional layers. Each convolutional layer in the dense block is accompanied by batch normalization and *ReLU* activation before it. Thus, when it comes to comparing dense and regular networks, the main distinction is that dense networks concatenate the output feature maps of each layer rather than sum them. This implies that the latter keeps the number of channels to be relatively smaller.

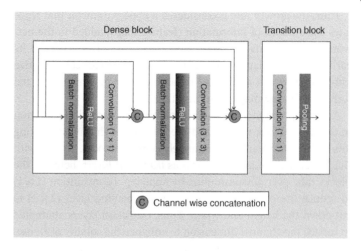

Figure 7.11 Illustration of the dense block.

As stated with ResNet, the aggregation of feature maps could not be achieved when their shapes are different irrespective of whether grouping is performed by addition or a concatenation. Therefore, DenseNet is structured into a stack of dense blocks where the shapes of the feature maps are kept constant within a block, but the number of channels varies between them. Since each convolutional layer generates a number of feature maps, the computation can be harder as we go deeper into the network. Hence, the structure of the dense block presented a bottleneck structure where convolution (1×1) is applied before a convolution (3×3), as illustrated in Figure 7.11. With the inclusion of the bottleneck layer in the dense block, the DenseNet can be referred to as BottleNeck DenseNet (DenseNet-B).

There is a direct correlation between the growth in output channels and the number of filters in a dense block, which is known as the *growth rate*. Since dense block concatenates feature maps, this channel dimension is growing at every layer. Given the number of input channels as F_I, L is the depth of dense block in terms of the number of convolutions, and the growth rate as g, the number of output channels F_o can be generally calculated as follows:

$$F_o = F_I + g \times L \tag{4}$$

Thus, the growth rate is considered a hyperparameter that regulates the amount of information (feature maps) added to the network by each convolutional layer. Every layer has access to its earlier feature maps, and, hence, to the shared commutative knowledge, which is updated by adding new information in the form of g feature maps of information.

Another problem to consider is that the concatenation operation in the dense block will expand the number of channels; stacking lots of them can lead to an extremely complex model. To deal with that, intermediate layers, known as *transition layers*, between the blocks take over downsampling by applying a convolution (1×1) to reduce the channel dimension, and a pooling layer (2×2) to cut down the height and width. Thus, transition layers attempted to reduce the channel dimension to enhance the solidity of DenseNet. Thus, when a dense block generates m feature maps that need to be reduced, the transition layer uses *compression factor* (θ) to perform this reduction. Rather than having m feature maps at a transition layer, it will have $\theta * m$ feature maps given that $0 < \theta < = 1$. If the value of θ is equal to one $(\theta = 1)$, the number of feature maps in transition layers continues unaffected. If $\theta < 1$, then the network can be called *DenseNet-C* and the value of θ is changed to 0.5. When both the layers of bottleneck and transition $(\theta < 1)$ are included, the network can be referred to as DenseNet-BC.

7.8 Temporal Convolutional Network

In the spectrum of deep learning, the concept of sequence modelling and predictive modeling has traditionally been coupled with recurrent neural networks. However, this concept has changed recently. Contrary to their frequent association with image recognition and vision tasks, CNN has been demonstrated to be a useful learner for predictive modeling and sequence modelling when the appropriate changes and updates are included. Thus, the research community believes that this method of thinking is out of date, and CNN should be considered as one of the key options for modelling sequential data, rather than the other way around. They were able to demonstrate that convolutional networks outperform recurrent networks in a wide range of tasks while avoiding the main limitations of recurrent models, such as the exploding gradients and/or vanishing gradient problem and an absence of memory retention, which are associated with them. Furthermore, taking the advantages of CNNs instead of the recurrent counterparts is envisioned as a promising solution for improving the modeling capabilities and enabling concurrent computation during the learning from sequential data. In this regard, TCN was proposed to add many advantages over traditional convolutional as well as recurrent networks and revolutionize the sequence modelling tasks in different application domains.

The TCN model is constituted of different building blocks, namely causal one-dimensional convolution, dilated convolution, residual blocks, etc. This section will go into detail about what these terms mean.

7.8.1 One-Dimensional Convolutional Network

The design of TCN is inherent in one-dimensional convolutional network, which receives input in the form of a three-dimensional tensor ($\text{batch}_{\text{size}} \times \text{input}_{\text{length}} \times \text{input}_{\text{size}}$) and similarly, generate three-dimensional tensor ($\text{batch}_{\text{size}} \times \text{input}_{\text{length}} \times \text{output}_{\text{size}}$) as output. Only the third dimension of the input and output tensors may vary for each layer of TCN due to the fact that all layers are sharing the same lengths of input and output.

In the univariate scenario, where one variable at a time is analyzed, the $\text{input}_{\text{size}}$ and $\text{output}_{\text{size}}$ will be one for both. On the other hand, in the multivariate scenario, where multiple variables are analyzed concurrently, $\text{input}_{\text{size}}$ and $\text{output}_{\text{size}}$ might be different because the targeted output might not contain every element of the input sequence.

For a one-dimensional convolutional layer, an input tensor of shape ($\text{batch}_{\text{size}}$, $\text{input}_{\text{length}}$, $\text{input}_{\text{channels}}$) is received, while output tensor of shape ($\text{batch}_{\text{size}}$, $\text{input}_{\text{length}}$, $\text{output}_{\text{channels}}$) is generated. For the sake of demonstration, let us examine how the output is calculated for a given sample (per batch) in a one-dimensional convolutional layer, while the same procedure applies to all samples in the batch. For convenience, let us begin with the most basic scenario, in which input$_{channels}$ and output$_{channels}$ both equal 1; thereby the convolutional layer will have one-dimensional input as well as one-dimensional output tensors as illustrated in Figure 7.12.

It is notable that the single element of the output is computed by selecting a window of successive elements with a length equal to kernel_size of input. A kernel vector of learnt weights and a subsequence from the input that share the same length are underdoing dot products to calculate the output. To compute the next output element, the same process is applied, but the next input subsequence is updated by shifting the selection window to the right by one element. It is important to keep in mind that the same kernel weights will be utilized to calculate every output element in each convolutional layer. Figure 7.13 shows an illustration of the calculation of two successive output elements and the corresponding input subsequences.

To ensure that the output of convolution keep the same input dimensions, zero padding is applied to inject extra zero-valued elements to the input tensor preserver the same input dimension.

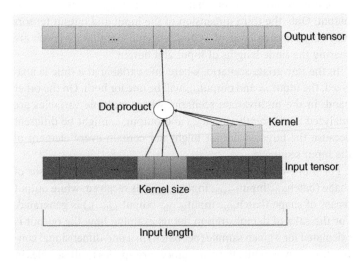

Figure 7.12 Illustration of one-dimensional convolution.

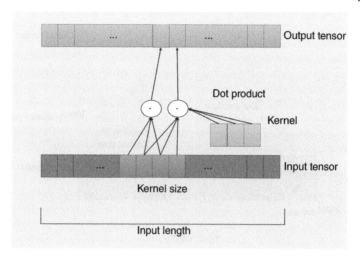

Figure 7.13 Illustration of calculation of output of one-dimensional convolution.

Consider, for a moment, the situation in which we have a number of input channels such as $input_{channels}$ is higher than one. In this situation, it is possible to repeat this process over and over again using various kernels for each input channel.

This makes the output of the convolutional layer contain $input_{channels}$ output vectors and the kernel weights of the convolutional layer take the shape of $kernel_{size} * input_{channels}$, which will generate intermediary output vectors whose count is equal in $input_{channels}$. Next, the intermediary output vectors are added to calculate the ultimate output vector. In some ways, this is the same as a two-dimensional convolution in which an input tensor ($input_{size}$, $input_{channels}$) and a kernel of shape ($kernel_{size}$, $input_{channels}$) as illustrated in Figure 7.14. The convolution is one-dimensional due to the fact that the window only moves along one axis. However, it simulates two-dimensional convolutions due to the fact that a two-dimensional kernel matrix was employed in each stage of the process.

For the illustrated example, the $input_{channels}$ is set to be 2. Now, rather than applying a kernel vector slipping over a one-dimensional input sequence, the network applies a kernel matrix

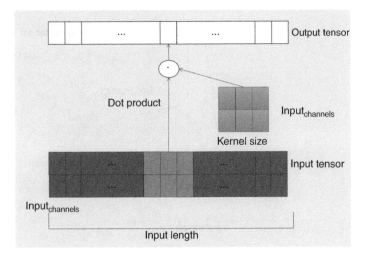

Figure 7.14 Illustration of calculation of output of multichannel convolution.

with dimension $\text{input}_{\text{channels}} \times \text{kernel}_{\text{size}}$ to slide over the multivariate series of length $\text{input}_{\text{length}}$.

In another scenario, when $\text{input}_{\text{channels}}$ and $\text{output}_{\text{channels}}$ are higher than 1, the above-mentioned calculations are just replicated for each output channel with a distinct kernel matrix. Then, the output vectors are then stacked on top of each other resulting in an output tensor of shape in the following step, the output vectors are piled on top of one another to produce an output tensor ($\text{input}_{\text{length}}$, $\text{output}_{\text{channels}}$). This way, the shape of the kernel matrix will be $\text{kernel}_{\text{size}} \times \text{input}_{\text{channels}} \times \text{output}_{\text{channels}}$. The values of the variable $\text{input}_{\text{channels}}$ and $\text{output}_{\text{channels}}$ change according to the position of the convolutional layer in the TCN. For example, in the first layer $\text{input}_{\text{channels}} = \text{input}_{\text{size}}$, while in the final layer, $\text{output}_{\text{channels}} = \text{output}_{\text{size}}$. In the intermediary layers, the number of channels can be determined by the number of convolutional filters.

7.8.2 Causal and Dilated Convolution

To make a convolutional layer causal, each output element i in $\{0, ..., \text{input}_{\text{length}} - 1\}$ must only rely on the input elements that come before index i such as $\{0, 1, 2, ..., i\}$. As previously stated, zero padding must be added to an input tensor in order to validate both output and input tensors sharing the same length. By applying zero padding on the left-hand side of the input tensor, the convolutional layer is guaranteed to be causal. To better grasp this, let us give a look at the rightmost element in the output sequence. Since there is no padding at the right-hand side of the input sequence, the last element it depends on is the last element of the input. On the other hand, when calculating the second rightmost element in the output sequence, it is notable that the kernel window is moved to the left by a single element. By induction, it could be demonstrated that the last dependency of each output element in the input sequence has the equivalent index as itself. Figure 7.15 illustrates an example for causal convolution with an $\text{input}_{\text{length}} = 4$ and a kernel size ($k = 3$).

It is notable that by applying zero padding of two entries, the output length of the convolution layer is identical to the input length while satisfying the causality rule. Generally, with no dilation, the number of zero-padding items necessary to make the length of the output identical to the input length is always equal to kernel size − 1.

A popular requirement in most sequence modeling tasks is that the value of a particular output element should take into account the current and previous input elements. This could be

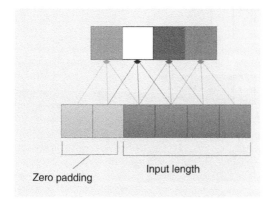

Figure 7.15 Illustration of an example of causal convolution.

accomplished once the receptive field has a size of *input length*. This phenomenon could be called "full dependency coverage." As demonstrated by single causal convolution, this behavior could be extended by stacking many causal layers on top of each other as shown in Figure 7.16.

It is notable that by stacking two convolutional layers with kernel size $k = 3$, the receptive field will have a size of 5. To generalize, for one-dimensional CNN consisting of n layers and having a kernel size k, the size of receptive field r is computed as follows:

$$r = 1 + n * (k - 1) \tag{5}$$

To identify the number of layers required for full coverage, the size of the receptive field can be set to be equal to *input_length* and the number of convolutional layers n can be calculated as follows:

$$n = \lceil (l - 1)/(k - 1) \rceil \tag{6}$$

This implies that, given a fixed kernel size, the number of layers necessary to fully cover the input is linear in the length of the input tensor, leading the network to be deeper, and thereby become computationally exhaustive because of the large number of parameters to be trained. Moreover, increasing the network depth has been

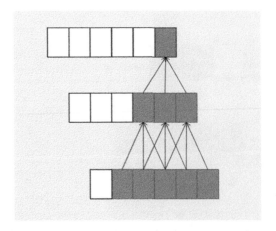

Figure 7.16 Illustration of stacked causal convolution.

demonstrated to cause degradation problems attributed to gradient vanishment. A possible remedy is to increase the size of the receptive field size while maintaining a smaller number of layers, which can be achieved by adding dilation to the convolutional layer (refer to Chapter 6). Recall that dilation can be defined as a distance between the input elements that are employed to calculate the output elements. This way, a standard convolutional layer can be viewed as a one-dilated layer because the input elements for any particular output element are contiguous. The readers could revisit Chapter 6 to know more about dilated convolutions. In general, for a given convolution layer, with dilation rate d and kernel size k, the size of receptive field r can be computed as follows:

$$r = 1 + d * (k - 1) \tag{7}$$

However, when d is constant, the number of layers are still linear in the length of the input tensor to achieve full receptive field coverage. As a solution to this problem, the value of d needs to grow exponentially with the number of stacked layers. To achieve this, a constant b is defined as the dilation baseline to enable calculating the dilation rate d, for each convolutional layer, as a function of the stacked layers in the network such that $d = b^i$. Figure 7.17

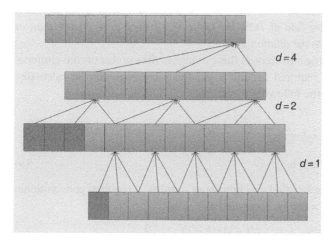

Figure 7.17 Illustration of temporal convolutional network with dilation base equal to one.

illustrates a network input_length = 10, a kernel size = 3 and a dilation_base = 2, which results in three dilated convolutional layers for full coverage of input sequences.

As expected, zero-padding entries are just required for calculating the last output element for each convolutional layer. Obviously, the rightmost output element is reliant on the complete input coverage. Every convolutional layer expands the size of the receptive field with $d * (k - 1)$. Therefore, the size of the receptive field r of a TCN can be calculated as follows:

$$r = 1 + \sum_{i=0}^{n-1}(k-1) - b^i = 1 + (k-1) \cdot \frac{b^n - 1}{b - 1} \tag{8}$$

Nevertheless, according to the value of b and k, the receptive field could encounter some "gaps." To illustrate the meaning of the term "gap," Figure 7.7 shows a convolutional network dilation base $b = 3$ and a kernel size $k = 2$:

As shown, the range covered by the receptive field exceeds the input_length. However, the receptive field exhibits some gaps such that some input elements are not considered at all when calculating the output element (inputs are shaded). To tackle this issue, the kernel size needs to be increased to $k = 3$ or the dilation base must be decreased such that $b = 2$. As a general rule, *to avoid gaps in a receptive field of TCN, the kernel size k need to be greater than or equal to the dilation base b.*

Taking into account these thoughts, the number of convolutional layers required for full dependency coverage can be calculated when the following is satisfied:

$$1 + (k-1) \cdot \frac{b^n - 1}{b - 1} \geq l$$

$$k \geq b \tag{9}$$

Once satisfied, the minimum number of required convolutional layers n can be computed as

$$n = \left\lceil \log_b \left(\frac{(l-1) \cdot (b-1)}{(k-1)} + 1 \right) \right\rceil \tag{10}$$

It can be noted that the number of layers become logarithmic instead of linear in the length of the input. This signifies a considerable enhancement that can be easily achieved without surrendering receptive field coverage. Specifying the number of zero-padding elements needed at each tier is the only task remaining to do. Given the hyperparameters b, k, and i, then the number of zero-padding elements p required for each convolutional layer are calculated as follows:

$$p = b^i \cdot (k-1) \tag{11}$$

7.8.3 Residual Blocks

The structural design of the TCN model illustrated in Figure 7.18 can be further improved by changing the basic building block of the TCN from a simple one-dimensional dilated causal convolutional layer to a residual block consisting of two layers having an identical

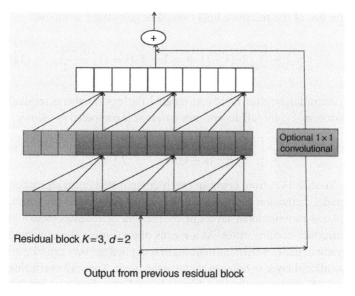

Figure 7.18 Illustration of temporal convolutional network with the residual connection.

dilation rate and a residual connection. The input of the residual block will be added to the output of the two convolutional layers to generate the input for the next block. For each residual block, except the first and the last blocks, the number of input and output channels will be the same and is equal to the number of convolutional filters. Since the first convolutional layer of the first residual block and the second convolutional layer of the last residual block might have the various number of input and output channels, the dimension of the residual tensor may need to be modified, which can be achieved by applying a 1×1 convolution to the residual connection.

Typically, the aforementioned changes could impact the calculation of the depth of TCN to achieve full coverage. Now, it is required to think about the number of residual blocks needed to reach a complete receptive field coverage. Inserting a residual block to a TCN implies adding twice as much size of receptive field than when inserting a fundamental causal convolutional layer, as it contains two such layers. Thus, following the earlier definition of i, b, and k, and given $k \geq b$, and n_{blocks} as the number of residual blocks, the size of the receptive field r could be calculated as follows:

$$r = 1 + \sum_{i=0}^{n-1} 2 \cdot (k-1) \cdot b^i = 1 + 2 \cdot (k-1) \cdot \frac{b^n - 1}{b-1} \qquad (12)$$

Accordingly, given input with length l, the least number of residual blocks n_{blocks} for full dependency coverage is computed as follows:

$$n_{\text{blocks}} = \left\lceil \log_b \left(\frac{(l-1) \cdot (b-1)}{(k-1) \cdot 2} + 1 \right) \right\rceil \qquad (13)$$

To shift TCN from being an overly complicated linear regression model, activation functions can be added either after the causal dilated convolutional layers or by the end of residual blocks to introduce nonlinearities. As a means of preventing the exploding gradient issue, weight normalization is applied to every causal convolutional layer in order to stabilize the input. To avoid overfitting in TCN, regularization is achieved by adding a dropout layer following the convolutional layers in each residual block. By putting all together, the final architecture if TCN can be viewed as displayed in Figure 7.19

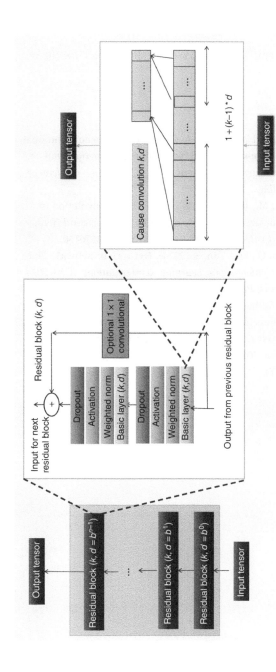

Figure 7.19 The final architecture of TCN.

7.9 Supplementary Materials

https://github.com/DEEPOLOGY-AI/DL-Book-Wiley-2022/tree/
main/Ch7

References

1 Simonyan, K. and Zisserman, A. (2015). Very deep convolutional networks for large-scale image recognition. *3rd International Conference on Learning Representations, ICLR 2015 – Conference Track Proceedings.*

2 Pang, Y., Sun, M., Jiang, X., and Li, X. (2018). Convolution in convolution for network in network. *IEEE Trans. Neural Netw. Learn. Syst.* https://doi.org/10.1109/TNNLS.2017.2676130.

3 Lin, M., Chen, Q., and Yan, S. (2014). Network in network. *2nd International Conference on Learning Representations, ICLR 2014 – Conference Track Proceedings.*

4 Szegedy, C., Vanhoucke, V., Ioffe, S. et al. (2016). Rethinking the inception architecture for computer vision. *Proceedings of the IEEE Computer Society Conference on Computer Vision and Pattern Recognition*, vol. 2016, 2818–2826. https://doi.org/10.1109/CVPR.2016.308.

8

Introducing Recurrent Neural Networks

8.1 Introduction

The previous chapters have debated two forms of data including tabular data and vision data, along with the main differences. In Chapter 5, we discussed the building of convolutional networks designed specially to make use of the regularity in the vision data, such that if the pixels of an image are permuted, it would be far more difficult to reason about the content of something that would look very similar to the background of a test pattern from the days of analog television. Most crucially, the earlier discussion implicitly assumed that the training samples are all derived from some distribution and independently and identically distributed (i.i.d.) data. Unfortunately, this is not the case for the vast majority of data. When you read this text, for example, the words are placed in a specific order, it would be quite difficult to grasp its meaning if the words were permuted at random. Image frames in a movie, voice signals in a conversation, and surfing behavior on a website are all organized in a sequential manner as well. As a result, it is reasonable to expect that specialized models for such data will do far better at characterizing them in general.

The idea that we can not only be given a sequence as input but that we would also be asked to continue the sequence raises another point of contention. Consider the following scenarios: the task is to continue the series 1, 3, 9, ..., the stock price time series

Deep Learning Approaches for Security Threats in IoT Environments,
First Edition. Mohamed Abdel-Basset, Nour Moustafa, and Hossam Hawash.
© 2023 The Institute of Electrical and Electronics Engineers, Inc.
Published 2023 by John Wiley & Sons, Inc.

analysis, the fever curve of a patient, or the acceleration required for a race car is extremely prevalent. Once again, we want models that are capable of dealing with this type of sequential data. In a nutshell, while convolutional neural networks (CNNs) are meant to rapidly model spatial interactions, recurrent neural networks (RNNs) were created to better model the dependencies in sequential data. RNNs combine state variables to store prior information, which is combined with the existing inputs to establish the present outputs. RNNs are used to predict future outcomes. Recurrent networks showed a broad acceptance in natural language processing (NLP) tasks. However, this field is out of the scope of this book. As a result, this chapter provides a strong emphasis on the fundamental concepts of building recurrent networks, the main challenge they face, and the possible solution. Furthermore, the chapter discusses the gradient calculation in the forward direction. Next, we debate the training of recurrent networks using the backpropagation through time (BPTT) algorithm. Finally, the chapter examines the vanishing and exploding gradient encountered during the training of recurrent networks.

8.2 Recurrent Neural Networks

A recurrent network is a family of deep networks that is structured as a special form of feedforward neural networks (FNNs) that uses the previous hidden state as memory, which captures and stores the contextual information (input) that the network has seen so far with connections between their hidden units. Each RNN layer represents a discrete time step, and the weights are shared between layers. The recurrent network may repeatedly create a useful summary of previous observations via connections among the hidden units, thus capturing relationships between events that take place over a long period of time in the data.

8.2.1 Recurrent Neurons

In previous chapters of this book, we have explored the main building of FFNs, in which the one-directional activations flow from the input to the output layer. The structure of a vanilla recurrent

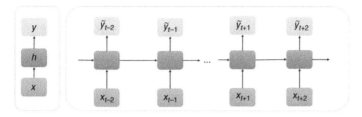

Figure 8.1 A simple recurrent neuron (left side), unrolled through time (right side).

network seems very much similar to FFNs, with the exception of having self-loop connections that pass the output back to the network. Figure 8.1 illustrates the building of the simplest probable recurrent network build with simply a single neuron accepting inputs, generating an output, and a self-loop connection that takes the output back to itself. This neuron is referred to as a recurrent neuron. The recurrent neuron receives two inputs at each time frame t (or step), namely the new input x_t as well as the output it generates at the preceding time step, $\tilde{y}_{t-1}$. This concept can be illustrated for this simple network along the time domain, as displayed on the right side of Figure 8.1, which is known as unrolling or unfolding the network through time. The output of a single recurrent neuron could be calculated as follows:

$$\tilde{y}_t = \phi\left(x_t \cdot W_x + \tilde{y}_{t-1} \cdot W_y + b\right) \tag{1}$$

where ϕ and b represent the activation function and the bias value, respectively.

In the same way, you could build a network consisting of one layer of recurrent neurons instead of just one. Each neuron in this layer can receive, at each time step t, two input vectors, one representing the current x_t and the other is the output vector from the earlier time step $\tilde{y}_{t-1}$, as illustrated in Figure 8.2. Bearing in mind that in this case, both the inputs and outputs are vectors rather than scalars in the case of the output of a scalar. Simply as with FNN, the output of the recurrent layer could be calculated whole in one shot for a complete mini-batch utilizing a vectorized variant of the previous equation:

$$\tilde{Y}_t = \phi\left(X_t \cdot W_x + \tilde{Y}_{t-1} \cdot W_y + b\right) \tag{2}$$

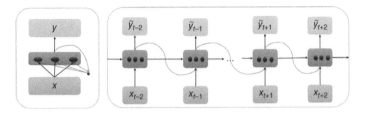

Figure 8.2 A simple recurrent layer (left side), unrolled through time (right side).

where $\tilde{Y}_t$ denotes $n_{\text{batch}} \times n_{\text{neuorn}}$ matrix comprising the output of recurrent layer at time step t; while n_{batch} and n_{neuron} representing the number of samples in the mini-batch and the number of neurons, respectively. X_t denotes $n_{\text{batch}} \times n_{\text{input}}$ matrix comprising the output of recurrent layer at time step t; while n_{input} representing the length of the input vector in terms of the number of features. W_x represent $n_{\text{input}} \times n_{\text{neurons}}$ matrix comprising the weight parameters for the input vector at time step t. W_y is an $n_{\text{neurons}} \times n_{\text{neurons}}$ matrix comprising the weight parameters for the output vector of length at time step $t-1$. For convenience, the weight matrices W_x and W_y are usually concatenated into a one matrix W of shape $(n_{\text{input}} + n_{\text{neurons}}) \times n_{\text{neurons}}$. Moreover, b denotes a bias vector of size n_{neurons}.

One should keep in mind that $\tilde{Y}_t$ is calculated as a function of X_t as well as $\tilde{Y}_{t-1}$, the value of $\tilde{Y}_{t-1}$ is calculated as a function of X_{t-1} and $\tilde{Y}_{t-2}$, the value of $\tilde{Y}_{t-2}$ is also calculated based on X_{t-2} and $\tilde{Y}_{t-3}$, and so on. This turn indicates that Y_t is a function of all the input samples starting from $t = 0$, such as $X_0, X_1, ..., X_t$. when it comes to the first-time step, i.e. $t = 0$, the network has no earlier outputs. Thus, it assumes the previous output to be all zeros.

8.2.2 Memory Cell

Given the fact that the output of a recurrent neuron in the previous time step $t - 1$ is kept to and used to calculate the output in the current time step t, and thereby the following steps, it could be said that the recurrent network has a kind of memory. In this context, the concept of a memory cell (or simply a cell is used to define the component of a neural network that maintains some network's hidden state throughout time steps. A fundamental or baseline form of the memory cell is the aforementioned recurrent neuron, but there are many complicated and compelling forms of cells that will be explored in the later part of this chapter. In most cases, the state of the memory cell, in particular, time step t is denoted h_t, where "h" is derived from the term "hidden," whereas h_t is a function of the input x_t at that time step as well as its previous state, such as $h(t) = f(h_{t-1}, x_t)$. Similarly, the output $\tilde{y}_t$ per time step t is calculated as a function of the two variables. In the case of the fundamental memory cells described so far, both the output $\tilde{y}_t$ and hidden state h_t are the same. However, in more complicated memory cells, this is not always applicable as illustrated in Figure 8.3.

8.2.3 Recurrent Neural Network

If you want to see a picture of RNNs in action, go no further than Figure 8.4. During the calculation of the current output, the hidden layer of the RNN uses the previous hidden state along with the present input element, which might be considered a self-looped link. Is this still a mystery to you? If you look at Figure 8.3, you can see an unrolled version of the "vanilla" RNN, with all of its layers laid out. The output is projected at time step $t = 1$ depending on the latest input element x and the previous concealed state a, as shown in the diagram. In the same way, at time step $t = 2$, the output is projected given the current input and the previously hidden state. The following is a mathematical formulation of the following graphic representation of RNN's working methodology:

$$h_t = f_h(X_t, h_{t-1}) \tag{3}$$

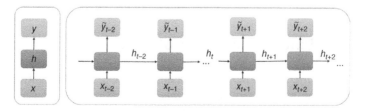

Figure 8.3 A simple recurrent neuron with a hidden state distinct from the output (left side), unrolled through time (right side).

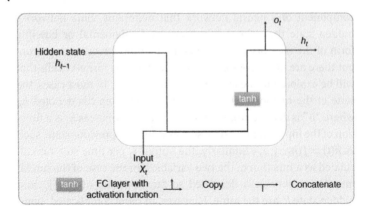

Figure 8.4 Illustration of the simple architecture of vanilla RNN cell.

$$\tilde{y}_t = f_o(h_t) \tag{4}$$

Just like for FNNs, the output of the recurrent layer can be computed in one shot for a complete mini-batch by placing all the inputs at time step t in an input matrix X_t.

Where f_h and f_o correspond to the tanh activation and softmax activation, respectively.

$$h_t = \tanh(X_t \cdot W_{xh} + h_{t-1} \cdot W_{hh} + b_h) \tag{5}$$

$$o_t = h_t W_{hy} + b_y \tag{6}$$

$$\tilde{y}_t = \text{softmax}(o_t) \tag{7}$$

where W_{xh}, W_{hh}, and W_{hy} are weight matrices for the input, recurrent connections, and the output, respectively.

8.3 Different Categories of RNNs

The recurrent networks can be classified into four main categories according to their structures of the input and/or output layers. These categories include one-to-one RNN, one-to-many RNN, many-to-one RNN, and many-to-many RNN, which are covered in more detail in this subsection.

8.3.1 One-to-One RNN

A type of recurrent network in which a single output value, at time step *t*, calculated as a function of single input, as illustrated in Figure 8.5. By definition and illustration, this is just the same as the vanilla neural network. Thus, the application or use cases of one-to-one recurrent networks span all applications of traditional FNN; thereby it is not a recommended choice for sequential modelling tasks. In the context of the internet of things (IoT) security, it can offer instance classification of tabular data based on network features corresponding to each sample in the IoT system.

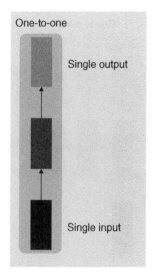

Figure 8.5 Computational graph of one-to-one recurrent neural network.

8.3.2 One-to-Many RNN

A type of recurrent network in which a single input is used to drive many hidden states and many outputs, as illustrated in Figure 8.6. This implies that a recurrent network can generate an output sequence from just one input. No matter how many hidden states the network shares over time, it can still accurately predict the output when only one input is provided. The one-to-many recurrent networks only share the previous hidden states $H(t-1)$ all over time steps instead of previous outputs $Y(t-1)$. When it comes to one-to-many problems, the networks should receive a fixed-size input and generate a variable length output, the network usually utilizes that fixed-size input to reset the hidden state and later allow the network to train and update the hidden state forward.

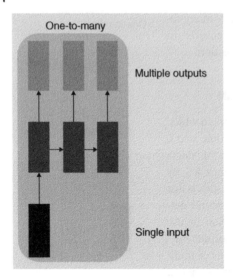

Figure 8.6
Computational graph
of the one-to-many
recurrent network.

A common use case of this type is image captioning, in which one image instance is fed to the network, as a static size input, to generate a sequence of words as an output, which are variable in length. In the first time step $t = 0$, the network predicts the word based only on the input image. When $t = 1$, the previous hidden state is utilized to approximate the subsequent element. Also, it continues for a number of steps and predicts the next word until a caption is generated.

8.3.3 Many-to-One RNN

A variant of the recurrent network in which a single output can be calculated as a function of the sequence of inputs and corresponding hidden states, as illustrated in Figure 8.7. Sentimental analysis can be is a popular use case for such form of network where a sequence of words constituting a sentence, fed to the network that later classify as either positive or negative sentiments. In IoT security, many-to-one network can be effectively applied for anomaly detection, in which a sequence of industrial samples over the time-domain is passed to the network to determine if they are

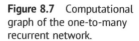

Figure 8.7 Computational graph of the one-to-many recurrent network.

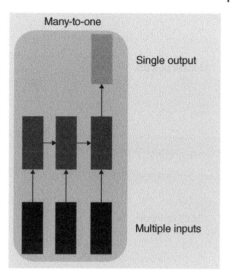

normal or anomalous. When it comes too many-to-one problem, the network make its final decision according to the final hidden state of this network, which encapsulate all of the learnt contextual representation from the whole sequence.

8.3.4 Many-to-Many RNN

A variant of the recurrent network in which a sequence of outputs can be calculated as a function of a sequence of inputs and corresponding hidden states, as illustrated in Figure 8.8. Both input sequences and output sequences can have either identical or different lengths. It can be viewed as a combination of many-to-one and one-to-many recurrent networks. The network accepts a variably sized input to perform encoding into a hidden state vector; then uses them to calculate a variably sized output. This kind of network is commonly used for machine translation as with Google Translate, whereas the input statement determines whether the output could have an identical or variable length. Another use case is the frame-level video in which you can expect an immediate output if you feed the neural network with every frame of a video.

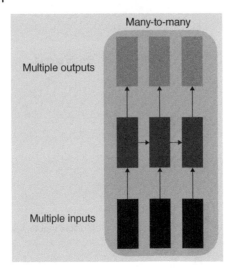

Figure 8.8 Illustration of the many-to-many recurrent network.

However, due to the fact that frames are typically interdependent, the network must propagate its hidden state from one frame to the next.

8.4 Backpropagation Through Time

In previous chapters, we have constantly discussed many concepts about the gradient calculations for training and updating the parameters, FNNs as well as CNNs. Generally, these concepts apply to recurrent networks where the network is training by repeatedly performing forward propagation and backpropagation. Forward propagation in an RNN is relatively straightforward. With the help of this part, you will be able to better understand how gradients are calculated for sequence models and why (and how) math works in this way.

When it comes to RNNs, BPTT is applied for training purposes [1]. An RNN's computational graph must be expanded one step at a time to discover the relationships between model variables and parameters (Figure 8.9). Then, using backpropagation and the chain rule, we can compute and store gradients. Due to the lengths of sequences, the interdependence can be quite long.

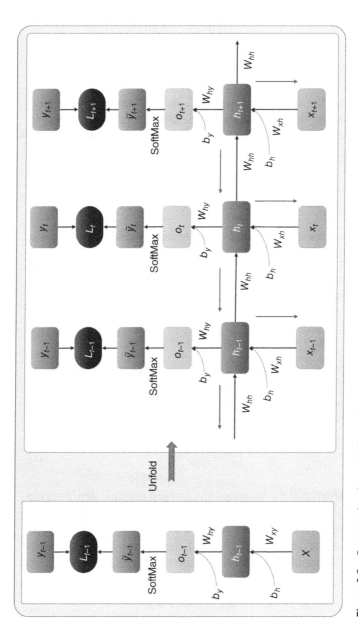

Figure 8.9 Computational graph illustrating the dependencies for a recurrent network during backpropagation.

In order to do BPTT to train a recurrent network, the loss function needs to be calculated first:

$$L(\tilde{Y}, Y) = \sum_{t=1}^{T} L_t(\tilde{y}_t, y_t) = -\sum_{t=1}^{T} y_t \log \tilde{y}_t = -\sum_{t=1}^{T} y_t \log \text{softmax}(o_t)$$

(8)

Since the weight parameter W_{yh} is shared across all the time sequences, the loss function can be differentiated with respect to it at each time step. Then sum up the results together:

$$\frac{\partial L}{\partial W_{hy}} = \sum_{t=1}^{T} \frac{\partial L_t}{\partial W_{hy}} = \sum_{t=1}^{T} \frac{\partial L_t}{\partial \tilde{y}_t} \frac{\partial \tilde{y}_t}{\partial o_t} \frac{\partial o_t}{\partial W_{yh}} = \sum_{t=1}^{T} (\tilde{y}_t - y_t) \odot h_t$$

(9)

whereas the derivative SoftMax can be easily proved to be $\dfrac{\partial o_t}{\partial W_{hy}} = h_t$

given that $o_t = h_t \cdot W_{yh} + b_y$ and $\odot$ denote the outer product of two vectors. In a similar way, the derivative of the loss function with respect to b_y could be computed as follows:

$$\frac{\partial L}{\partial b_y} = \sum_{t=1}^{T} \frac{\partial L_t}{\partial b_y} = \sum_{t=1}^{T} \frac{\partial L_t}{\partial \tilde{y}_t} \frac{\partial \tilde{y}_t}{\partial o_t} \frac{\partial o_t}{\partial b_y} = \sum_{t=1}^{T} (\tilde{y}_t - y_t)$$

(10)

Moreover, consider using the L_{t+1} to represent the output calculated at time step $t+1$ such that $L_{t+1} = -y_{t+1} \log y_{t+1}$. By taking into account the time step from t to $t+1$, let's go through the details of calculating the gradient of the loss with respect to W_{hh}:

$$\frac{\partial L_{t+1}}{\partial W_{hh}} = \frac{\partial L_{t+1}}{\partial \tilde{y}_{t+1}} \frac{\partial \tilde{y}_{t+1}}{\partial h_{t+1}} \frac{\partial h_{t+1}}{\partial W_{hh}}$$

(11)

It seems that the equation considers just one time step (from t to $t+1$). However, the hidden state h_{t+1} somewhat depends also on h_t in accordance with the recursive formulation (Eq. (11)). Therefore, at the time step from $t-1$ to t, the network can further calculate the partial derivative with respect to W_{hh} as follows:

$$\frac{\partial L_{t+1}}{\partial W_{hh}} = \frac{\partial L_{t+1}}{\partial \tilde{y}_{t+1}} \frac{\partial \tilde{y}_{t+1}}{\partial h_{t+1}} \frac{\partial h_{t+1}}{\partial h_t} \frac{\partial h_t}{\partial W_{hh}}$$

(12)

This way, in the time step $t + 1$, the network could compute the derivatives and further take advantage of BPTT from time step $t + 1$ to time step 1 to calculate the overall gradient with respect to W_{hh}:

$$\frac{\partial L_{t+1}}{\partial W_{hh}} = \sum_{k=1}^{t+1} \frac{\partial L_{t+1}}{\partial \tilde{y}_{t+1}} \frac{\partial \tilde{y}_{t+1}}{\partial h_{t+1}} \frac{\partial h_{t+1}}{\partial h_k} \frac{\partial h_k}{\partial W_{hh}} \tag{13}$$

bearing in mind that the $\dfrac{\partial h_{t+1}}{\partial h_k}$ by itself is a chain rule. For instance, $\dfrac{\partial h_3}{\partial 1} = \dfrac{\partial h_3}{\partial 2} \dfrac{\partial h_2}{\partial 1}$. Also, one could notice that since the network is calculating the derivative of a vector function with respect to another vector, the result is a matrix (known as the Jacobian matrix) whose elements are all pointwise gradients. The above formula can be rewritten as the following gradient:

$$\frac{\partial L_{t+1}}{\partial W_{hh}} = \sum_{k=1}^{t+1} \frac{\partial L_{t+1}}{\partial \tilde{y}_{t+1}} \frac{\partial \tilde{y}_{t+1}}{\partial h_{t+1}} \left(\prod_{j=k}^{t} \frac{\partial h_{j+1}}{\partial h_k} \right) \frac{\partial h_k}{\partial W_{hh}} \tag{14}$$

where

$$\prod_{j=k}^{t} \frac{\partial h_{j+1}}{\partial h_k} = \frac{\partial h_{t+1}}{\partial h_k} = \frac{\partial h_{t+1}}{\partial h_t} \frac{\partial h_t}{\partial h_{t-1}} \cdots \frac{\partial h_{k+1}}{\partial h_k} \tag{15}$$

Aggregating the derivatives with respect to W_{hh} over the entire time steps during the backpropagation phase can finally lead to the following gradient with respect to W_{hh}:

$$\frac{\partial L}{\partial W_{hh}} = \sum_{t=1}^{T} \sum_{k=1}^{t+1} \frac{\partial L_{t+1}}{\partial \tilde{y}_{t+1}} \frac{\partial \tilde{y}_{t+1}}{\partial h_{t+1}} \left(\prod_{j=k}^{t} \frac{\partial h_{j+1}}{\partial h_k} \right) \frac{\partial h_k}{\partial W_{hh}} \tag{16}$$

Followingly, let us calculate the derivative of loss with respect to the gradient with respect to W_{xh}. Likewise, by taking into account the time step $t + 1$ that denotes only the contribution from X_{t+1}, the network drives the gradients with respect to W_{xh} as follows:

$$\frac{\partial L_{t+1}}{\partial W_{xh}} = \frac{\partial L_{t+1}}{\partial \tilde{y}_{t+1}} \frac{\partial \tilde{y}_{t+1}}{\partial h_{t+1}} \frac{\partial h_{t+1}}{\partial W_{xh}} \tag{17}$$

Since h_t and X_t both contribute to h_{t+1}, the network needs to backpropagate to h_t as well. Thus, by considering the contribution from the time step, the previous formula can be rewritten as

$$\frac{\partial L_{t+1}}{\partial W_{xh}} = \frac{\partial L_{t+1}}{\partial \tilde{y}_{t+1}} \frac{\partial \tilde{y}_{t+1}}{\partial h_{t+1}} \frac{\partial h_{t+1}}{\partial W_{xh}} + \frac{\partial L_{t+1}}{\partial \tilde{y}_{t+1}} \frac{\partial \tilde{y}_{t+1}}{\partial h_{t+1}} \frac{\partial h_{t+1}}{\partial h_t} \frac{\partial h_t}{\partial W_{xh}}$$

(18)

Therefore, summing up all the contributions from $t+1$ to 1 through backpropagation, the network could calculate the gradient at the time step $t+1$ as follows:

$$\frac{\partial L_{t+1}}{\partial W_{xh}} = \sum_{k=1}^{t+1} \frac{\partial L_{t+1}}{\partial \tilde{y}_{t+1}} \frac{\partial \tilde{y}_{t+1}}{\partial h_{t+1}} \frac{\partial h_{t+1}}{\partial h_k} \frac{\partial h_k}{\partial W_{xh}}$$

(19)

$$\frac{\partial L}{\partial W_{hh}} = \sum_{t=1}^{T} \sum_{k=1}^{t+1} \frac{\partial L_{t+1}}{\partial \tilde{y}_{t+1}} \frac{\partial \tilde{y}_{t+1}}{\partial h_{t+1}} \frac{\partial h_{j+1}}{\partial h_k} \frac{\partial h_k}{\partial W_{xh}}$$

(20)

Recall that $\dfrac{\partial h_{j+1}}{\partial h_k}$ is a chain rule in itself, again!

8.5 Challenges Facing Simple RNNs

Two of the common problems related to the training of vanilla recurrent networks using gradient-based methods and backpropagation include vanishing gradients and exploding gradients. In this section, we explore how these problems affect the training of RNNs.

8.5.1 Vanishing Gradient

Driven by the behavior of BPTT, the recurrent network calculates the derivative of the loss function in terms of weights and biases. Every time the network propagates backward, it repeats this calculation till convergence. There are two aspects that impact the magnitude of gradients – weights and derivatives of activation functions that the gradient goes through. It is known that the derivative of hyperbolic tangent is bounded to one. It is also known that multiplying any two values in range between zero and one $(0, 1)$ results in a smaller fractional number. Typically, the parameters of the network are initialized with a small number.

Therefore, the multiplication of the derivatives and weight parameters during the backpropagation are fundamentally the multiplication of small fractional values. Thus, doing so at every backpropagation step, the gradient of vanilla RNN becomes infinitesimally small resulting in a final number that the computing machine cannot deal with. This is what we can briefly call the vanishing gradient problem. In vanilla RNNs, vanishing gradients originate from the repetitive backpropagation through recurrent connections. More explicitly, it takes place because of the recursive derivative the network needs to calculate as in Eq. (15).

At this point, let us explore one of these terms by calculating the derivative of h_{j+1} with respect to h_j where diag transforms a vector into a diagonal matrix for the reason that this recursive partial derivative is a Jacobian matrix:

$$\frac{\partial h_{j+1}}{\partial h_j} = \text{diag}\left(\phi_h'\left(X_{j+1} \cdot W_{xh} + h_j \cdot W_{hh} + b_h\right) \cdot W_{hh}\right)$$

(21)

Therefore, if the network would like to backpropagate through $t - k$ time steps, this gradient will be

$$\prod_{j=k}^{t} \frac{\partial h_{j+1}}{\partial h_k} = \prod_{j=k}^{t} \text{diag}\left(\phi_h'\left(X_{j+1} \cdot W_{xh} + h_j \cdot W_{hh} + b_h\right) \cdot W_{hh}\right)$$

(22)

As you can notice, the network is multiplying the weights and derivatives of the activation function ϕ_h' at each time step t. This repeated multiplication of these two leads to a very small number and triggers the vanishing gradients' dilemma.

The vanishing gradients do not only encounter in the recurrent networks, but they also take place in a broad range of deep networks. The deep nature of recurrent networks (through time) is the reason that makes this family of networks more popular with such a problem. To further explain, once the gradient gets vanished in the recurrent network, the earlier hidden states have no contribution to the content of subsequent hidden states, implying that there are no long-term dependencies learned. A variety of methods have been shown beneficial for evading the vanishing gradient problem such as appropriate initialization of the network parameter. Another recommended solution is to use the ReLU activation function as an alternative to hyperbolic tangent or sigmoid activation functions in vanilla RNN. This is because the derivative of the ReLU is a constant of either zero or one. So, it is not as expected to suffer from vanishing gradients.

8.5.2 Exploding Gradient

In a similar way, when the parameters of the vanilla recurrent network are initialized with a big number, the gradients will grow to be very huge at every step. During backpropagating, the network has to multiply a large number together at every time step, which, in turn, results in infinity. This is called the exploding gradient dilemma. However, many possible solutions have been proposed to alleviate this problem, which are summarized in the following subsections.

8.5.2.1 Truncated Backpropagation Through Time (TBPTT)

The key problem in BPTT stems from the fact that updating the weight parameters necessitates propagating forward through the whole sequence to calculate loss, then again backpropagating through the whole sequence to calculate gradients. The minor variation of the BPTT algorithm, known as truncated BPTT (TBPTT) [2], was introduced to address this problem by performing forward and backward propagations over pieces of sequences rather than the whole sequence. This algorithm sets up some maximum number of time steps n along which error can be propagated, in which the network has $t - n$ steps, hence reducing the number of time steps factored into the total error gradient throughout backpropagation. These supports prevent the gradient from growing exponentially beyond n steps. This idea is similar to utilizing minibatches in gradient descent, whereas the gradients are computed for each iteration, but the parameters are updated occasionally in batches. This concept enables reducing the complexity of the training practice and enables removing possible noise from the updates of parameters. However, it is worth mentioning that the TBPTT encounters another problem, which is that the network is unable to learn long-term interdependencies as with BPTT due to the constraint on the flow of the gradient caused by truncation.

8.5.2.2 Penalty on the Recurrent Weights W_{hh}

This solution [3] simply applies regularization to guarantee that the spectral radius of the W_{hh} does not go beyond one, which in itself is a necessary requirement for gradients not to explode.

The downside of this solution is that the model is constrained to a straightforward regime, and all inputs must die off exponentially fast in time. It is commonly applied to train a generator model and also give up the capability to learn long-range dependencies.

8.5.2.3 Clipping Gradients

A method to bypass the exploding gradient trouble by rescaling downgradients whenever they go beyond a predefined threshold. In particular, the gradients are normalized according to a vector norm (say, $L2$) and thereby clipped to a certain range. Assuming g represents the gradient of the loss with respect to W as follows:

$$g = \frac{\partial L}{\partial W} \tag{23}$$

Then, the gradients are normalized using the $L2$ norm, that is, $\|g\|$. Once the normalized gradient exceeds the specified threshold, the gradient can be updated as follows:

$$g = \frac{\text{threshold}}{\|g\|} g \tag{24}$$

The downside of this solution is that it introduces an additional hyperparameter, namely the threshold.

8.6 Case Study: Malware Detection

Malware describes malicious software offenders transmitting to contaminate different IoT devices or even the whole network of organization. There are many types of malicious software that are designed to cause harm to computer systems and compromise user security. Malware is any program or piece of code that secretly works against the users' best interests and engages in harmful activities. Malware targets a wide range of IoT devices, including servers, desktops, laptops, smartphones, and digital cameras, in order to gain unauthorized access, steal complex data, and interrupt the standard functioning of the system. It exploits target system vulnerabilities, such as a bug in legitimate software (e.g. a browser or web application plugin) that can be hijacked. Data theft, extortion, and network system paralysis are all possible outcomes of malware infiltration.

When it comes to internet-connected devices, malware is a major cause of concern. Malware is the root cause of most internet problems, including spam e-mails and denial of service attacks. Thus, infected machines are frequently interconnected to establish botnets, and a large number of attacks are made against these networks by malevolent, attacker-controlled individuals. Common malware families include spyware, ransomware, and Trojan horse. Anti-malware tools are always evolving to keep up with the ever-changing threat landscape. One solution to tackle the problem of malware protection is to identify and analyze the malicious software. Malware behavior analysis is a conventional solution to this problem. This line of work carefully follows the model of malware families, which also indicates the pattern of malicious behavior.

Deep learning has been shown as a great achievement in automating and improving the capability of malware detection, hence improving the overall security of IoT devices and systems. The main concepts explained for the recurrent networks in the previous sections will be implemented for technically explored malware detection from the real-world dataset. The details about the used datasets and type of malware considered are described in detail in the following section.

8.7 Supplementary Materials

https://github.com/DEEPOLOGY-AI/DL-Book-Wiley-2022/tree/main/Ch8

References

1 Werbos, P.J. (1990). Backpropagation through time: what it does and how to do it. *Proc. IEEE* https://doi.org/10.1109/5.58337.

2 Pearlmutter, B.A. (1995). Gradient calculations for dynamic recurrent neural networks: a survey. *IEEE Trans. Neural Netw.* 6 (5): 1212–1228. https://doi.org/10.1109/72.410363.

3 Doya, K. (1992). Bifurcations in the learning of recurrent neural networks. *[Proceedings] 1992 IEEE International Symposium on Circuits and Systems*, vol. 6, 2777–2780. https://doi.org/10.1109/ISCAS.1992.230622.

9

Dive Into Recurrent Neural Networks

9.1 Introduction

The previous chapter introduced the main concepts and elementary knowledge about recurrent neural networks (RNNs), which provide a robust solution to model interdependencies in sequential data. The mathematical and practical findings demonstrated that recurrent networks still face many gradient problems that limit their ability to effectively deal with sequence learning problems in complex internet of things (IoT) environments. The notable limitation of recurrent networks resides in their numerical instability. Even though gradient clipping could provide a tricky solution to alleviate this issue, the vanilla RNN is unable to retain the sequential information in its memory state in case of the too long input sequence.

To combat this, a set of improved variants of the recurrent network was designed based on some gating mechanisms to keep the information in memory if it is necessary. These gates help the network by learning the information that should be retained and the ones that should be discarded.

This chapter provides a deep dive into such widely used recurrent networks, starting with *long short-term memory* (LSTM). The detailed description of the building blocks of LSTM is explored to exactly grasp how LSTM overcomes the shortcomings of vanilla

Deep Learning Approaches for Security Threats in IoT Environments,
First Edition. Mohamed Abdel-Basset, Nour Moustafa, and Hossam Hawash.
© 2023 The Institute of Electrical and Electronics Engineers, Inc.
Published 2023 by John Wiley & Sons, Inc.

RNN. Going ahead, the chapter explores the *gated recurrent units* (GRUs) in terms of design principles, working methodology, and steps of the calculation, and also describes the main points of similarities and differences with LSTM and vanilla RNN.

Moving forward, we discuss the convolutional LSTM (ConvLSTM) as an advanced variant of LSTM that exploits the spatial learning capabilities to afford efficient modeling of spatiotemporal representations in spatial-temporal sequences.

Moreover, the chapter provides a basic understanding of deep recurrent networks that stack multiple recurrent hidden layers. By the end of the chapter, the main idea of bidirectional recurrent networks is investigated to understand how past and future information can contribute to sequential modeling.

9.2 Long Short-Term Memory (LSTM)

The LSTM was early proposed in 1973 by Sepp Hochreiter and Jürgen Schmidhuber [1]. Since then, it has progressively enhanced over the years by a number of research studies [2, 3]. LSTM is a variant of a vanilla recurrent network that resolves the issue of vanishing gradient and maintains information in the memory as long as it is necessary. Essentially, the simple cells in the vanilla recurrent network are replaced with LSTM cells in the hidden units, as illustrated in Figure 9.1.

When the LSTM cell is treated as a black box, it could be applied very much like the simple cell in a vanilla recurrent network.

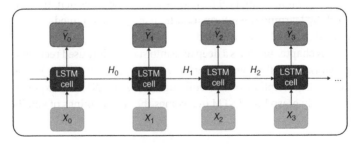

Figure 9.1   An illustration of the generic structure of the LSTM model.

However, it could effectively model the sequential data much better, while achieving faster training converge. When considered as a black box, the LSTM cell behaves just like a conventional cell, except that the corresponding state, at time step t, is divided into two types of states, one being the hidden state H_t and the other being the memory state C_t. For convenience, the hidden state H_t can be believed to be the short-term state and memory state C_t to be the long-term state. When the box is opened, the LSTM is mainly designed to enable the network to learn the information to be saved to the long-term state C_t, the information to be thrown away, as well as the information to be read from it. As the long-term state C_t is designed to move across the LSTM cell from left to right, passing through a *forget gate*, to drop some memorized information, and then passing through an *input gate* adds some new information memories. Besides, once the addition of new information is completed, the long-term state is copied and filtered by the *output gate* to generate the short-term state H_t. However, this is too broad a description of the LSTM cell. So, let us figure out how the LSTM is structured and how it functions step by step.

9.2.1 LSTM Gates

Questionably, the design of the LSTM cell was derived from logic gates in computer architecture. The architecture of LSTM presents a *memory cell* (or simply *cell*) to store long-term states that share the same shape with the hidden state engineered in some way for recording supplementary information. Memory cells are regarded by some researchers and practitioners as a distinct subtype of the hidden state. To gain control over the memory cell, LSTM architecture necessitates a number of gates each serving a different purpose. In particular, some gate is required to determine the part of memory information to be read and output from the memory cell. This can be identified as the *output gate*. One more gate is necessary to regulate the addition of new entries into the memory. As its name implies, this is named the *input gate*. Moreover, a *forget gate* is also essential to control a mechanism for erasing the content of the cell. The motive for this gated design stems from the fact that the network needs a committed mechanism for determining

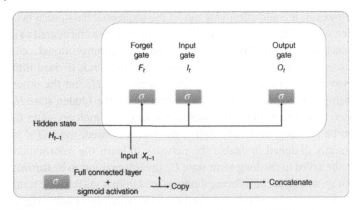

Figure 9.2 Illustration of the gating operations in an LSTM cell.

whether or not inputs in the hidden state should be recalled or ignored.

Similar to the cell of a recurrent network, the input data passed to the LSTM cell is composed of two components, namely the previous hidden state at time step $t-1$ and the present sequential input at time step t, as illustrated in Figure 9.2. This twofold input is concurrently passed to the aforementioned three gates. Each gate is implemented using a fully connected layer that is activated with a sigmoid function, and function to process the received input and generate the corresponding output values. Accordingly, the output of input, forget as well as the output gates lie in (0, 1).

In mathematical terms, n is given as batch size, d as the number of inputs, and h as the number of hidden units. Hence, the input is $X_t \in \mathbb{R}^{n \times d}$, the previous hidden state $H_{t-1} \in \mathbb{R}^{n \times h}$. At time step t, the input gate is denoted as $I_t \in \mathbb{R}^{n \times h}$, which is responsible for determining whatever information must be kept in the cell state, and it is calculated as follows:

$$I_t = \sigma(X_t \cdot W_{xi} + H_{t-1} \cdot W_{hi} + b_i), \tag{1}$$

where σ is a sigmoid function, and W_{xi} and W_{hi} denote the weight parameters of the input gate for its connections for the input vector and previous hidden state, respectively. $b_i \in \mathbb{R}^{1 \times h}$ denote the bias parameters of the input gate. At time step t, the forget gate is denoted as $F_t \in \mathbb{R}^{n \times h}$, which decides the information that needs to be removed from the cell state, and it is computed as follows:

$$F_t = \sigma\left(X_t \cdot W_{xf} + H_{t-1} \cdot W_{hf} + b_f\right) \tag{2}$$

where W_{xf} and W_{hf} denote the weight parameters of forget gate for its connections for the input vector and previous hidden state, respectively. $b_f \in \mathbb{R}^{1 \times h}$ denotes the bias parameters of forget gate. The output gate, at time step t, is denoted as $O_t \in \mathbb{R}^{n \times h}$, which is accountable for choosing what information must be taken from the cell state to generate as an output, and it is calculated as follows:

$$O_t = \sigma(X_t \cdot W_{xo} + H_{t-1} \cdot W_{ho} + b_o) \tag{3}$$

where W_{xo} and W_{ho} denote the weight parameters of the output gate for its connections for the input vector and previous hidden state, respectively. $b_o \in \mathbb{R}^{1 \times h}$ denotes the bias parameters of the output gate.

9.2.2 Candidate Memory Cells

To this point, we simply learned how all three gates run in an LSTM cell. Let us understand how the LSTM cell uses these gates to essentially update the cell state by inserting significant new information and removing information that is not needed from the cell state. In this regard, to record all the new information that can be added to the long-term cell state, the LSTM cell creates a new vector termed a *candidate memory* cell to store the candidate state or internal state vector $\widetilde{C}_t \in \mathbb{R}^{n \times h}$. The *candidate* memory cell is structured and functions in a similar way as with the three stated gates (i.e. full connected layers). However, the output is calculated based on tanh activation, meaning it lies in the range $(-1, 1)$. The *candidate* memory cell has the typical responsibility of analyzing the current input X_t and the preceding hidden state H_{t-1}. In a rudimentary cell of the vanilla recurrent network, there is not anything else besides this layer, and its output is passed directly to $\widetilde{Y}_t$ and H_t. On the contrary, the output of the LSTM cell output does not go directly, but rather it is partly saved in the long-term state. In mathematical terms, the

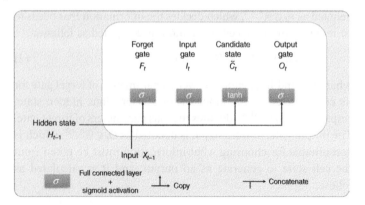

Figure 9.3 Illustration of calculation of the candidate state in an LSTM cell.

output of the candidate memory cell $\widetilde{C}_t$, at time step t, is computed as follows:

$$\widetilde{C}_t = \tanh\left(X_t \cdot W_{xc} + H_{t-1} \cdot W_{hc} + b_c\right) \tag{4}$$

where W_{xc} and W_{hc} denote the weight parameters of the input and the previous hidden state, respectively. $b_c \in \mathbb{R}^{1 \times h}$ denotes the bias parameters of the input gate. As illustrated in Figure 9.3, the candidate memory cell receives that twofold input $[X_t, H_{t-1}]$ as with the gates stated earlier, and also at the same time.

9.2.3 Memory Cell

The LSTM here seeks to develop a mechanism to regulate the addition or disregard of the information to the cell state by deciding if the candidate state contains the related information or not. Since the input gate is responsible for deciding to add new information or not, the element-wise multiplication of the candidate states $\widetilde{C}_t$ and I_t will obtain important information that has to be added to the memory. That is, it is known that the input gate returns to zero if the information is not needed and one if the information is needed. This way, when the multiplication gives zero, it implies that the information in the candidate state $\widetilde{C}_t$ is not needed and the LSTM cell does not choose to update the cell state. In contrast, when the multiplication result is one, it implies the LSTM adds the information in $\widetilde{C}_t$ to the cell state.

To decide whether to remove unnecessary information from the previous cell state, the forget gate comes into play. So, if the LSTM cell multiplies with the previous cell state C_{t-1}, and forget gate, F_t, then it can retain only relevant information in the cell state.

Imagine that $F_t = 0$. Then the multiplication result is zero, which means the knowledge in the cell state C_{t-1} is not required and ought to be forgotten. In contrast, if $F_t = 1$, then the multiplication result is one, which suggests that information in the previous cell state C_{t-1} is required and must not be eliminated. By applying the pointwise multiplication technique described earlier, the network comes up with an updated formula as follows:

$$C_t = F_t \odot C_{t-1} + I_t \odot \widetilde{C}_t \tag{5}$$

This way, when the input gate is forever roughly *zero*, the forget gate is forever roughly one, and the earlier memory cells C_{t-1} will be recorded across time and fed to the present time step. The main advantage of this structural design is to relieve the problem of the vanishing gradient problem, thereby empowering the network to capture long-term interdependencies in the input sequences. Following this design step, the architecture of an LSTM cell can be illustrated in Figure 9.4.

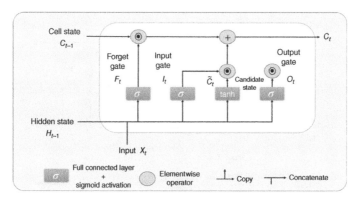

Figure 9.4 Illustration of calculation of the candidate state in an LSTM cell.

9.2.4 Hidden State

The residual thing to know about LSTM is how it defines and calculates the hidden state $H_t \in \mathbb{R}^{n \times h}$. When it comes to this point, the role of the output gate comes into work. The current hidden state can be calculated as basically a gated form of the tanh of the content of the memory cell, which means that the value of the hidden state H_t is forever closed in the interval $(-1, 1)$.

$$H_t = O_t \odot \tanh(C_t) \tag{6}$$

Each time the output gate approaches one, the LSTM actually routes all memory information through to the forecaster. In contrast when it approximates to zero, the LSTM preserves all the information simply within the memory cell and does not perform any extra processing. Following this design step, the final architecture of the LSTM cell can be illustrated in Figure 9.5.

To sum up, an LSTM cell could learn to identify a valuable input (via the input gate), save it in the memory cell (long-term state), learn to maintain it as long as it is required (via the forget gate), and learn to obtain it at whatever time it is required. This, in turn, explains the reason that makes LSTM remarkably effective at capturing long-term interdependencies in sequential data, such as long texts, time series, network traffic, sensor measurement, inertial data, WiFi data, and so on.

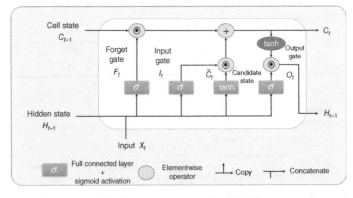

Figure 9.5 Illustration of calculation of the hidden state in an LSTM cell.

9.3 LSTM with Peephole Connections

It is worth noting that there exist numerous variants of the fundamental LSTM architecture described earlier. A popular one is building peephole connections that enable the gates of LSTM cells to not just receive twofold input $[X_t, H_{t-1}]$, but they also receive the long-term state (cell) at the previous time step C_{t-1}. This concept was proposed by Felix Gers and Jurgen Schmidhuber [4]. To make things simpler, the structure of the LSTM cell supplemented with "peephole connections" is illustrated in Figure 9.6. Following this idea, the formula of input, update, and output can be respectively written as follows:

$$I_t = \sigma(C_{t-1} \odot W_{cI} + X_t \cdot W_{xi} + H_{t-1} \cdot W_{hi} + b_i) \qquad (7)$$

$$F_t = \sigma(C_{t-1} \odot W_{cf} + X_t \cdot W_{xf} + H_{t-1} \cdot W_{hf} + b_f) \qquad (8)$$

$$O_t = \sigma(C_t \odot W_{co} + X_t \cdot W_{xo} + H_{t-1} \cdot W_{ho} + b_o) \qquad (9)$$

Remarkably, the LSTM cell supplemented with "peephole connections" from its memory cells to its multiplicative gates could learn the outstanding difference between sequences of spikes divided by either 50 or 49 discrete time steps.

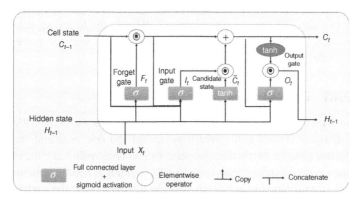

Figure 9.6 Illustration of the architecture of an LSTM cell with "Peephole Connections."

9.4 Gated Recurrent Units (GRU)

In the previous section, a detailed description is provided of the LSTM cell and how it uses various gating mechanisms to deal with the problem of the issue of vanishing gradient faced in the vanilla recurrent network. However, one cloud noticed that the design of the LSTM cell has a huge number of parameters since it includes many states and gating mechanisms. Thus, while backpropagating the LSTM model, we need to update a lot of parameters in each training step. This increases our training time. To address this limitation, the gated recurrent unit was proposed by Kyunghyun Cho et al. [5], which functions as a streamlined edition of the LSTM network. However, unlike the LSTM network, the design of GRU cells used exactly two gates and one hidden state.

The key difference between GRU and vanilla recurrent network is that the former allows for gating of the hidden state as with LSTM. This implies that the network has to develop some mechanisms to regulate the update and the erasing of the hidden state. As with LSTM, some gates can be used to implement these mechanisms and address the aforementioned limitations of the recurrent network. In doing so, if the first input element is of excellent significance, the GRU network could learn not to update the hidden state once this input is observed. Similarly, it could learn to skip inappropriate temporary observations. Additionally, the network could also learn to reset the latent state every time required. To dive into a detailed interpretation of the GRU cell, the following subsection will explore its constituting components and the corresponding functionality step by step.

9.4.1 CRU Cell Gates

As with the LSTM cell, the first component to know about the GRU cell is the control gates, which are called the *reset gate* and the *update gate*. In particular, the reset gate is responsible to control the amount of information that the GRU cell might need to remember from the previous hidden state. In a similar way, the update gate is responsible for regulating the degree to which the new hidden state is simply a copy of the old hidden state.

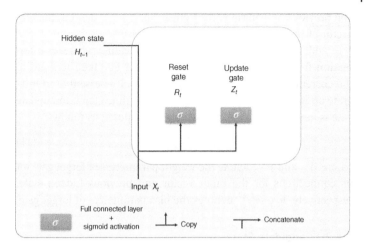

Figure 9.7 Illustration of computation of the gating mechanisms in a GRU cell.

Like the cell of LSTM and vanilla recurrent network, the input data fed into the GRU cell, at time step t, is made of two parts, namely the preceding hidden state $t - 1$ and the current input at the time step t, as illustrated in Figure 9.7. This twofold input is passed to the two gates at the same time. Again, the two gates are designed via fully connected layers that are activated with a sigmoid function, and function to process the received input and generate the corresponding output values. Accordingly, the output of the reset and forget gate is always in the interval (0, 1).

Mathematically speaking, n is given as the batch size, d as the number of inputs, and h as the number of hidden units. Hence, the input is $X_t \in \mathbb{R}^{n \times d}$ and the previous hidden state $H_{t-1} \in \mathbb{R}^{n \times h}$. The reset takes over deciding the amount of information that GRU cell can forget. At time step t, the reset gate is denoted as $R_t \in \mathbb{R}^{n \times h}$ and is calculated as follows:

$$R_t = \sigma(X_t \cdot W_{xr} + H_{t-1} \cdot W_{hr} + b_r) \tag{10}$$

where σ is a sigmoid function, and W_{xr} and W_{hr} denote the weight parameters of the reset gate for its connections for the input vector and previous hidden state, respectively. $b_r \in \mathbb{R}^{1 \times h}$ denotes the bias vector of the input gate.

In addition, the update gate facilitates deciding whatever information from the previous state H_{t-1} could be taken forward to the current H_t. As described in LSTM cells, it is essential to integrate an input gate and a forget gate. So, at time step t, the update gate is denoted as $Z_t \in \mathbb{R}^{n \times h}$, which is computed as follows:

$$Z_t = \sigma(X_t \cdot W_{xz} + H_{t-1} \cdot W_{hz} + b_z) \tag{11}$$

where W_{xz} and W_{hz} denote the weight parameters of forget gate for its connections for the input vector and previous hidden state, respectively. $b_z \in \mathbb{R}^{1 \times h}$ denotes the bias parameters of forget gate.

9.4.2 Candidate State

In this step, the reset gate is used to remove information that is not required. So, this gate $R_t \in \mathbb{R}^{n \times h}$ can be exploited to create a candidate *hidden state* or simply a *candidate state*, which holds only the necessary information. The *candidate state* $\widetilde{H}_t \in \mathbb{R}^{n \times h}$ at time step t can be calculated as follows:

$$\widetilde{H}_t = \tanh(X_t \cdot W_{xh} + (R_t \odot H_{t-1}) \cdot W_{hh} + b_h) \tag{12}$$

where W_{xh} and W_{hh} denote the weight parameters of the *candidate hidden state* for its connections for the input vector and the previous hidden state, respectively. $b_z \in \mathbb{R}^{1 \times h}$ denotes the bias parameters of forget gate. The symbol $\odot$ denotes the Hamdard product.

Till now, the GRU cell just calculated the *candidate state*. However, it still needs to integrate the role of the update gate. Unlike the vanilla recurrent network, the GRU cell is capable to reduce the influence of the hidden states from the previous time step $t-1$ via the elementwise multiplication (Eq. (8)). When the reset gate R_t encountered entries approximating one, the GRU acts as the vanilla recurrent networks. In contrast, when the reset gate R_t encountered an entry approximating to zero, the candidate hidden state is the result of a fully connected layer with X_t as the input, which implies that any present hidden state is, therefore, *reset* to defaults. Figure 9.8 shows the flow of computation once the reset gate is applied.

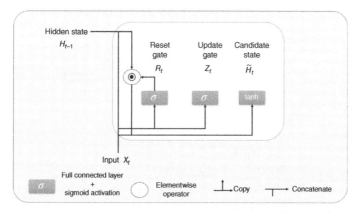

Figure 9.8 Illustration of computation of the candidate state in a GRU cell.

9.4.3 Hidden State

As the last step, the CRU cell integrates the update gate Z_t to define the degree to which the hidden state at the current time step t is just a copy of the hidden state at the previous time step H_{t-1} by calculating the amount of information to be considered from the candidate state $\tilde{H}_t$. In particular, the update gate Z_t achieves this task merely by computing the elementwise convex permutations between both $\tilde{H}_t$ and H_{t-1}. This way the new hidden state of the GRU cell can be calculated as follows:

$$H_t = Z_t \odot H_{t-1} + (1 - Z_t) \odot \tilde{H}_t \tag{13}$$

Every time the update gate Z_t approximates to one, the CRU cell basically maintains the hidden state from the earlier time step. This way, the new input information X_t is essentially overlooked, efficiently jumping time step t in the dependence chain. On the other hand, every time Z_t approximates zero, the current hidden state H_t is likely to be close to the candidate state $\tilde{H}_t$. Figure 9.9 displays the flow of computing when the updated gate is effectuated in the GRU cell. The structural designs of the GRU cells offer a solution to avoid the vanishing gradient problem in recurrent networks and better model the interdependencies in input sequences.

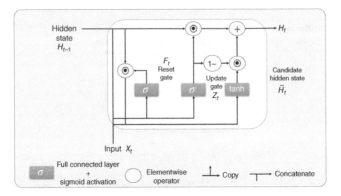

Figure 9.9 Illustration of computation of the hidden state in a GRU cell.

9.5 ConvLSTM

ConvLSTM is a type of LSTM that was proposed by Shi et al. [6] for spatiotemporal video frame prediction. It has convolutional operation in both the input-to-state and state-to-state transitions. The ConvLSTM defines the future state of a particular cell in the grid by the inputs and earlier states of its local neighbors. The main motive for the design of ConvLSTM is to combine the advantages of the LSTM for sequential modeling and convolutions for modeling the spatial correlations in data. ConvLSTM adapted the inner gate controllers of the LSTM cell to use the convolution operation, denoted as $*$, rather than using simple matrix multiplication in case of full connected gates. Thus, in ConvLSTM cells, the formula for calculating input gate, forget gate, output gate, and candidate state can be rewritten as follows:

$$I_t = \sigma\left(X_t * W_{xi} + H_{t-1} * W_{hi} + C_{t-1} \odot W_{cI} + b_i\right) \qquad (14)$$

$$F_t = \sigma\left(X_t * W_{xf} + H_{t-1} * W_{hf} + C_{t-1} \odot W_{cf} + b_f\right) \qquad (15)$$

$$O_t = \sigma\left(X_t * W_{xo} + H_{t-1} * W_{ho} + C_{t-1} \odot W_{co} + b_o\right) \qquad (16)$$

$$\tilde{C}_t = \tanh\left(X_t * W_{xc} + H_{t-1} * W_{hc} + b_c\right) \qquad (17)$$

The main difference between the distinct ConvLSTM cell and the LSTM cell is that the matrix multiplication between weight matrices W and inputs X is replaced with convolution operation.

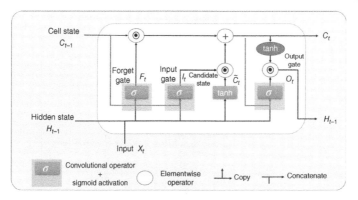

Figure 9.10 Illustration of internal computation of different gates in a ConvLSTM cell.

This means that the wight parameters are now learnable using a group of filters/kernels. Like LSTM, a matrix multiplication is performed between kernels' weight parameters and previous hidden state H_{t-1}. Accordingly, the input X, hidden state H, call state, the gates I, F, and O turned to be three-dimensional tensors, whose first dimension is the number of channels, and the last two dimensions are the height and width of the spatial maps. Figure 9.10 illustrates the structure of the ConvLSTM cell.

The ConvLSTM was demonstrated to perform better than earlier purely LSTM when dealing with spatiotemporal data because of its extra capability of being able to model the spatial correlations as well. In terms of the number of parameters, ConvLSTM hugely decreases them compared to an LSTM implemented with a fully connected layer. This is completely analogous to how the number of parameters in a convolutional network varies from a fully connected network.

9.6 Unidirectional vs. Bidirectional Recurrent Network

A typical state in a recurrent network (vanilla RNN, GRU, or LSTM) relies on past and current events. While this is a conventional scenario, it is not the only one that might be encountered in sequence modeling. There could be circumstances wherever a

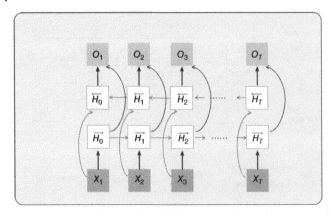

Figure 9.11 Illustration of the architecture of the bidirectional recurrent neural network.

prediction depends on past, current, and future events. To enable straight (past) and reverse (future) traversal of input, the structural design of recurrent networks that have been seen so far need to be modified. Mercifully, this seems simple from the conceptual point of view. In particular, the targeted look-back ability necessitates the recurrent network to process from the last entries iterating back to the first entries rather than processing the input in the forward mode starting from the first entry. *Bidirectional recurrent network* was proposed in 1997 by Schuster and Paliwal to achieve this goal by expanding the one-directional recurrent network with an additional hidden layer that flexibly fed the information in a backward direction. Figure 9.11 illustrates the structural design of a bidirectional recurrent network as a combination of two one-directional recurrent networks – one moves forward, beginning from the start of the data sequence, and the other moves backward, starting from the end of the data sequence with one hidden layer.

Mathematically speaking, n is given as the batch size, d as the number of inputs, and h as the number of hidden units. Given the forward and backward hidden states as $\overrightarrow{H_t} \in \mathbb{R}^{n \times d}$ and

$\overleftarrow{H_t} \in \mathbb{R}^{n \times h}$, respectively, at time step t, $\overrightarrow{H_t} \in \mathbb{R}^{n \times d}$ and $\overleftarrow{H_t} \in \mathbb{R}^{n \times h}$ can be calculated as follows:

$$\overrightarrow{H_t} = \phi \left(X_t * W_{xh}^f + H_{t-1} * W_{hh}^f + b_h^f \right) \tag{18}$$

$$\overleftarrow{H_t} = \phi \left(X_t * W_{xh}^b + H_{t-1} * W_{hh}^b + b_h^b \right) \tag{19}$$

where ϕ is the hidden layer activation function. $W_{xh}^f \in \mathbb{R}^{d \times h}$, $W_{hh}^f \in \mathbb{R}^{h \times h}$, $W_{xh}^b \in \mathbb{R}^{d \times h}$, and $W_{hh}^b \in \mathbb{R}^{h \times h}$ denote the weight parameters of the forward and backward layers, respectively. $b_h^f \in \mathbb{R}^{1 \times h}$ and $b_h^b \in \mathbb{R}^{1 \times h}$ denotes the biased parameters of the forward and backward layers, respectively.

Following, both the forward hidden state $\overrightarrow{H_t}$ and the backward hidden state $\overleftarrow{H_t}$ are concatenated to calculate the hidden state $H_t \in \mathbb{R}^{n \times 2h}$ to be passed to the output layer. In the case of deep bidirectional recurrent networks, the information of the hidden state H_t is given as *input* to the following bidirectional layer. At the end of the network, the output is calculated as

$$O_t = H_t \cdot W_{hq} + b_q \tag{20}$$

where $W_{hq} \in \mathbb{R}^{2h \times q}$ and $b_q \in \mathbb{R}^{1 \times q}$ denote the weight and bias parameters of the output layer, respectively. One of the crucial characteristics of a bidirectional recurrent network is that it exploits the information from both directions of the sequence to approximate the output. In other words, the past and future information are taken into account during the prediction of a certain output. The training of *bidirectional recurrent networks* is the same as one-directional ones that use the BPTT algorithm. The BPTT algorithm unrolls the network and calculates errors at every time step. Then, roll up the network and update weights.

In a *bidirectional recurrent network*, however, since there are forward and backward passes taking place at the same time, updating the weights for the two processes could take place at the same point in time.

9.7 Deep Recurrent Network

In earlier parts, you can observe that deep neural networks generally contain numerous hidden layers. This is why they are called "deep." Likewise, a deep recurrent network is designed by stacking multiple hidden layers. However, an interesting question in this case is how the network calculates the hidden states. As stated before, the current hidden state is usually computed by taking inputs and the preceding hidden state. But this did not tell how the hidden states in the next layers are computed. To make things simpler, the general structure of deep recurrent networks is illustrated in Figure 9.12. For example, to calculate the hidden state H_1^2, the recurrent cell takes as input, the previous hidden state H_0^2, and the output of previous layer H_1^1. Therefore, when dealing with the deep recurrent network, the hidden state at the non-first layers is calculated by taking the previous hidden state and the previous layer's output.

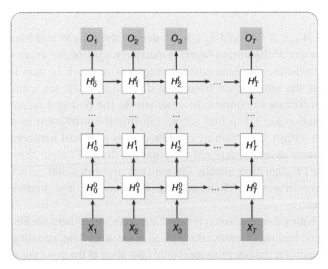

Figure 9.12 Illustration of the architecture of the deep recurrent neural network.

Mathematically speaking, n is given as batch size, d as the number of inputs, h as the number of hidden units, l as the index of the layer in the range $[1, L]$ where L is the number of hidden layers, and q is the number of outputs. Hence, the input will be $X_t \in \mathbb{R}^{n \times d}$, the hidden state will be $H_t^l \in \mathbb{R}^{n \times h}$ of the l-th layer, and the output layer variable will be $O_t \in \mathbb{R}^{n \times q}$. Assuming that $H_t^0 = X_t$, then at time step t, the hidden state of each layer can be calculated as follows:

$$H_t^l = \phi^l \left(H_t^{l-1} \cdot W_{xh}^l + H_{t-1}^l \cdot W_{hh}^l + H_t^{l-1} \cdot b_h^l \right) \qquad (21)$$

where ϕ^l denotes the activation function in layer l; H_{xh}^l and H_{hh}^l denote the weight parameters of input and hidden state connections in layer l, respectively. $b_h^l \in \mathbb{R}^{1 \times h}$ denotes the bias parameters in layer l. Finally, the computation of the output layer is just depending on the hidden state of the final hidden layer:

$$O_t = H_t^L \cdot W_{hq} + b_q \qquad (22)$$

where W_{hq} and b_q denote the weight and bias parameters of layer L, respectively. As with the deep neural network, the hyperparameters L and h denote the number of hidden layers and units. To put it another way, they can be defined by the developer. Moreover, these concepts and calculations could be easily applied to all variants of recurrent networks by replacing the hidden state computation with that from an LSTM cell or a GRU cell.

9.8 Insights

When it comes to training improved recurrent networks discussed in the previous sections, one should notice that they all are difficult to train for the reason that they necessitate many computational resources, which is the worst nightmare for IoT communities that eventually confine the applicability of these solutions. In brief, LSTM uses four fully connected layers in each cell and for each sequence time step. As stated earlier, linear layers involve a high number of trainable parameters, which necessitate large amounts of memory resources to be trained. In fact, they cannot use a lot of computing units frequently for the reason that the system does not have sufficient memory bandwidth to feed the computational units. As a result, these variants of recurrent networks are likely to face many challenges when it comes to being used in a resource-constrained IoT system.

A tricky solution to this problem lies in replacing the linear layers with convolutional ones as with ConvLSTM. This can be attributed to the fact that convolution operation necessitates lower memory bandwidth requirements, as the input maps can be used in several convolution operations in parallel, and convolution parameters are comparatively small. One alternative to these heavily trained networks is the temporal convolutional network (TCN), which has outperformed canonical recurrent networks across a broad range of tasks and datasets while demonstrating longer effective memory. One can refer to Chapter 7 for more information about TCNs.

Moreover, the LSTM network and its variants became so popular because they offer a solution to the problem of vanishing gradients. However, LSTM is unable to completely eliminate that problem because of the fact that information keeps flowing between cells to be evaluated. Additionally, the cell has come to be somewhat complicated given the extra features being brought into the picture. Furthermore, the LSTM network and its variants are still suffering from overfitting issues. Input dropout and recurrent dropout can be applied to not eliminate the activations between time steps instead of layers.

9.9 Case Study of Malware Detection

Given the case study (malware detection) presented in the previous chapter, the main topics covered in the previous sections (e.g. LSTM, GRU, ConvLSTM, etc.) are practically validated and implemented for detecting malware in the real-world IoT. The details about the type of malware regarded in the case study, the datasets employed to train and evaluate the model, and other related tricks can be found in the supplementary materials of this chapter.

9.10 Supplementary Materials

https://github.com/DEEPOLOGY-AI/DL-Book-Wiley-2022/tree/main/Ch9

References

1 Hochreiter, S. and Schmidhuber, J. (1997). Long short-term memory. *Neural Comput.* 9 (8): 1735–1780. https://doi.org/10.1162/neco.1997.9.8.1735.

2 Sak, H., Senior, A., and Beaufays, F. (2014). Long short-term memory recurrent neural network architectures for large scale acoustic modeling. *Proceedings of the Annual Conference of the International Speech Communication Association, INTERSPEECH.* https://doi.org/10.21437/interspeech.2014-80.

3 Hofmann, M. and Mader, P. (2021). Synaptic scaling – an artificial neural network regularization inspired by nature. *IEEE Trans. Neural Netw. Learn. Syst.* https://doi.org/10.1109/TNNLS.2021.3050422.

4 Gers, F.A. and Schmidhuber, J. (2000). Recurrent nets that time and count. https://doi.org/10.1109/ijcnn.2000.861302.

5 Cho, K., Van, B., Gulcehre, C. et al. (2014). Learning phrase representations using RNN encoder–decoder for statistical machine translation. *EMNLP 2014 – 2014 Conference on Empirical Methods in Natural Language Processing, Proceedings of the Conference.* https://doi.org/10.3115/v1/d14-1179.

6 Shi, X., Chen, Z., Wang, H. et al. (2015). Convolutional LSTM network: a machine learning approach for precipitation nowcasting. *Proceedings of the 28th International Conference on Neural Information Processing Systems*, vol. 1 (NIPS'15), 802–810. Cambridge, MA: MIT Press.

10

Attention Neural Networks

10.1 Introduction

A primate's visual system's optic nerve receives a huge amount of sensory input, considerably beyond the brain's capacity for processing it all. It is good to know that not all stimuli are equal. The ability of monkeys to focus and concentrate their minds on certain parts of their visual surroundings, such as food and adversaries, is a result of the development of focalization and awareness. When it comes to survival, the ability to focus on just a small portion of the data is critical to human evolution.

Since the late nineteenth century, researchers in cognitive science have been focusing on attention. In this chapter, we will take a look at a common framework for understanding how people pay attention to images on the screen. Models based on the attention signals found in this paradigm will be developed. Furthermore, the kernel regression of 1964 is an excellent example of machine learning that uses attention mechanisms in a straightforward manner. Moving forward, this chapter will dive into attention methods that have been comprehensively employed for the design of attention-based intelligence solutions.

By the end of this chapter, we explore popular self-attention methods as an extension of multi-head attention. Then, the transformer neural network established solely upon attention mechanisms is explained in detail.

Deep Learning Approaches for Security Threats in IoT Environments,
First Edition. Mohamed Abdel-Basset, Nour Moustafa, and Hossam Hawash.
© 2023 The Institute of Electrical and Electronics Engineers, Inc.
Published 2023 by John Wiley & Sons, Inc.

10.2 From Biological to Computerized Attention

Thank you for taking the time to read this chapter. You are reading this chapter and pay no attention to others because you have a limited supply of attention. As a result, human attention is paid with an occasion expense, much like money. To guarantee that your time and attention are well spent, the authors have worked hard to generate a high-quality book. Life and any work's exceptionality can only be achieved if you pay attention to what you are doing.

Human attention is a restricted, valued, and rare commodity that can be traded as a result of the focus of economics on the distribution of rare resources. It has spawned a slew of business strategies to make use of it. In the case of video- or audio-streaming services, humans have two options, the first is to pay attention to the advertisements, and the other is to hide the advertisement by paying some money. To progress in the gaming world, humans can either pay attention to take part in gaming challenges, which appeal to new gamers or pay money to instantaneously come to be powerful. There is no such thing as a free lunch.

Overall, while humans have plenty of information at their disposal, humans can pay limited attention. A human's optical nerve gets information at a rate of 10^8/s when analyzing a visual scene, considerably above the rate at which the human brain can comprehend it all. As it turns out, early humans were already aware of the fact that not all sensory inputs are made equivalent. The ability of human brains to focus on only a small portion of the information available has helped humans to live, grow, and socialize.

10.2.1 Biological Attention

A two-component structure has arisen and permeated the visual world to describe in what way human attention is carried out. William James, known as the "Father of American Psychology," first proposed this concept in the 1890s [1]. Subjects use both nonvolitional and voluntary cues to strategically direct their attention. This nonvolitional cue relies on the saliency and prominence of things in the surrounding environment to provide the information.

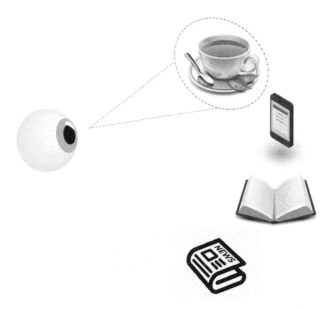

Figure 10.1 Utilizing the nonvolitional cue according to saliency, attention is unwillingly turned to the cup of tea.

Figure 10.1 illustrates a situation in which you have four objects in front of somebody: a cup of tea, a mobile phone, a book, and a newspaper. The coffee or tea has a distinct color from those patterns on the rest of the stationery. That is to say, the tea itself spontaneously and unintentionally draws attention due to its prominence in this visual situation. Figure 10.1 shows how to place the fovea (the macula's brightest spot) on the cup of tea.

When you drink tea, he/she feels energized and ready to read. Figure 10.2 shows how you should turn your head and focus your eyes to read the text. Unlike Figure 10.1, the task-dependent selection differs from the tea-biased situation in which the tea encourages you to select according to saliency. This style of attention is more intentional because of employing a volitional cue according to varying selection principles. It is also more effective when the individual actively participates in the process.

Figure 10.2 Illustration of the task-oriented volitional cue, attention is turned to the book under the volitional mechanism.

10.2.2 Queries, Keys, and Values

Motivated by the volitional and nonvolitional attention signals that characterize attentional implementation, this section dives into the details of the methodology of incorporating these two attention signals to develop attention mechanisms.

First, think about a straightforward situation in which only non-volitional inputs are provided. A nonparameterized maximum or average pooling or parameterized fully connected layer can be adopted for biasing selection toward sensory information. The addition of volitional cues distinguishes attention processes from those pooling layers or fully connected layers. In this regard, volitional cues are referred to as "query." Attention mechanisms employ attention pooling to impact the selection of sensory inputs (e.g. intermediary patterns) in response to a particular query. In view of that, the term "value" is used to represent an element in these sensory inputs. Broadly speaking, each sensory input has a

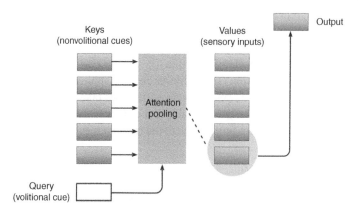

Figure 10.3 Illustration of attention mechanisms based on attention over a set of values.

form of nonvolitional cue called "key," such that every value has a key. Figure 10.3 illustrates the methodology of building attention pooling to enable the supplied query to interact with keys, aiming to direct the bias selection over values.

Attention mechanisms can be designed in a variety of ways. For example, reinforcement learning is likely to be used to develop an attention model that is not differentiated. However, because of the supremacy of the framework (Figure 10.3), it can be settled as the baseline attention model in this chapter.

10.3 Attention Pooling: Nadaraya–Watson Kernel Regression

In the previous section, you have learned about the primary components of attention mechanisms. To recap, attention pooling is the result of the interplay between queries and keys. When values are selectively gathered by attention pooling, an output is generated. This section goes into more depth on attention pooling so that it could be easy to understand the way in which these mechanisms work practically. In particular, in 1964, the Nadaraya–Watson (NW) kernel regression method was presented as a straightforward yet comprehensive demonstration of attention mechanisms in machine learning [2].

For the sake of simplicity, given a regression problem in which data consists of pairs of input–output $\{(x_1, y_1), ..., (x_n, y_n)\}$, the model seeks to train a function f that achieves better mapping of input x to output, such that $\hat{y} = f(x)$. To begin with, let us take into account the most trivial regression estimator that estimates the output for a new example by averaging over all of the training results as follows:

$$f(x) = \frac{1}{n}\sum_{i=1}^{n} y_i \tag{1}$$

As noticed, the inputs x_i are not included in the average pooling. As an improvement to this calculation, Nadaraya and Waston (in 1964) proposed to score the output y_i based on their locations of the corresponding inputs:

$$f(x) = \frac{1}{n}\sum_{i=1}^{n} \frac{\mathcal{K}(x - x_i)}{\sum_{j=1}^{n} \mathcal{K}(x - x_j)} y_i \tag{2}$$

where $\mathcal{K}$ denotes a *kernel*. This formula is known as *Nadaraya–Watson kernel regression*. To further understand the kernels, call to mind the attention mechanisms in Figure 10.3. From the attention standpoint, general *attention pooling* can be driven by updating the aforementioned formula:

$$f(x) = \frac{1}{n}\sum_{i=1}^{n} \alpha(x, x_i)\, y_i \tag{3}$$

where x and (x_i, y_i) represent the query and key-value pair, respectively. In this way, attention pooling is calculated by weighted averaging of value y_i. The *attention weight* $\alpha(x, x_i)$ is allocated to the respective y_i according to the relations between a key x_i and a query x, which is scored with α. The attention weights of each particular query across all the key-value pairs follow a legal probability distribution, which means they are positive values and sum up to one. A Gaussian kernel (GK) should be taken into account in order to get a sense of the way by which attention is pooled. This kernel can be declared as follows:

$$K(u) = \frac{1}{\sqrt{2\pi}} \exp\left(-\frac{u^2}{2}\right) \tag{4}$$

The substitution of the Gaussian kernel into Eq. (3) yields the following:

$$
\begin{aligned}
f(x) &= \frac{1}{n}\sum_{i=1}^{n} \frac{\exp\left((-1/2)\left((x-x_i)w\right)^2\right)}{\sum_{j=1}^{n} \exp\left((-1/2)\left((x-x_j)w\right)^2\right)} y_i \\
&= \frac{1}{n}\sum_{i=1}^{n} \mathrm{Softmax}\left(-\frac{1}{2}\left((x-x_i)w\right)^2\right) y_i
\end{aligned}
\tag{5}
$$

This means that when a key x_i is nearer to a particular query x, it would obtain more attention by means of a *bigger attention score* given to the corresponding value y_i.

As noticed, NW regressor is a nonparametric method; so, it is regarded as a form of nonparametric attention pooling.

Nonparametric NW kernel regression has the advantage of uniformity and can converge to the best solution when it has enough data. However, it can be parameterized by incorporating a particular learnable parameter w that can be learned into attention pooling. To do so, the parameter w is multiplied by the calculated distance between the key x_i and query x. Thus, Eq. (5) will be slightly updated as follows:

$$
\begin{aligned}
f(x) &= \frac{1}{n}\sum_{i=1}^{n} \frac{\exp\left((-1/2)\left(x-x_i\right)^2\right)}{\sum_{j=1}^{n} \exp\left((-1/2)\left(x-x_j\right)^2\right)} y_i \\
&= \frac{1}{n}\sum_{i=1}^{n} \mathrm{Softmax}\left(-\frac{1}{2}\left(x-x_i\right)^2\right) y_i
\end{aligned}
\tag{6}
$$

10.4 Attention-Scoring Functions

Beforehand, the interactions between queries and keys were modeled with a GK. Given the scoring function of attention as the exponent of the GK, the outcome of that function was passed to a

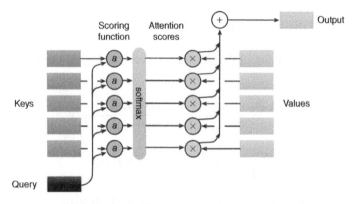

Figure 10.4 Illustration of the calculation of the output of attention pooling as weighted combination/average.

SoftMax function to generate attention scores in the form of a probability distribution over the key-value pairs. These attention scores are simply summed to provide a final output. Consequently, the attention weights are acquired from the key-paired values. Finally, it is easy to see that the result of attention pooling is merely the summation of their attention scores.

On a broad scale, the above-mentioned methods could be used to instantiate the framework of attention mechanisms (refer to Section 10.1). Given that the scoring function is denoted as a, Figure 10.4 demonstrates that a weighted combination of key-value pairs is the outcome of attention pooling. In this context, since attention scores are probabilistic in nature, the weighted combination of them is inherently a weighted mean.

In mathematical terms, (k_1, v_1), ..., (k_m, v_m) represent a set of pairs of keys and values such that $k \in \mathbb{R}^k$ and $v \in \mathbb{R}^v$, m denotes the number of pairs, and $q \in \mathbb{R}^q$ represents the query. The attention pooling f can be computed by taking weighted combinations of pairs as follows:

$$f(q, (k_1, v_1), ..., (k_m, v_m)) = \sum_{i=1}^{m} \alpha(q, k_i)v_i \qquad (7)$$

where the scoring function a is calculated for the key k and query q by mapping both vectors into a scalar. Then, the generated output is fed to the SoftMax function to calculate the final attention score as follows:

$$\alpha(q, k_i) = \text{SoftMax}\left(a(q, k_i)\right) = \frac{\exp\left(a(q,k_i)\right)}{\sum_{j=1}^{m} \exp\left(a(q,k_j)\right)} \tag{8}$$

It is notable that the behavior of attention pooling can vary depending on the adopted scoring function. Thus, this section explores the implementation of more complex attention mechanisms using different variants of scoring functions.

10.4.1 Masked Softmax Operation

We recall that the probability distribution is produced as attention weights via the softmax function. However, there are some instances in which attention pooling should receive only some values instead of all of them. For example, consider having a padded text sequence that contains some extraordinary tokens that have no value. Specifying a suitable sequence length when calculating softmax allows us to focus the attention on just profound tokens as values and exclude those that fall outside of that scale. This can be achieved through the masked softmax function, which masks any number more than the permissible length as zero.

10.4.2 Additive Attention (AA)

Generally speaking, additive attention can be employed as a scoring function in case vectors of queries and keys are not of the same lengths. Provided a key $k \in \mathbb{R}^k$ and query $q \in \mathbb{R}^q$, the additive scoring function can be calculated as follows:

$$a(q, k) = w_v^T \tanh\left(w_q q + w_k k\right) \tag{9}$$

where $w_q \in \mathbb{R}^{h \times q}$ and $w_k \in \mathbb{R}^{h \times k}$ are trainable parameters. This can be easily implemented by concatenating the query and the key and passing them to multilayer perceptron with one hidden layer containing h of hidden neurons.

10.4.3 Scaled Dot-Product Attention

Another form of the scoring function is basically the dot product which has lower computational complexity. Nevertheless, this scoring function necessitates the vectors of key and query sharing identical dimensions denoted as d. For both query and key vectors, all the elements are assumed to have a mean equal to zero and variance equal to one, such that they are autonomous random variables. A mean of zero and a variance of d could be obtained as a result of the dot product of query and key vectors. To guarantee obtaining a unit variance in the output of the dot product irrespective of vector length, a scaling operation is added by dividing that output by $\sqrt{d}$, thereby the scoring function is called *scaled dot-product attention (SDA)* and is calculated as follows:

$$a(q, k) = \frac{q^T k}{\sqrt{d}} \tag{10}$$

Practically speaking, it is common to consider the minibatch calculation for the effectiveness purpose, in particular, calculating the attention score of a set of n queries and a set of m key-value pairs, wherever the vectors of queries and keys have the lengths of d and v, respectively. This way the SDA can be calculated for $Q \in \mathbb{R}^{n \times d}$ and $K \in \mathbb{R}^{m \times v}$ as follows:

$$\text{SoftMax}\left(\frac{QK^T}{\sqrt{d}}\right) \in \mathbb{R}^{n \times v} \tag{11}$$

10.5 Multi-Head Attention (MHA)

As a practical matter, there are some cases that necessitate the network to aggregate representations from a variety of behaviors of the same attention mechanism (e.g. short-term vs. long-term dependencies) in sequential input bases on the same group of key-value pairs and queries. The attention method could benefit from using alternative patterns of key-value pairs and queries in conjunction. As a remedy, rather than executing one attention pooling, a number of h linear projections could be applied to independently

transform queries, keys, and values. The generated set of *h* estimated key-value pairs and queries, which are passed to attention
pooling autonomously. After that, the number of *h* outcomes generated from the attention pooling are concatenated and passed to a
later layer to be linearly projected again to generate the final
output.

Attention pooling is then used to feed that set of *h* key-value pairs
and queries into attention pooling at once. A number of *h* outputs
of attention pooling are concatenated and later processed in a linear operator (layer) to generate the definitive outcome. That model
is known as the MHA mechanism, in which the attention pooling
has a number of *h* heads one for each output. Typically, trainable
linear transformations can be implemented by means of fully connected layers. Figure 10.5 illustrates the concept of multi-head
attention.

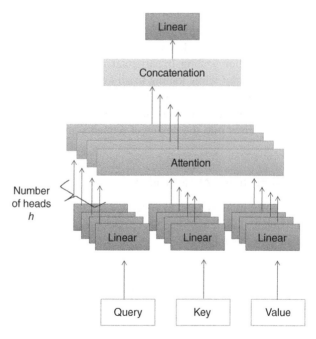

Figure 10.5 Illustration of MHA, where the output of attention heads is
linearly projected after being concatenated.

In mathematical terms, having a key $k \in \mathbb{R}^{d_k}$ *and* query $q \in \mathbb{R}^{d_q}$, and value $v \in \mathbb{R}^{d_v}$, each head h_i ($i = 1, ..., h$) is calculated as follows:

$$h_i = f\left(w_i^q q, w_i^k k, w_i^v v\right) \qquad (12)$$

where f is the attention pooling, like SDA or AA. The concatenation of h heads attention outputs are linearly projected transformation via learnable parameters $W_o \in \mathbb{R}^{p_o \times h p_v}$ as follows:

$$W_o \begin{array}{c} h_1 \\ \vdots \\ h_n \end{array} \qquad (13)$$

10.6 Self-Attention Mechanism

Convolutional and recurrent networks are broadly used for sequence-modeling applications. However, the same sequential input elements can be used as key-value pairs and queries if we input them into attention pooling. In particular, each query creates a single attention output while joining to all key-value combinations. Self-attention (also known as intra-attention) is achieved since the queries, keys, and values all originate from the same location. This section dives into the details of sequence modeling in more detail.

10.6.1 Self-Attention (SA) Mechanism

Having a sequential input $x_1, ..., x_n$ in which $x_i \in \mathbb{R}^d$ for all $1 < i < n$, the output sequence of self-attention shares the same length $y_1, ..., y_n$, and is calculated as follows:

$$y_i = f(x_i, (x_1, x_1), ..., (x_n, x_n)) \qquad (14)$$

where f denotes attention pooling as defined in the earlier part of this chapter. A d-dimensional vector represents each element in an input or output sequence; thus, we can evaluate different mapping topologies for n inputs compared to convolutional and recurrent networks, and self-attention in particular. This comparison will focus on the computational burden, sequential processes, and longest path lengths of these two solutions. A shortened path between every mixture of sequential places turns it possible to discover long-term relationships inside the sequence, but sequential processes prohibit parallelization.

Given K as the size of the kernel of convolutional operation, n as the input length, d as the number of input and output channels, the convolution operation has a time complexity of $O(knd^2)$. As illustrated in Figure 10.6, the convolutional network is hierarchical. Therefore, there are $O(1)$ functions and the extreme length of the path is $O(n/k)$. For instance, x_1 and x_5 are residing in the convolutional receptive field in case of $K = 3$ as shown in Figure 10.6. To perform a hidden state update in a recurrent network, a $d \times d$ weight matrix is multiplied by d-dimensional hidden state leading to time complexity of $O(d^2)$. For recurrent layer, given that the sequence has a length n, the time complexity becomes $O(nd^2)$. As illustrated in Figure 10.6, there exist $O(n)$ sequential functions that could not be parallelizable while having $O(n)$ as the highest path length. In self-attention, the key-value pairs and queries have a shape of $n \times d$ tensor. Think about SDA in which $n \times d$ matrix is

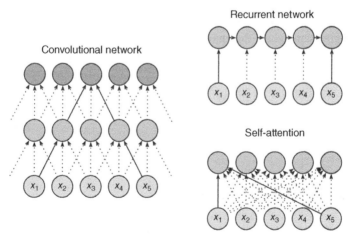

Figure 10.6 Illustration of comparison between the self-attention, recurrent network, and convolutional network.

multiplied by a $d \times n$ tensor, giving an output of $n \times n$ tensor that undergoes multiplication with $n \times d$ tensor. Consequently, the time complexity of self-attention can be defined as $O(n^2 d)$. Figure 10.6 shows that each input element is completely linked to any other input element via self-attention. Thus, computing could be parallelized with $O(1)$ procedures and the with $O(1)$ as the highest path length. Overall, convolutional network and self-attention both benefit from parallel processing, although self-attention has the smallest possible path size. For extended sequences, self-attention is impossible because of the quadratic complexity of the computation required.

10.6.2 Positional Encoding

Different from the recurrent network, self-attention abandons sequential processes in favor of parallel computations. It is possible to add relative or absolute positioning information to the input representations by using information from the sequence order. Two options are available for designing positional encodings: fixed positional encodings or trainable positional encodings. Going forward, this subsection shows how to calculate rigid positional encoding using Sin and Cos functions. Assuming there is some input representation $X \in \mathbb{R}^{n \times d}$ includes the embeddings (with d dimension) for a number of sequences equal to n. The positional embedding $p \in \mathbb{R}^{n \times d}$ is used to generate positional encoding $X + P$, both sharing identical dimension, where the embedding element at the i-th row and the $(2j)$-th column or the $(2j - 1)$-th column is computed as follows:

$$p_{i,2j} = \sin \left(\frac{i}{10\,000^{2j/d}} \right) \tag{15}$$

$$p_{i,2j+1} = \cos \left(\frac{i}{10\,000^{2j/d}} \right) \tag{16}$$

10.7 Transformer Network

In the previous sections, self-attention was contrasted with convolutional and recurrent networks, the findings demonstrated its ability to be parallelized as well as the shortest highest path length.

Consequently, it is interesting to use self-attention to develop a complete deep learning model. Different from the previous models that combine self-attention and depend on recurrent layers for input representation, the transformer network was proposed exclusively established on attention mechanisms without the inclusion of any recurrent and convolutional layers. Although transformer network was originally designed for text data sequence to sequence modeling, however, they have revolutionized the intelligence-driven application across different application domains such as computer vision, natural language processing (NLP), and time-series, analysis [4].

Figure 10.7 illustrates the structural design of the transformer network as a form of encoder–decoder model. The transformer,

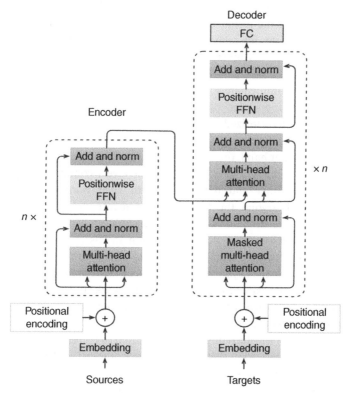

Figure 10.7 Illustration of the structural design of transformer network.

as we can see, consists of an encoder and a decoder. It could be noted that the transformer network consists of two main building modules, namely an encoder and a decoder. Unlike Bahdanau attention [3], the sequence embeddings of inputs of either encoder or decoder are passed to are included with positional encoding prior to passing to the stacked self-attention layers in the encoder or decoder.

The general structure of the encoder part is composed of a sequence of numerous identical layers, where each layer has two sublayers, namely an MHA followed by a position-wise feedforward network (FNN).

In particular, the key-value pairs and queries of self-attention of any encoder layer are actually the outcome of the preceding encoder layer. Motivated by the residual network, the transformer network uses the residual connection to link these sublayers. In the transformer, for each element $X \in \mathbb{R}^d$ in the input sequence, the network needs sublayer$(X) \in \mathbb{R}^d$ so as to make residual connection $x + $ sublayer$(x) \in \mathbb{R}^d$ achievable. Layer normalization is then added immediately after the residual connection. Consequently, the encoder part of the transformer generates d-dimensional vectorized features corresponding to each element in sequential input.

On the other hand, the decoder modules of the transformer network are composed of a pile of similar layers connecting in a residual manner and normalized with layer normalizations. Above and beyond the two sublayers mentioned during the encoding, the decoder adds the third sublayer between them, which is called encoder–decoder attention. In this layer, the query vectors are received from the outcomes of the earlier decoding module, while the keys and values are received from the outcomes of the encoder part of the transformer network. In the decoder, query vectors, keys, and values of self-attention are all obtained from the outcomes of the preceding decoding layer. Nevertheless, each point in the decoding part is permitted to merely pay attention to all locations in the decoder fit for that location. To ensure that the prediction is exclusively based on data that has been generated, the transformer network uses a technique called masked attention.

10.8 Supplementary Materials

https://github.com/DEEPOLOGY-AI/DL-Book-Wiley-2022/tree/main/Ch10

References

1 James, W. (2007). *The Principles of Psychology*, vol. 1. Cosimo, Inc.

2 Watson, G.S. (1964). Smooth regression analysis. *Sankhyā Indian J. Stat. Ser. A* 359–372.

3 Bahdanau, D., Cho, K., and Bengio, Y. (2014). Neural machine translation by jointly learning to align and translate. *arXiv preprint arXiv:1409.0473*.

4 Vaswani, A., Shazeer, N., Parmar, N. et al. (2017). Attention is all you need. In: *Advances in Neural Information Processing Systems* (ed. I. Guyon, U. Von Luxburg, S. Bengio, et al.), 5998–6008.

11

Autoencoder Networks

11.1 Introduction

In the early parts of this book, different families of *deep neural networks (DNNs)* were introduced to perform discriminative learning by mappings from data instances to labels. This includes convolutional neural networks (CNNs) and recurrent neural networks (RNNs). In a similar way, this chapter dives deep into a family of deep networks known as "autoencoders," which are designed to find the most compressed representation of input data.

Like the earlier chapters, the input data can exist in three main formats, namely tabular data, visual data, and sequence data. An autoencoder network seeks to learn a representation to perform useful transformations on the input data. So, it can be trained to reduce and encode data efficiently before recreating it in a form that is closest to the input vector. Human labeling is not necessary for autoencoders because the coding can be learned autonomously from the data alone. As a result, autoencoders fall under the category of algorithms for unsupervised learning.

Autoencoders have the ability to learn improved and low-dimensional representations from the input data, called coding, with no supervision at all. The dimension of these representations is typically lower than the dimension of input data, rendering the

Deep Learning Approaches for Security Threats in IoT Environments,
First Edition. Mohamed Abdel-Basset, Nour Moustafa, and Hossam Hawash.
© 2023 The Institute of Electrical and Electronics Engineers, Inc.
Published 2023 by John Wiley & Sons, Inc.

autoencoders a powerful tool for dimensionality reduction. More essentially, autoencoders can effectively function as a robust feature detector, qualifying them to be exploited for unsupervised pretraining of deep learning models.

This chapter begins by investigating the main principles of building autoencoders in terms of main components, structural design, training, optimization, loss, and so on. Moving forward, more improved variations of autoencoders will be investigated along with how they differ from each other. For example, *denoising autoencoders (DAEs)* which learn to eliminate noise in the input data, sparse autoencoders to learn from sparse inputs, *convolutional autoencoders (CAEs)*, which use convolutional layers, and so many others.

Last but not least, *autoencoders* are capable of randomly generating new samples that seem very analogous to the original data, meaning that can act as a *generative model*. Thus, by the end of the chapter, you will learn about an exciting category of autoencoders, known as variational autoencoders (VAEs), that can be used for generating synthetic data from the actual training data.

11.2 Introducing Autoencoders

By simply attempting to reproduce the input, an autoencoder may figure out its representation or code. Using an autoencoder, on the other hand, is more complicated than simply copying the input to the output. To avoid this, the neural network would not have been able to discover any structure in the input data.

The input distribution is encoded into a low-dimensional tensor by an autoencoder, often in the form of a vector. The latent representation, code, or vector is a term used to describe this hidden structure. The encoding portion of the operation is completed here. The decoder component will recover the original input from the latent vector after it has been decoded.

11.2.1 Definition of Autoencoder

An autoencoder is an interesting unsupervised learning algorithm. Different from other deep networks, the goal of the autoencoder is

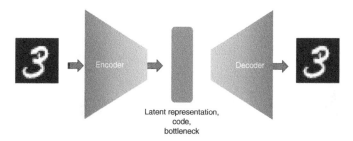

Latent representation,
code,
bottleneck

Figure 11.1   Illustration of generic autoencoder for reconstructing input image.

to rebuild the given input such that the generated output is identical to the input [1]. To do so, the autoencoder is composed of two significant modules termed the encoder and the decoder. The role of the encoder is to encode the input by learning the latent representation of the input, and the role of the decoder is to reconstruct the input from the latent representation produced by the encoder. "Code" or "bottleneck" is another name for the latent representation. As illustrated in Figure 11.1, the encoder module receives an image and input then trains to learn the latent representation of that input. Follow, the latent representation is passed to decoder takes that seek to reconstruct the input image.

To dive more into the autoencoder, let us begin with a simple vanilla autoencoder constructed with just two layers as illustrated in Figure 11.2. It is notable that it consists of an input layer, a hidden (acting as encoder) layer, and an output layer (acting as a decoder). There are two stages in this process: first, the encoding stage learns an important representation of the input as the bottleneck. Then the decoding stage exploits the bottleneck to reassemble the input [2].

If we were to ask ourselves, "What is the logic behind encoding the input and then decoding it?," "What is the point of simply reconstructing the input?" Image denoising and data compression are just a few examples of how autoencoder might be put to use. Because the autoencoder seeks to reconstruct the inputs, the number of nodes in the input and output layers should be the same. Given are a dataset consisting of 50 features and a vanilla

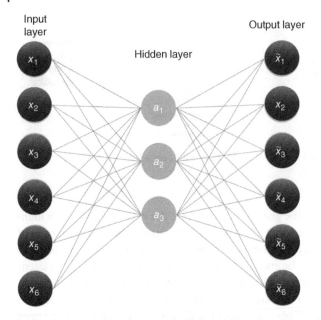

Figure 11.2   Illustration of the architecture of vanilla autoencoder.

autoencoder with 50 input units, 25 hidden units, and 50 output units. Once the data is fed into autoencoders, it seeks to learn the most significant features in the dataset, which limits them to only 25 features and creates a latent representation. This way, only the essential information is contained in the latent representation. In order to get the original input, the decoder uses the latent representation. If the decoder is able to recreate the original input, then the encoder has magnificently learned the encodings or representations of the given input (50 feature dataset).

As a result, the encoder is primarily concerned with learning how to minimize the dimensionality of the data while maintaining the important information. When it comes to dimensionality reduction approaches, principal component analysis (PCA) and autoencoders are most common alogorithms. However, in PCA, the data is projected into a low-dimension space by applying a set of using linear transformations and deleting the features that are not needed in the analysis. The distinction between PCA and an autoencoder is that PCA reduces dimensionality by using a linear transformation, whereas the autoencoder reduces dimensionality by using a nonlinear transformation [3–5].

Beyond dimensionality reduction, autoencoders can also be used to reduce the amount of noise in photos, music, and other media. For example, it is known that an encoder in an autoencoder can minimize the number of dimensions in a dataset by learning only what is essential. As a result, when an autoencoder is fed noisy input data (in any format), the encoder only learns the information it needs from the image to generate a latent representation. As a result of the encoder learning only what it needs to represent an image, it removes noise information from the latent representation because noise is regarded as unnecessary information.

A bottleneck has been created, which is a pictorial representation that does not include any noise information. The decoder reconstructs the input picture from the encodings produced by the encoder when this learned representation of the encoder, that is, the bottleneck, is provided to it. The reconstructed image will have no noise because the encodings have no noise.

One might think of autoencoders as a way to reduce the complexity of input data by mapping it to a lower level of abstraction. It is known as a latent representation or bottleneck because it contains just the most meaningful and important elements of the input. An autoencoder selects a reconstruction error as the loss function because its job is to reconstruct its input. Thus, it is interesting to measure how much of the input is correctly reconstructed by the decoder. Mean squared error (MSE) loss can be used to measure the performance of autoencoders in terms of the reconstruction error.

11.2.2 Structural Design

Beyond the above discussions, this section dives deeper into the structure of autoencoders. Encoder $g_\varphi(\cdot)$ and decoder $f_\theta(\cdot)$ make up the structure of autoencoders, as we have just seen, and they are both critical to its operation. Let us take a closer look at each of them:

- **Encoder:** The encoder g_φ consisting of one or more neural layers receives some input x and returns the corresponding low-dimensional latent representation z. This can be mathematically represented as follows:

$$z = g_\varphi(x) \tag{1}$$

$$\tilde{z} = \phi(\varphi x + b) \tag{2}$$

where φ represents the parameter of the encoder.

• **Decoder:** The latent representation z is fed into the decoder $f_\theta(\cdot)$, consisting of one or more neural layers, which learn to produce output $\tilde{x}$ by reconstructing the original input. This can be mathematically represented as follows:

$$\tilde{x} = f_\theta(z) \tag{3}$$

$$\tilde{x} = \phi(\theta z + b) \tag{4}$$

where θ represents the parameter of the decoder.

The autoencoder needs to learn the optimal parameters, θ and φ, for both encoder and decoder, correspondingly, by minimizing some loss function that estimates the difference between the actual input and reconstructed input, which is known as reconstruction loss. For example, MSE is a common function to calculate the reconstruction loss in autoencoders.

$$L(\theta, \varphi) = \frac{1}{n}\sum_{i=1}^{n} \left(x - f_\theta\left(g_\varphi(x)\right)\right)^2 \tag{5}$$

where n represents the number of training samples.

In some cases, the dimension of the latent representation, in an autoencoder, is less than the dimension of the encoder's input, and this is referred to as *undercomplete autoencoder*. The lower dimension of latent representation means that undercomplete autoencoders try to learn and retain the only important, differentiating, and valuable features of the input and eliminate the useless ones. On the other hand, if the dimension of the latent representation is larger than or equal to the dimension of the encoder's input, the autoencoders will simply make a copy of input without extracting, or learning any valuable features, and this is commonly referred to as *overcomplete autoencoders*. Figures 11.3 and 11.4 present an illustration of both undercomplete and overcomplete autoencoder,

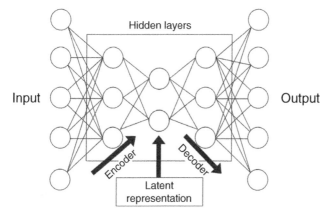

Figure 11.3 Illustration of the architecture of undercomplete autoencoders.

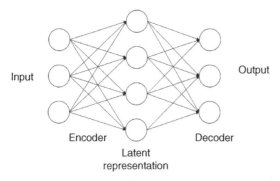

Figure 11.4 Illustration of the architecture of overcomplete autoencoders.

respectively. From a structural perspective, the number of hidden neurons in the undercomplete autoencoders is less than the number of neurons in the input layer. Meanwhile, the number of hidden neurons in overcomplete autoencoders is larger than the number of units in the input layer.

Therefore, by reducing the number of neurons in the hidden layer (latent representation), the autoencoder could better learn the valuable representations in the input. Autoencoders can also have any number of hidden layers.

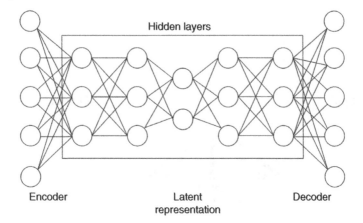

Figure 11.5 Illustration of the architecture of deep autoencoders.

An autoencoder consisting of just one hidden layer (such as the vanilla neural network) is called a vanilla autoencoder, when a small number of hidden layers (such as feedforward neural network [FNN]), it is called shallow autoencoder. Autoencoders consisting of many numbers of hidden layers (such as DNN) are known as deep autoencoders (Figure 11.5) since the input layer is activated by using nonlinear activation functions.

11.3 Convolutional Autoencoder

In the last part, the autoencoders have been described in detail, where the encoder and decoder modules are designed with simple shallow or deep neural networks. However, a question often arises in this regard. Is it possible to design an autoencoder with a convolutional network instead of a feedforward network?

Since it is known that a convolutional network has shown robust spatial feature extraction and exhibits many advantages over DNN (as discussed in previous chapters), it will be a powerful learner to encoder spatial inputs and subsequently reconstruct them in an autoencoder.

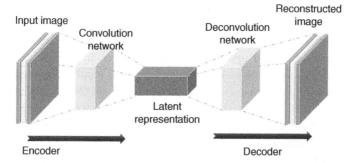

Figure 11.6 Illustration of the generic architecture of convolutional autoencoders.

Therefore, this section introduces a new variant of autoencoders called convolutional autoencoders that use convolutional networks as the basic building blocks for both encoder and decoder modules. In particular, this means the encoder is implemented using convolutional layers, while the decoder is implemented with transposed convolutional layers, instead of a feedforward network. The architecture of convolutional autoencoders is illustrated in Figure 11.6.

Convolutional layers in encoders perform convolution operations and extract significant information from the image as indicated in Figure 11.7, which we feed into the encoder. After that, maximum pooling layers can be used to preserve only the most crucial aspects of the image. The latent representation learned is

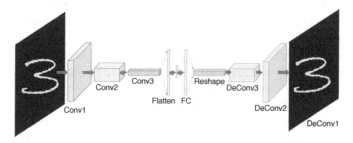

Figure 11.7 Illustration of the convolutional autoencoders for the reconstruction of handwritten digits.

extracted and learned by performing a series of convolutional and max-pooling procedures. After that, the latent representation is passed to deconvolutional decoders that perform a sequence of deconvolution and upsampling operations that, in turn, reconstruct the input image. Bear in mind that the input is assumed to be in image format. However, the same concept can be applied to different types of data and dimensional spaces, i.e. one-dimensional convolutional layers and three-dimensional convolutional layers, etc.

Unlike convolutional networks, convolutional autoencoders are not trained end-to-end to learn filters and integrate features for the purpose of classifying their input. Rather, they are trained only to learn filters capable to extract features that could be applied to reconstruct the input.

A convolutional autoencoder works well with high-dimensional input because the number of parameters necessary to generate an activation map are always the same regardless of the input's size. In contrast to vanilla autoencoders, which totally ignore the multidimensional structure due to the fact that the multidimensional input must be unrolled into a single vector. Thus, convolutional autoencoders are general-purpose feature extractors.

11.4 Denoising Autoencoder

Another version of the autoencoder is known as a denoising autoencoder (DAE). A primary function of these filters is to remove background noise from input data such as images, tabular data, and other formats. The denoising autoencoders are able to rebuild the original uncorrupted input from the corrupted input that we feed it. Interestingly, this section looks at how denoising autoencoders deal with noise removal. DAEs use stochastic noise to corrupt input before feeding it to an autoencoder, rather than feeding it as raw input. By retaining only, the most significant data, the encoder learns to represent the input and then maps the compressed representation to the latent space. When the encoder receives the contaminated input, it will learn that noise is unneeded information and delete it from the encoder's representation while learning the input's representation. In this way, encoders learn the most efficient representation of the input by retaining just the most relevant information and mapping the learnt representation to the latent space.

Followingly, the decoder learns to reconstruct the input using the cleaned feature representation acquired by the encoding operation. Given that the latent representation does not include any noise, the decoders reconstruct the input without noise. In this methodology, the denoising autoencoder is applied as a denoising tool in a wide range of applications. A typical denoising autoencoder is illustrated in Figure 11.8. There are two steps involved in this process: first, we introduce a little noise to the input, and then we send it to an encoder, which learns how to represent it without that noise, and then we use that representation to decode it back.

Mathematically speaking, x is given as input that is corrupted with some noise to obtain a corrupted input x^{noisy} as follows:

$$x^{\text{noisy}} = x + \text{noise} \tag{6}$$

Then, the corrupted input x^{noisy} is encoded as follows:

$$z = g_\varphi\left(x^{\text{noisy}}\right) \tag{7}$$

$$z = \phi\left(\varphi x^{\text{noisy}} + b\right) \tag{8}$$

The latent representation z is decoded as follows:

$$\widetilde{x} = f_\theta(z) \tag{9}$$

$$\widetilde{x} = \phi(\theta z + b) \tag{10}$$

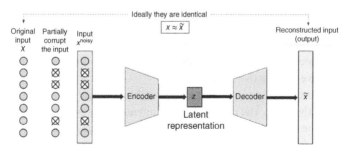

Figure 11.8 Illustration of the architecture of denoising autoencoders.

11.5 Sparse Autoencoders

Autoencoders are already known to be capable of learning to rebuild their input. However, if we make the number of nodes in the hidden layer bigger than the number of nodes in the input layer, it will learn an identity mapping, which is not desirable because it simply replicates the input in its entirety.

Increasing the number of nodes in the hidden layer aids in the learning of a strong latent representation. In contrast, when the hidden layer contains more nodes, the autoencoder attempts to replicate the input completely, resulting in the overfitting of the training data. In order to address the issue of overfitting, a new restriction can be imposed on the loss function of the autoencoder, which is referred to as the sparsity constraint or sparsity penalty. Hence, the loss function with sparsity penalty could be formulated as follows:

$$L = \|\tilde{x} - x\|_2^2 + \beta(\text{sparsity condition}) \tag{11}$$

where the expression $\|\tilde{x} - x\|_2^2$ denotes the reconstruction loss between the actual input and reconstructed counterpart. The symbol β denotes the sparsity constraint to alleviate the problem of overfitting as discussed in the following subsection.

It is possible to stimulate only a few neurons in the hidden layer by applying a sparsity restriction. When neurons are activated and deactivated based on the input, they learn to extract significant information from the input. Autoencoders could learn a resilient latent representation because they have a sparse penalty that prevents them from copying the input perfectly to the output.

As illustrated in Figure 11.9, the hidden layer of sparse autoencoders has more units than the input layer, but only a few units in the hidden layer are active. Unshaded neurons indicate the ones that have been active so far.

A neuron yields one when it is in an active state and zero when in an inactive state. The design of sparse autoencoders sets the majority of the hidden neurons to an inactive state. It was identified in earlier chapters that the sigmoid activation function squeezes the value between zero and one. Hence, when it is used, the network

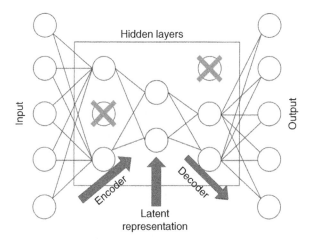

Figure 11.9 Illustration of the architecture of sparse autoencoders.

attempts to maintain the values of neurons approximately to zero. Typically, for each hidden neuron, the average activation value should be maintained close to zero, around 0.05, but not exactly zero, and this value is known as sparsity parameter ρ. The sparsity parameter is typically set to be $\rho = 0.05$.

So, as the first step, the average activation $\bar{\rho}_j$ of a j-th hidden neuron is calculated as follows:

$$\bar{\rho}_j = \frac{1}{n} \sum_{i=1}^{n} \left[a_j^h x^i \right] \tag{12}$$

where $\bar{\rho}_j$ represents the average activation of the j-th neuron in the hidden layer h. n represents the number of training instances. a_j^h represents the activation of j-th neuron in the hidden layer. x^i represents the i-th training example. $a_j^h x^i$ represents the activation of the j-th neuron in the hidden layer h for the i-th training example.

The objective, here, is to keep the average activation value, $\bar{\rho}_j$, of the j-th neurons close to parameter ρ, such that

$$\bar{\rho}_j \approx \rho \approx 0.05 \tag{13}$$

This way, the sparse autoencoder punishes the value of $\bar{\rho}_j$, which is differing from ρ. To do so, the Kullback–Leibler (KL) divergence is broadly applied for measuring the disparity between the two probability distributions. Basically, by confining the mean activation of neural nodes over a group of instances, the network encourages the nodes (in each layer) to activate for only subset of the data instances. The ρ denote the Bernoulli random variable distribution that could be leveraged the KL to contrast the perfect distribution ρ with the noted distributions over all hidden layer nodes $\bar{\rho}_j$. This can be mathematically calculated as follows:

$$KL = \sum_{j=1}^{l^h} \log \frac{\rho}{\bar{\rho}_j} + (1-\rho) \log \frac{1-\rho}{1-\bar{\rho}_j} \tag{14}$$

where l^h represents the hidden layer h, and j represents the j-th neurons in the hidden layer h. The above formula is essentially the sparsity constraint or sparse penalty. Therefore, with this sparsity constraint, all the neurons cannot be active simultaneously, and on average, they are set to 0.05.

This way, the loss function can rewrite as follows:

$$L = \|\tilde{x} - x\|_2^2 + \beta KL \tag{15}$$

Therefore, sparse autoencoders enable having a larger number of units in the hidden layer than the input layer but evade the problem of overfitting with the assistance of the sparsity constraint in the loss function.

11.6 Contractive Autoencoders

Similar to sparse autoencoders, contractive autoencoders include a new regularization term for the loss function. Small differences in training data can affect the accuracy of encodings. Using contractive autoencoders, our encodings are more tolerant of minor changes in our training dataset, such as the presence of tiny noise. This section discovers the contractive autoencoders, where a new term called the regularizer or penalty term is introduced to the loss function of the autoencoder to punish too many features or representations that are very sensitive to the input.

The loss function of this variant of autoencoder could be mathematically expressed as follows:

$$L = \|\tilde{x} - x\|_2^2 + \lambda \left\| j_f(x) \right\|_F^2 \tag{16}$$

The term $\|\tilde{x} - x\|_2^2$ symbolizes the reconstruction loss and the term $\lambda \left\| j_f(x) \right\|_F^2$ denotes the regularization or penalty term and it is essentially the *Frobenius norm* of the *Jacobian matrix*. In particular, the Frobenius norm, sometimes known as the *Hilbert–Schmidt norm*, of a matrix is calculated as the square root of the sum of the absolute square of its value. A matrix containing a partial derivative of the vector-valued function is known as the *Jacobian matrix*.

Therefore, evaluating the Frobenius norm of the Jacobian matrix indicates the regularization term is the sum of squares of the whole partial derivatives of the neurons in the hidden layer with respect to the input. This can be mathematically expressed as follows:

$$\lambda \left\| j_f(x) \right\|_F^2 = \sum_{ij} \left(\frac{\partial h_j(x_i)}{\partial x_i} \right)^2 \tag{17}$$

This seems like gradients of loss function as it computes the partial derivative of the hidden layer with respect to the input. What if a sigmoid activation function is used? Then the partial derivative of the hidden layer with respect to the input can be calculated as follows:

$$\lambda \left\| j_f(x) \right\|_F^2 = \sum_j \left(h_j(1 - h_j) \right)^2 \sum_i \left(W_{ji} \right)^2 \tag{18}$$

Adding the penalty term to the loss function enables lessening the sensitivity of the model to the changes in the input and makes the autoencoder more resilient to the outliers. Therefore, contractive autoencoders decrease the sensitivity of the model to the slight differences in the training data.

11.7 Variational Autoencoders

VAEs are interesting variants of autoencoders that differ from the previously mentioned autoencoders in such that they are generative models that imply they learn to generate new data just similar to generative networks [6].

Given a dataset containing network traffic flows of different cyberattacks, when VAE is trained on this data, it learns to generate new practical traffic samples that are not seen in the data. VAEs have a variety of applications for the reason of their generative nature and some of them involve generating images, music, and so on. But what makes VAEs generative and what is the difference between them and other autoencoders?

Generally, any model can be declared as generative when it is able to learn the distribution of the inputs. For example, suppose you have a dataset containing handwritten digits. To generate new handwritten digits, the model must be able to learn the distribution of the digits in the training data. By learning the distribution of the digits available in the training data, the VAEs can learn valuable characteristics such as digit stroke, dimensions, and others. After the model encodes these features in its distribution, it could generate new handwritten digits by sampling from the learned distribution. Similarly, when we have a dataset of IoT security, learning the distribution of the faces in the dataset helps us learn various properties such as network users, applications, peak usage times, traffic routing, and so on. Once the model learns and encodes these characteristics in its distribution, it can generate a new data sample simply by sampling from the learned distribution.

Therefore, in VAEs, rather than mapping the encodings from the encoder immediately to the latent representation space, it maps the encodings to a distribution; generally, it is a Gaussian distribution. The latent representations are sampled from this distribution and later feed to a decoder to learn to reconstruct the input.

As illustrated in Figure 11.10, an encoder maps its input to a distribution, and a latent vector is sampled from this distribution and fed directly to the decoder to reconstruct an image:

The mean and covariance matrices could be used to parameterize their *Gaussian distribution*. Therefore, the encoder can be applied to generate its encoding and maps it to a mean vector and standard deviation vector that almost follows the Gaussian distribution. Driven from such distribution, a latent vector is sampled and decoded to reconstruct an input. This concept can be easily interpreted from Figure 11.11.

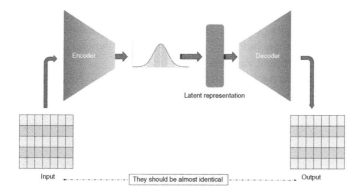

Figure 11.10 Illustration of the generic architecture of variational autoencoders.

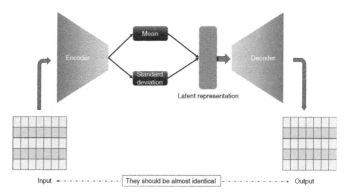

Figure 11.11 Illustration of the architecture of variational autoencoders with Gaussian distribution.

VAEs refer to the encoder and decoder as "recognition model" and "generative model," respectively. Having gained a basic grasp of VAEs, let us dive deeper into their workings in the following part.

Before moving deeper, some important notations should be defined as follows:

$p_\theta(x)$ denotes the distribution of the input data, where θ denotes the parameters to be determined during the training. z represents the latent representation, which encodes all the features of the input by sampling from the distribution. $p(x, z)$ represents the joint distribution of the input and their features. $p(z)$ denotes the distribution of the latent variable.

According to the Bayesian theorem, the distribution of the input data can be expressed in the following formula:

$$p_\theta(x) = \int p_\theta(z \mid x)\, p(x)dz \qquad (19)$$

The previous calculation enables calculating the probability distribution of the input data. However, the problem lies in calculating $p_\theta(z \mid x)$ as calculating it is intractable. Therefore, a tractable way to estimate the $p_\theta(z \mid x)$ should be found. To do so, the concept of *variational inference was introduced*. As opposed to deducing the distribution of $p_\theta(z \mid x)$ immediately, another distribution $q_\varphi(z \mid x)$ is adopted approximate to it, for example, a Gaussian distribution, i.e. $q_\varphi(z \mid x)$, which is essentially a parameterized neural network to estimate the value of $p_\theta(z \mid x)$. In this regard, $q_\varphi(z \mid x)$ is essentially a probabilistic encoder of VAE, which generates a latent vector z based on input x. $p_\theta(z \mid x)$ is the probabilistic decoder that seeks to reconstruct the input given the latent representation z. Figure 11.12 provides an illustration of the above notations and concepts seen so far.

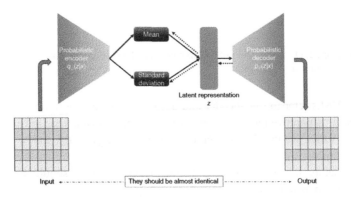

Figure 11.12 Illustration of the variational *inference* in variational autoencoders.

Since $q_\varphi(z \mid x)$ is used to approximate $p_\theta(z \mid x)$. Thus, the projected value of $q_\varphi(z \mid x)$ must be close to $p_\theta(z \mid x)$. Given that they both are distributions, KL divergence can be used to estimate how $q_\varphi(z \mid x)$ diverges from $p_\theta(z \mid x)$, and then the network should minimize the divergence.

So, the loss function of VAEs can be written as follows:

$$L = -\mathbb{E}_{z \sim Q}[\log (p_\theta(x \mid z))] + D_{\mathrm{KL}}\Big(q_\varphi(z \mid x) \big\| p_\theta(z \mid x)\Big)$$

(20)

where $\mathbb{E}_{z \sim Q}[\log (p_\theta(x \mid z))]$ indicates the reconstruction loss of the decoder, which takes the latent representation z to generate reconstructed input x.

VAEs encounter the problem of training with gradient descent. Recall, a sampling operation is performed to generate a latent representation. Since a sampling procedure is not differentiable, there will be no gradients to calculate. That is, when the network backpropagates to minimize the loss, it cannot calculate the gradients of the sampling operation as illustrated in Figure 11.12.

So, to combat this, *reparameterization trick* was proposed to introduce a new parameter known as *epsilon*, which is randomly sampled from a unit Gaussian, which is given as follows:

$$\epsilon \sim \mathcal{N}(0, 1)$$

(21)

In this way, the latent representation can be calculated as follows:

$$z = \mu + \sigma \odot \epsilon$$

(22)

The reparameterization trick is illustrated in Figure 11.13. The reparameterization trick works for other kinds of distributions too, not only Gaussian. In the multivariate Gaussian case, we make the model trainable by learning the mean and variance of the distribution, μ and σ, explicitly using the reparameterization trick, while the stochasticity remains in the random variable.

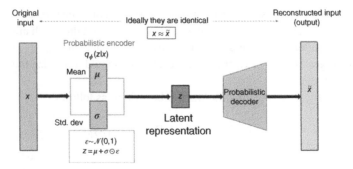

Original input ········ Ideally they are identical ········ Reconstructed input (output)

$x \approx \tilde{x}$

Probabilistic encoder $q_\phi(z|x)$

Mean μ

Std. dev σ

$\varepsilon \sim \mathcal{N}(0,1)$
$z = \mu + \sigma \odot \varepsilon$

z

Latent representation

Probabilistic decoder

x $\tilde{x}$

Figure 11.13 Illustration of reparameterization trick in variational autoencoders.

11.8 Case Study

Vulnerabilities in digital systems, including the IoT system, are discovered on occasion. It is possible for an attacker to gain access to, damage, or compromise a system through one of these security weaknesses. National vulnerability database, for example, keeps track of all of the world's known vulnerabilities (NVD). There is a continuing search for new vulnerabilities in software products by both software providers and independent security researchers. It is the duty of the software vendor to swiftly produce a patch that addresses the security risk – users of the software can then apply the patch to ensure their own security.

Zero-day (or 0-day) attacks are software vulnerabilities exploited before the vendor is aware of them. Because there is no patch available at that time, attackers can take advantage of the vulnerability with impunity because there are no defenses in place. As a result, zero-day vulnerabilities pose a significant danger to security. For an attacker to take advantage of a zero-day vulnerability, they require a method of delivery. There are many circumstances in which the delivery technique is a socially engineered email – an email or other message that appears to be from a recognized or legal correspondence but is, in fact, sent by an attacker. By clicking on a link or accessing a malicious file, the message hopes to trick the user into triggering the exploit.

An attacker uses a zero-day vulnerability to attack a system using a zero-day exploit. They are extremely harmful since they are more likely to succeed than assaults on known weaknesses. When a vulnerability is released publicly on day zero, businesses have not had time to patch it, allowing for an exploit to be carried out. The strategic deployment of zero-day exploits by some advanced cybercriminal gangs makes them even more deadly. For high-value victims, such as healthcare or banking industry or government organizations, these groups deploy zero-day exploits. As a result, the exploit has a greater possibility of being undetected for a longer period of time. Updates are still required, even after a patch has been developed. Otherwise, attackers can use a zero-day vulnerability until a fix is released. To this end, the experimental part of this section will concentrate on investigating the potential of the abovementioned autoencoders to precisely detect and identify zero-day attacks in IoT environments.

11.9 Supplementary Materials

https://github.com/DEEPOLOGY-AI/DL-Book-Wiley-2022/tree/main/Ch11

References

1 Hinton, G.E. and Salakhutdinov, R.R. (2006). Reducing the dimensionality of data with neural networks. *Science (80-)* https://doi.org/10.1126/science.1127647.

2 Goodfellow, I., Bengio, Y., Courville, A., and Bengio, Y. (2016). Deep Learning, vol. 1. Cambridge: MIT press.

3 Goodfellow, I., Bengio, Y., and Courville, A. (2016). *Deep Learning*. MIT Press.

4 Nielsen, M.A. (2015). *Neural Networks and Deep Learning*, vol. 25. San Francisco, CA: Determination Press.

5 Goodfellow, I., Bengio, Y., and Courville, A. (2016). Autoencoders. *Deep Lear.* 1: 493–515.

6 Kingma, D. and Welling, M. (2013). Auto-encoding variational bayes. *arXiv preprint arXiv:1312.6114*.

12

Generative Adversarial Networks (GANs)

12.1 Introduction

The previous chapters of this book have covered forecasting things by simply mapping a set of input samples to a particular output. This is known as discriminative learning because, as it enables, for example, distinguishing between images of cats and dogs. Discriminative learning is demonstrated through classification and regression models. The introduction of deep-learning models optimized through backpropagation has revolutionized the concept of discriminative learning on huge and complex data. Accuracy in the classification of high-resolution photos has gone from unusable to human level (with some caveats) in just five or six years. For the sake of time, we will not go on and on about all the other amazing things deep neural networks can achieve in terms of discrimination. Accuracy in the classification of high-resolution photos has gone from unusable to human-level in the last ten years. For the sake of time, we will not go on and on about all the other amazing things deep learning can achieve in terms of discrimination.

However, there is more to machine learning than merely resolving discriminative problems. Suppose we have a large dataset with no labels, and we want to develop a model that summarizes the data's features in the most efficient way possible. A model like this would allow us to pick instances of synthetic data that were distributed similarly to the training data. As an example, we would wish to be able

Deep Learning Approaches for Security Threats in IoT Environments,
First Edition. Mohamed Abdel-Basset, Nour Moustafa, and Hossam Hawash.
© 2023 The Institute of Electrical and Electronics Engineers, Inc.
Published 2023 by John Wiley & Sons, Inc.

to create a photorealistic image that seems like it could have originated from the same collection of photos of faces. For this method of learning, we use the term "generative modeling."

By 2014, a generative adversarial network (GAN) was proposed by Goodfellow et al. as an intelligent deep-learning approach that could take the advantage of discriminative learners to build a well-behaved generative learner. GANs are fundamentally based on the premise that a data generator is excellent if it is incapable of distinguishing between real and false data. from a statistical standpoint, that is termed a two-sample test, which is a test to determine if X and $\tilde{X}$ were taken from the same distribution.

The major distinction between GANs and statistical tests lies in that the GAN applies this concept in a practical manner. In particular, instead of simply training a model to tell "hello, these two sets of data do not appear as they originated from one distribution," they utilize a two-sample test to deliver training indicators to a generative model. The data generator can be improved so that it provides a more accurate representation of real data. The classifier must be deceived, at the very least. It does not matter how advanced our deep neural network classifier is.

To this end, this chapter dives into the details of the standard GAN model [1] as the baseline member of the family of generative deep networks. Apart from autoencoders, generative techniques, on the other hand, can produce novel and useful results that could be used to produce random encodings. By covering the principles of GANs, we give a look at such early GANs and show how to obtain satisfactory training. Later, this chapter concentrates on two well-known generative models, namely deep convolutional GAN (DCGAN) [2] and conditional GAN (CGAN) [3].

12.2 Foundation of Generative Adversarial Network

While we are on the subject of GANs, here are some examples of GANs and their guiding principles. GANs are incredibly powerful as proven by their capacity to use latent space interpolation to create new human faces that are not based on real individuals.

With the help of two opposing but collaborating networks (i.e. the discriminator and the generator), GANs can learn how to construct input distributions (also called a critic). In order to fool the discriminator, the generator must keep finding new ways to fabricate the input data instances. In the meantime, the discriminator is trained to differentiate the generated samples from the genuine ones. The capacity of the discriminator to discriminate between synthetically created and actual data will deteriorate as the project progresses. After removing the discriminator, the generator could be adapted to generate convincing data samples, which are not encountered earlier.

The basic premise of GANs is simple; nevertheless, it is worth mentioning that training the generator–discriminator network to a decent level is a difficult task. The challenge lies in the ability of the GAN model to stably train the above-mentioned competing networks by achieving a nutritious contest between the discriminator and generator such that they could learn instantaneously.

The parameters of the objective function update faster since they are computed from the discriminator output. The generator no longer obtains sufficient gradient updated information to converge once the discriminator gets converged faster, and therefore, this fails. GANs are still subject to full or partial modal collapse, a circumstance in which the generator generates essentially identical outputs for distinct latent encodings.

To understand the main notion behind generator-discriminator training, Figure 12.1 illustrates a real-world example of the interaction process between counterfeiter and police specialist. The police officers receive much training to detect if the cash dollar is real or counterfeit at the academy. Officers learn how to spot counterfeit currency by comparing it to actual banknotes. The counterfeiter, on the other hand, will occasionally, attempt to fool the public into believing that she/he has published genuine cash dollars. As a first step, the police would then inform the counterfeiter how it is that their currency is phony. The counterfeiter sharpens her/his abilities once more and tries to make new phony cash dollars, bringing this feedback into consideration. Despite the fact that it is expected, the police are permitted to identify the counterfeit money and explain why the cash dollars are counterfeit.

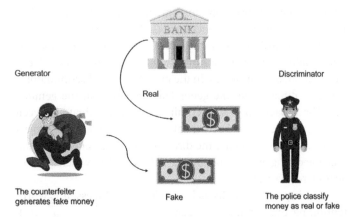

Generator

Real

Discriminator

The counterfeiter
generates fake money

Fake

The police classify
money as real or fake

Figure 12.1 Illustration of the concepts of discriminator and generator with a real-world example of creating fake dollars to deceive the police think they are real.

This cycle can go on endlessly, but eventually, the counterfeiter will have perfected the art of making fake money to the point where even the most experienced police officers will have difficulty telling the difference between the real dollars and the fake ones. Because the money is no longer recognizable as counterfeit, the counterfeiter can continue to print money forever without being apprehended by the police.

The structural design of the GAN model is illustrated in Figure 12.2, with a couple of networks, one acting as a generator and the other as a discriminator. The generator takes noise as input and produces synthesized data as an output. The discriminator's input will be either actual or synthetic data in the meanwhile. Counterfeit data is obtained from the generator, whereas genuine data is produced from true sampling data. All legitimate data is labeled as one (implying that it has a hundred percent of probability of being correct), but all synthesized data is labeled as zero (that is, it has a zero chance of being true). GANs are still included in the category of unsupervised deep learning because the labeling operation is automatedly performed during the training.

The primary purpose of the discriminator part is to use the provided dataset to learn to differentiate authentic samples from bogus

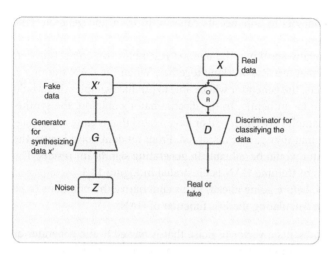

Figure 12.2 Illustration of the architecture of the GAN model consisting of generator G and discriminator D.

samples. Only the discriminator parameters will be changed during this stage of generative training. To train the discriminator, the input samples are compared to the actual samples and then the discriminator is trained to estimate how comparable the given data is to the real data. In other words, it acts as a binary classifier to model and foresees how close a given set of input data is to the real data on a confidence scale of zero to one.

On a regular basis, the generator claims that it produces real samples, and accordingly, it will advocate that the GAN classifies them as authentic data. However, the discriminator is expected to classify fake samples with a label closer to zero after they got it.

On the basis of a label, the optimizer calculates updates to the parameters of the generator. When it comes to new data, it also considers its own predictions. The discriminator is unsure about its predictions. So, the GAN considers that as well. At this point, the GAN model propagates the gradients backward from the discriminator's final layer all the way to the generator's input layer. Nevertheless, in most cases, the parameters of the discriminator are kept unchanged throughout this stage of training. As its parameters are updated and improved, the generator will then make use of the gradients to enhance its capacity to train and generate fake samples.

Generally speaking, the method resembles two competing networks that are also working together. When the GAN training is complete, the generator will be able to produce samples that would seem to be authentic. In the discriminator's opinion, the synthesized samples are either real or have a label that is close to one, signaling that they can be discarded. From random noise inputs, the generator would be valuable in generating significant results. The process of training GAN is illustrated in Figure 12.3.

Now, before going ahead, let us summarize the notations to be used in calculating the loss function of GAN:

- z represents a vector of noise that is passed to the generator as input. It is randomly sampled from uniform distribution denoted as p_z such that $z \sim p_z(z)$.
- x represents an input sample to the discriminator and it is sampled from real data distribution or distribution of our training set denoted as p_{data} such that $x \sim p_{data}(z)$.
- It is easy to interpret that both the generator G and discriminator D are networks that update their parameters through backpropagation. We now need to find the optimal generator parameter, θ^G, and the discriminator parameter, θ^D.

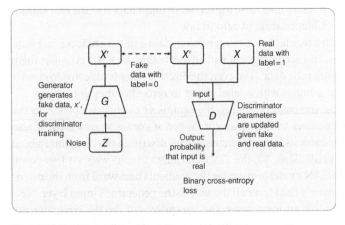

Figure 12.3 Illustration of the discriminator training as a binary classifier in the GAN model.

To calculate the loss function of the discriminator, it is important to recall that the role of the discriminator lies in categorizing the generated samples either as genuine or counterfeit. So, it could be observed that the discriminator can be trained by optimizing a cross-entropy cost function as follows:

$$L^{(D)}\left(\theta^G, \theta^D\right) = -\mathbb{E}_{x \sim p_{\text{data}}} \log D(x) - \mathbb{E}_{z \sim p_z(z)} \log\left(1 - D(G(z))\right)$$

(1)

The loss is equal to the negative sum of two terms. The first term represents the expectation of appropriately recognizing genuine samples, $D(x)$, while the second term denotes the expectation of one minus the proper recognition of artificial samples, $1 - D(G(z))$. The log has no impact on where the local optimum is located.

Throughout the training, the discriminator receives two minibatches of data. First, x represents the original data obtained from the training set (in other words, $x \sim p_{\text{data}}$), which is labeled as one. Second, $x' = G(z)$, which represents the artificial samples synthesized by the generator, is labeled as zero.

To reduce the objective function, the optimizer updates the parameters of the discriminator, $\theta^{(D)}$, by propagating the loss gradients for accurately discriminating the actual samples, $D(x)$, from the artificial ones, $1 - D(G(z))$. Accurately discovering genuine samples can be expressed as $D(x) \rightarrow 1$, while properly categorizing phony samples can be expressed as either $D(G(z)) \rightarrow 0$ or $(1 - D(G(z))) \rightarrow 1$. In this equation, z represents a vector of random noise that is fed to the generator to synthesize the artificial samples. These two terms make a contribution to the cost function being minimized.

When it comes to the generator training, both the cost function of the generator and that of the discriminator are treated as a zero-sum game by the GAN model. This way, the cost function of the generator is just the same as the cost function of the discriminator but with a negative sign. This can be mathematically formulated as follows:

$$L^{(G)}\left(\theta^G, \theta^D\right) = -L^{(D)}\left(\theta^G, \theta^D\right)$$

(2)

The previous formula could be more appropriately redesignated to take a form of a value formula:

$$v^{(G)}\left(\theta^G, \theta^D\right) = -L^{(D)}\left(\theta^G, \theta^D\right) \tag{3}$$

The above loss formula should be minimized from the standpoint of the generator. The value function should be maximized from the discriminator's perspective. As a result, the training condition generator could be expressed as a min-max game:

$$\theta^{(G)*} = \arg\min_{\theta^{(G)}} \max_{\theta^{(D)}} v^{(G)}\left(\theta^G, \theta^D\right) \tag{4}$$

The network will occasionally attempt to deceive the discriminator by imagining that the generated artificial data is genuine and labeled as one. The updates of the gradient are propagated to the parameters of the discriminator by the optimizer to treat this artificial data as genuine by maximization with regard to $\theta^{(D)}$. Simultaneously, the parameters of the generator are updated by the optimizer by minimization with regard to $\theta^{(G)}$, aiming to deceive the discriminator during the generator. Practically speaking, the GAN parameters would not be updated if the discriminator is certain that the generated data is phony. To make matters worse, as they have progressed to the generator layers, gradient updates have gotten smaller and smaller. To put it another way, the generator is not converging as expected.

To combat this, the loss function of the generator can be reformulated as follows:

$$L^{(G)}\left(\theta^G, \theta^D\right) = -\mathbb{E}_z \log\left(D(G(z))\right) \tag{5}$$

By training the generator, the loss function easily maximizes the likelihood of the discriminator being willing to believe the generated samples are genuine. The above formula is entirely based on heuristics and has become zero-sum no more. The generator is shown in Figure 12.4 throughout the training. As illustrated, the parameters of the generator are updated only after the entire GAN model completes the training, and this can be attributed to the fact that the discriminator flows the gradients back to the

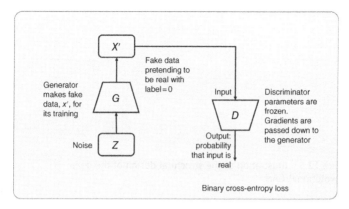

Figure 12.4 Illustration of the generator training as a binary classifier in the GAN model.

generator. However, during adversarial training, the trainable parameters of discriminator weights are only momentarily kept unchanged.

Both generator and the discriminator can be effectively developed using an appropriate model design consideration. For example, when dealing with image data, a convolutional network or vision transformers will be the perfect choice for building both discriminator and generator. In the case of sequential data, generator and discriminator are likely to be built and implemented with recurrent networks or attention networks.

12.3 Deep Convolutional GAN

By understanding the principles behind GANs and how GANs can be built with common network layers (discussed in previous chapters). GANs are famously difficult to train, which sets them apart from other networks. Even a tiny modification in the building of a generator or discriminator can cause the model to encounter unstable training. This section explores an early and common variant of GANs based on a convolutional network. It is called deep convolutional GAN.

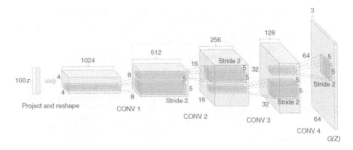

Figure 12.5 Illustration of the structural design of the deep convolutional GAN.

In particular, deep convolutional GAN is a well-known and effective implementation of GAN that makes use of strided convolution and transposed convolution to implement the discriminator and generator, correspondingly. The structural building of each network in deep convolutional GAN is mainly dependent on convolution only and did not involve any max-pool or linear/dense layers. Figure 12.5 illustrates the structure of the generator in deep convolutional GAN according to the reference paper.

The design of deep convolutional GAN is very simple and sticks to the following design principles:

- Instead of MaxPooling2D or UpSampling2D, use strides greater than one and convolution with strides greater than one. This way the convolutional layer can easily update the size of feature maps.
- Dense layers are avoided; hence, convolutions were used in all network levels. However, only the input layer of the generator is implemented with a dense/linear layer for receiving the z-dimensional vector of noise. The output of that dense layer is reshaped and used as the input for the subsequent convolutions.
- To stabilize the learning process, it may be useful to normalize the input of each layer to have a mean of zero and a variance of one. Thus, deep convolutional GAN applied batch normalization (BN) layers across different levels of both networks except for the input layer of the discriminator and output layer of the generator.
- For activation purposes, a rectified linear unit (ReLU) function is applied in the overall generator's layers with exception of the last

layer, which employs tanh activation. Sigmoid activation can also use the output layer of the generator instead of tanh because it generally results in more stable training.

- In all layers of the discriminator, use Leaky ReLU. Unlike ReLU, when the input is less than zero, leaky ReLU generates a small gradient rather than generating zeros for all activations.

To begin with, z-dimensional vectors of random noise, drawn from a uniform distribution $[-1, 1]$, are passed as an input to the generator that reshapes it into two-dimensional tensors that are passed to a stack of transposed convolutions to generate counterfeit images. When the adversarial network is trained, the discriminator aims to identify counterfeit images and real ones, but, in this way, it unintentionally teaches the generator to create images that are almost identical to true ones. The implementation of the original deep convolutional GAN employs a different kernel size in different layers of the network. This allows it to start increasing the convolution's responsive field size and expressive power. Typically, transposed convolutional layers are stacked to build the generator as it acts as the reverse of the standard convolutional layer. For instance, if a convolutional layer extracts feature maps from an image, the transposed convolution enables the creation image from given feature maps. The RMSprop optimizer is used by both discriminator and adversarial networks.

It is worth mentioning that the fake images generated by the deep convolutional GAN are completely unintentional. The generator has no choice but to specify the class of image it will generate. The structural design of deep convolutional GAN did not afford any method for requesting the network to generate a specific class of image. As presented in the later section, a conditional variant of GAN [3] can be used to solve this problem.

12.4 Conditional GAN

As described in previous sections, GANs are able to generate samples ranging from simple grayscale images to complex video streams, and this applies to other forms of data. Nevertheless, though the domain of samples is controlled to train the GAN to mimic the training data, we are still unable to identify some attributes of synthesized samples from the generators. For example, the deep convolutional GAN is trained to synthesize sensible-seeing images, but it was unable to predetermine the class of images to be generated. As remarkable as the data generated progressively in the previous GAN, we have no control over what data to be generated. Thus, there is no means to control the generator to synthesize some data instances based on any associated features.

In a trivial task of hand digit recognition, where samples belong to just one of ten classes of digits, this concern may seem trivial. When the network seeks to generate an image with the number nine, the generator continues generating samples till the targeted number is reached. When it comes to more complex adversarial tasks, for instance, human faces generation task. Even though remarkable samples are synthesized in GAN, the generator cannot regulate which face to generate. The standard GAN has no mechanism to charge the generator to produce, say, a face of a female or male, while disregarding other characteristics like age, color, emotional expressions, etc.

The capacity to determine whatever form of information to be generated paves the way for a massive range of different applications. As a fairly artificial example, think about the situation in which officers are solving a murder thriller, and an eyewitness refers to the killer as a young man with blue eyes. In order to speed up the process, rather than hiring a painter, we can input the features into a computer program and employ it to generate a variety of faces that meet the criteria. The person who most strongly matches the criminal would be identified by our eyewitness. Moving ahead, one may think about countless applications for which the capacity to engender a data instance meets predefined criteria.

To combat this, conditional GAN, or CGAN for simplicity, is a type of GAN that involves the conditional generation of data instances by a generator model. A conditional setup is used in CGANs, which means that both the generator and discriminator are contingent on auxiliary input from other modalities (such as class labels or data). As a consequence, by being fed varied contextual information, the perfect model can learn a multimodal mapping from inputs to outputs. Two main benefits could be gained by this design. First, convergence will take place more quickly. Second, it enables customizing the generator's output by providing a label for the image you would like to generate.

In *conditional GAN*, both the discriminator and generator are conditioned in the course of training by utilizing some supplementary information, which can be, theoretically, anything, like tags, textual explanation, class labels, etc. To make things simpler, this section considers conditioning the discriminator and generator, in CGAN, using class label information. The condition is represented by a one-hot vector of the class label.

In the course of training CGAN, the conditional generator is trained to generate realistic samples for each label in the training set, while the conditional discriminator learns to differentiate phony example-label couples from genuine sample-label couples.

Different from deep convolutional GAN presented in the previous section, the conditional discriminator is trained merely to receive actual, corresponding couples and deny a couple of incompatible images and a couple of samples containing an artificial sample.

A good example of that is the CGAN trained for generating images of handwritten digits, the conditional discriminator must learn to deny the couple (three, four), irrespective of whether the sample (image with number three) is genuine or phony, for the reason that it did not agree with the given label. Moreover, the conditional discriminator ought to learn to refuse all sample-label couples where the image is phony, even if the sample and label are matched

Consequently, fooling the conditional discriminator in CGAN, it is not just requiring the generator to generate samples almost identical to the realistic sample, but it must also produce samples matching given labels. Once the conditional generator is completely trained, the CGAN is enabled to decide the sample it needs to synthesize by giving it the required label.

Except for the additional one-hot vector input, CGAN is similar to DCGAN. The encoded label information is integrated as an input to the generator. The conditional discriminator varies from the previous discriminator by adding a dense layer to reshape the encoded label so that it can be passed to the successive layers.

The basic concept of a CGAN remains similar to that of a deep convolutional GAN, with the exception that the discriminator and generator inputs are conditioned on the class labels, y. By integrating that condition in the CAN, the loss functions of the network can be formulated as follows:

$$L^{(D)}\left(\theta^G, \theta^D\right) = -\mathbb{E}_{x \sim p_{\text{data}}} \log D(x \mid y) - \mathbb{E}_z \log\left(1 - D(G(z \mid y'))\right)$$

$$(6)$$

$$L^{(G)}\left(\theta^G, \theta^D\right) = -\mathbb{E}_z \log\left(1 - D(G(z \mid y'))\right) \tag{7}$$

It is possible that the loss functions should be written as

$$L^{(D)}\left(\theta^G, \theta^D\right) = -\mathbb{E}_{x \sim p_{\text{data}}} \log D(x \mid y) - \mathbb{E}_z \log\left(1 - D(G(z \mid y') \mid y')\right)$$

$$(8)$$

$$L^{(G)}\left(\theta^G, \theta^D\right) = -\mathbb{E}_z \log\left(1 - D(G(z \mid y') \mid y')\right) \tag{9}$$

The discriminator's new loss function seeks to decrease the error in forecasting real photos from the dataset and fake photos from the generator given their one-hot labels. Figure 12.6 depicts the training of the discriminator.

The generator's new loss function reduces the discriminator's accurate estimate of fake photos conditioned on the stipulated one-hot labels. Given its one-hot vector, the generator learns how

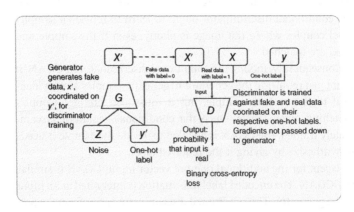

Figure 12.6 Illustration of discriminator training in the conditional GAN model.

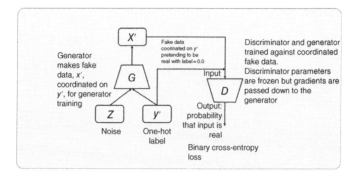

Figure 12.7 Illustration of generator training in the conditional GAN model.

to start generating the specific sample, which can hoodwink the discriminator. The training of the generator is depicted in Figure 12.7.

12.5 Supplementary Materials

https://github.com/DEEPOLOGY-AI/DL-Book-Wiley-2022/tree/main/Ch12

References

1 Goodfellow, I., Pouget-Abadie, J., Mirza, M. et al. (2020). Generative adversarial networks. *Commun. ACM* 63(11): 139–144.

2 Radford, A., Metz, L., and Chintala, S. (2016). Unsupervised representation learning with deep convolutional generative adversarial networks. *arXiv preprint arXiv:1511.06434*.

3 Mirza, M. and Osindero, S. (2014). Conditional generative adversarial nets [Online]. http://arxiv.org/abs/1411.1784 (November 2014).

13

Dive Into Generative Adversarial Networks

13.1 Introduction

Since the emergence of generative adversarial networks (GANs) in 2014 [1], their prominence has skyrocketed. GANs have been demonstrated to be effective generative models capable of generating new data that appears real. Many of the subsequent deep learning studies introduce measures to identify the challenges and implications of the existing GAN.

GANs are legendary for being hard to train and susceptible to mode collapse. Mode collapse occurs when the generator produces identical outcomes even though the loss functions have already been optimized. With mode collapse, the generator may only produce numbers four and nine in the perspective of MNIST numbers because they appear alike. The Wasserstein GAN (WGAN) [2] takes this issue by trying to argue that by easily changing the GAN loss formula by relying on Wasserstein 1, also known as the earth mover's distance (EMD), stable training and mode collapse can be avoided.

The concern of stability, however, is not the only concern with GANs. Additionally, there is a growing necessity to enhance the perceptual quality of the generated pictures. The least squares GAN (LSGAN) [3] presented discussing both of these issues at the same time. The general concept is that throughout training, sigmoid cross-entropy loss results in a vanishing gradient. As a result, the image quality suffers. The least squares loss method does not

Deep Learning Approaches for Security Threats in IoT Environments,
First Edition. Mohamed Abdel-Basset, Nour Moustafa, and Hossam Hawash.
© 2023 The Institute of Electrical and Electronics Engineers, Inc.
Published 2023 by John Wiley & Sons, Inc.

produce vanishing gradients. When compared to vanilla GAN-generated pictures, the eventually resulting pictures have higher perceptual quality. CGAN presented a methodology for conditioning the generator's outcome. Such like, if we needed digit eight, we would contain the conditioning label in the generator's input. The auxiliary classifier GAN (ACGAN) [4] introduced a manipulated conditional algorithm prompted by CGAN, resulting in higher perspicacious quality and a variety of outcomes. This chapter covers the aforementioned variants of generative networks in more detail.

13.2 Wasserstein GAN

As previously stated, GANs are legendarily difficult to train. The two networks' opponent goals, the discriminator, and the generator, can easily lead to training destabilization. The discriminator tries to correctly distinguish between fake and real data. In the meantime, the generator makes every effort to fool the discriminator. The generator parameters will struggle to optimize if the discriminator learns quicker than the generator. However, if the discriminator learns more slowly, the gradients may disappear before having reached the generator. In the worst-case scenario, if the discriminator is unable to converge, the generator will not receive any useful feedback.

The intrinsic uncertainty of a GAN, according to WGAN, is due to its loss function, which is based on the Jensen–Shannon (JS) distance. The goal of a GAN is for the generator to learn how to convert from one source distribution (such as noise) to an approximated target distribution (like MNIST numbers). The loss function in the initial conception of a GAN is minimizing the length between the target distribution and its approximate. The issue is that there is no seamless path to minimize this JS distance for some pairs of distributions. As a result, the training will struggle to converge.

Throughout the following part, we will start investigating three distance functions and evaluate which of them might be a good substitute for the JS distance function, which is better suited for GAN optimization.

13.2.1 Distance Functions

Investigating the loss functions of a GAN can help you understand its consistency when training. We will look at the popular distance or divergence functions between two probability distributions to help us understand GAN loss functions.

The distance between p_{data} for true data distribution and p_g for generator data distribution is of concern to us. The goal of GANs is to make $p_g \rightarrow p_{\text{data}}$. The divergence functions are summarized as follows:

- *Kullback–Leibler (KL)*

$$D_{\text{KL}}\left(p_{\text{data}} \parallel p_g\right) = \mathbb{E}_{x \sim p_{\text{data}}} \log \frac{p_{\text{data}}(x)}{p_g(x)} \neq D_{\text{KL}}\left(p_g \parallel p_{\text{data}}\right)$$

$$= \mathbb{E}_{x \sim p_g} \log \frac{p_g(x)}{p_{\text{data}}(x)}$$

$$(1)$$

- *Jensen–Shannon (JS)*

$$D_{js}\left(p_{\text{data}} \parallel p_g\right) = \frac{1}{2} \mathbb{E}_{x \sim p_{\text{data}}} \frac{\log\left(p_{\text{data}}(x)/p_g(x)\right)}{2} = D_{js}\left(p_g \parallel p_{\text{data}}\right)$$

$$(2)$$

- *Earth Mover's Distance (EMD) or Wasserstein 1*

$$W\left(p_{\text{data}}, p_g\right) = \inf_{\gamma \in \prod(p_{\text{data}}, p_g)} \mathbb{E}_{x \sim p_{\text{data}}} [\parallel x - y \parallel] \quad (3)$$

where $\prod(p_{\text{data}}, p_g)$ is the set of all joint distributions $\gamma(x, y)$ whose marginals are p_{data} and p_g.

Mostly in expectation – maximization tasks, we'll use Kullback–Leibler (KL) divergence, or D_{KL}, in the loss function to determine how far our neural network model prediction deviates from the true distribution function. As indicated in the above formula, D_{KL} is not symmetric because $D_{KL}(p_{data} \| p_g) \neq D_{KL}(p_g \| p_{data})$. JS, also known as D_{JS}, is a D_{KL}-based divergence. D_{JS}, on the other hand, is symmetrical and finite, unlike D_{KL}. In the later section, we will show how optimization of GAN loss functions is the same as optimization D_{JS}.

EMD is a measure of how much mass $\gamma(x, y)$ should be transported by $d = \| x - y \|$ for the probability distribution p_{data} in order to match the probability distribution p_g. $\gamma(x, y)$ is a joint distribution in the space of all possible joint distributions. To reflect the strategy for transporting masses to match the two probability distributions, $\gamma(x, y)$ is also known as a transport plan. Given the two probability distributions, there are numerous transportation options. In general, inf denotes a low-cost transportation strategy.

Figure 13.1, for example, depicts two simple discrete distributions, x and y, wheras x has masses m_i for $i = 1, 2, 3$, and 4 at locations x_i for $i = 1, 2, 3$, and 4. Meanwhile, y has masses m_i for $i = 1$ and 2 at locations y_i for $i = 1$. The arrows show the simplest

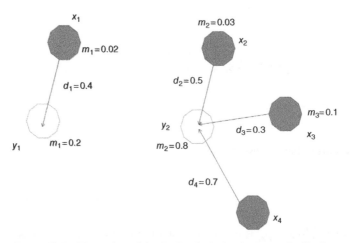

Figure 13.1 Illustration of the EMD calculation between distribution x and distribution y.

transport plan to move each mass x_i by d_i to match the distribution y. The EMD is calculated as follows:

$$\text{EMD} = \sum_{i=1}^{4} x_i d_i = 0.2(0.4) + 0.3(0.5) + 0.1(0.3)$$
$$+ 0.4(0.7) = 0.54 \tag{4}$$

The EMD in Figure 13.1 can be interpreted as the least amount of effort required to move the pile of dirt x to fill the holes y. While the inf can be deduced from the figure in this example, in most cases, especially in continuous distributions, exhausting all possible transport plans is intractable.

13.2.2 Distance Function in GANs

We will now calculate the optimum discriminator given any generator from the loss function. We will go over the following equation:

$$L^{(D)} = -\mathbb{E}_{x \sim p_{\text{data}}} \log D(x) - \mathbb{E}_z \log \left(1 - D(\mathcal{G}(z))\right) \tag{5}$$

The previous equation can also be demonstrated as sampling from the generator distribution rather than noise distribution:

$$L^{(D)} = -\mathbb{E}_{x \sim p_{\text{data}}} \log D(x) - \mathbb{E}_{x \sim p_g} \log \left(1 - D(x)\right) \tag{6}$$

To discover the minimum $L^{(D)}$

$$L^{(D)} = -\int_x p_{\text{data}}(x) \log(x)\, dx \; - \int_x p_g(x) \log\left(1 - D(x)\right) dx \tag{7}$$

$$L^{(D)} = -\int_x \left(p_{\text{data}}(x) \log(x) + p_g(x) \log\left(1 - D(x)\right)\right) dx \tag{8}$$

The concept within the integral is of the form $y \to a \log y + b \log (1 - y)$, with the recognized highest value at $\dfrac{a}{a + b}$ for $y \in [0, 1]$ for any $a, b \in \mathbb{R}^2$ not for $\{0, 0\}$. Because the integral has no effect on the location of the highest value (or the lowest value of $L^{(D)}$) in this formula, the best discriminator is

$$D^*(x) = \frac{p_{\text{data}}}{p_{\text{data}} + p_g} \tag{9}$$

Therefore, as a result, based on the optimum discriminator, the loss function is as follows:

$$L^{(D^*)} = -\mathbb{E}_{x \sim p_{\text{data}}} \log \frac{p_{\text{data}}}{p_{\text{data}} + p_g} - \mathbb{E}_{x \sim p_g} \log \left(1 - \frac{p_{\text{data}}}{p_{\text{data}} + p_g}\right)$$

$$L^{(D^*)} = -\mathbb{E}_{x \sim p_{\text{data}}} \log \frac{p_{\text{data}}}{p_{\text{data}} + p_g} - \mathbb{E}_{x \sim p_g} \log \left(\frac{p_g}{p_{\text{data}} + p_g}\right)$$

$$L^{(D^*)} = 2\log 2 - D_{\text{KL}} \left(p_{\text{data}} \,\|\, \frac{p_{\text{data}} + p_g}{2}\right) - D_{\text{KL}} \left(p_g \,\|\, \frac{p_{\text{data}} + p_g}{2}\right)$$

$$L^{(D^*)} = 2\log 2 - 2D_{\text{js}} \left(p_{\text{data}} \,\|\, p_g\right)$$

$$(10)$$

We can see from this equation that the ideal discriminator's loss function is a constant minus twice the JS divergence between the true distribution, p_{data}, and any generator distribution, p_g. Reducing $L^{(D^*)}$ implies maximizing $D_{\text{js}}(p_{\text{data}} \,\|\, p_g)$ or the discriminator should accurately distinguish between fake and real data.

Whereas we can reliably assert that the ideal generator occurs when the generator distribution equals the true data distribution:

$$\mathcal{G}^*(x) \rightarrow p_g = p_{\text{data}} \quad (11)$$

The above basically confirms that the generator's goal is to deceive the discriminator by learning the real data distribution. We can efficiently arrive at the ideal generator by reducing D_{JS} or by making $p_g \rightarrow p_{\text{data}}$. Provided an ideal generator, the ideal discriminator should be as follows:

$$D^*(x) = \frac{1}{2} \text{ with } L^{(D^*)} = 2\log 2 = 0.60 \quad (12)$$

The issue is that when the two distributions do not overlap, there is no smooth function that can help bridge the gap between them. Gradient descent will not converge training GANs. Assume, for example, that

$$p_{\text{data}} = (x, y) \text{ where } x = 0, \, y \sim U(0, 1) \quad (13)$$

$$p_g = (x, y) \text{ where } x = \theta, \, y \sim U(0, 1) \quad (14)$$

The uniform distribution is denoted by $U(0, 1)$. Each distance function's divergence is described as follows:

$$
\begin{aligned}
D_{\text{KL}}\left(p_{\text{data}} \parallel p_g\right) &= \mathbb{E}_{x=0, y \sim U(0,1)} \log \frac{p_{\text{data}}(x, y)}{p_g(x, y)} \\
&= \sum 1 \log \frac{1}{0} = +\infty
\end{aligned}
\tag{15}
$$

$$
\begin{aligned}
D_{\text{KL}}\left(p_g \parallel p_{\text{data}}\right) &= \mathbb{E}_{x=\theta, y \sim U(0,1)} \log \frac{p_g(x, y)}{p_{\text{data}}(x, y)} \\
&= \sum 1 \log \frac{1}{0} = +\infty
\end{aligned}
\tag{16}
$$

$$
\begin{aligned}
D_{\text{JS}}\left(p_{\text{data}} \parallel p_g\right) &= \frac{1}{2} \mathbb{E}_{x=0, y \sim U(0,1)} \log \frac{p_{\text{data}}(x, y)}{p_{\text{data}}(x, y) + p_g(x, y)/2} \\
&+ \frac{1}{2} \mathbb{E}_{x=\theta, y \sim U(0,1)} \log \frac{p_g(x, y)}{p_{\text{data}}(x, y) + p_g(x, y)/2} \\
&= \frac{1}{2} \sum 1 \log \frac{1}{1/2} + \frac{1}{2} \sum 1 \log \frac{1}{1/2} = \log 2
\end{aligned}
\tag{17}
$$

$$
W\left(p_{\text{data}}, p_g\right) = |\theta|
\tag{18}
$$

Because D_{JS} is constant, the GAN will not have enough gradient to direct $p_g \rightarrow p_{\text{data}}$. We will also discover that D_{KL}, or reverse D_{KL}, is ineffective. However, with $W(p_{\text{data}}, p_g)$, we can have a smooth function to achieve $p_g \rightarrow p_{\text{data}}$. Because D_{JS} keeps failing in circumstances where two distributions have little to no overlap, the EMD or Wasserstein 1 appears to be a more logical loss function for optimizing GANs.

In the following section, we will look at how to use the EMD or the Wasserstein 1 distance function to create an alternative loss function that will motivate reliable GAN training.

13.2.3 Wasserstein Loss

There is one more hurdle to clear before using EMD or Wasserstein 1. It is impossible to exhaust the space of $\prod(p_{\text{data}}, p_g)$ in order to find $\gamma \in \prod (p_{\text{data}}, p_g)$. Its Kantorovich–Rubinstein dual is presented as a solution:

$$W\left(p_{\text{data}}, p_g\right) = \frac{1}{k} \text{sub}_{\|f\|_L \le k} \mathbb{E}_{x \sim p_{\text{data}}}[f(x)] - \mathbb{E}_{x \sim p_g}[f(x)]$$

(19)

EMD, $\text{sub}_{\|f\|_L \le 1}$, is the supremum (roughly, maximum value) of all K-Lipschitz functions: K-Lipschitz functions satisfy the constraint: $f : x \to \mathbb{R}$

$$|f(x_1) - f(x_2)| \le K \mid x_1 - x_2 \mid$$

(20)

For all x_1, $x_2 \in \mathbb{R}$. K-Lipschitz functions, the derivatives are confined but they are almost always distinguishable (for example, $f(x) = |x|$ has confined derivatives and is continuous but not distinguishable at $x = 0$).

The above equations can be remedied by locating a family of K-Lipschitz functions $\{f_w\}_{w \in W}$:

$$W\left(p_{\text{data}}, p_g\right) = \max_{w \in W} \mathbb{E}_{x \sim p_{\text{data}}}[f_w(x)] - \mathbb{E}_{x \sim p_g}[f_w(x)]$$

(21)

The above equation can be altered in the perspective of GANs by sampling from the z-noise distribution and replacing f_w with the discriminator function, D_w:

$$W\left(p_{\text{data}}, p_g\right) = \max_{w \in W} \mathbb{E}_{x \sim p_{\text{data}}}[D_w(x)] - \mathbb{E}_z[D_w(\mathcal{G}(z))]$$

(22)

In which we are using bold characters to emphasize the applicability to multidimensional samples. The final issue is determining how to locate the family of functions, $w \in W$. The potential alternative is to trim the weights of the discriminator w between lower and upper bounds (such as −0.01 and 0.01) at each gradient upgrade:

$$w \leftarrow \text{clip}(w, -0.01, 0.01)$$

(23)

The discriminator is constrained to a small parameter space by the low values of w, ensuring Lipschitz continuity.

We can base our new GAN loss functions on the last two equations. EMD, also known as Wasserstein 1, is the loss function that

Table 13.1 A comparison between the loss functions of a GAN and a WGAN.

Network	Loss functions
GAN	$L^{(D)} = -\mathbb{E}_{x \sim p_{\text{data}}} \log [D(x)] - \mathbb{E}_z \log [1 - D(\mathcal{G}(z))]$ $L^{(G)} = -\mathbb{E}_z \log [D(\mathcal{G}(z))]$
WGAN	$L^{(D)} = -\mathbb{E}_{x \sim p_{\text{data}}} [D_w(x)] - \mathbb{E}_z [D_w(\mathcal{G}(z))]$ $L^{(G)} = -\mathbb{E}_z [D_w(\mathcal{G}(z))]$ $w \leftarrow \text{clip}(w, -0.01, 0.01)$

the generator strives to minimize and the cost function that the discriminator strives to maximize or minimize $-W(p_{\text{data}}, p_g)$:

$$L^{(D)} = -\mathbb{E}_{x \sim p_{\text{data}}}[D_w(x)] - \mathbb{E}_z[D_w(\mathcal{G}(z))] \tag{24}$$

$$L^{(G)} = -\mathbb{E}_z[D_w(\mathcal{G}(z))] \tag{25}$$

The first term in the generator loss function vanishes because it is not directly optimizing with regard to the truth data.

The differential between the loss functions of a GAN and a WGAN is shown in Table 13.1, where the expressions are refined for $L^{(D)}$ and $L^{(G)}$ for clarity:

To further understand how to use these loss functions to train a WGAN, you can follow the steps as in Algorithm 13.1.

Algorithm 13.1   WGAN

Require: α, the learning rate. c, the clipping parameter. m, the batch size. n_{critic}, the number of the critic (discriminator) iterations per generator iteration.

Require: w_0, initial critic (discriminator) parameters. θ_0, initial generator parameters:

Step 1. while θ has not converged do

Step 2. for $\theta = 1, ..., n_{\text{critic}}$ do

Step 3. Sample a batch $\{x^{(i)}\}_{i=1}^{m} \sim p_{\text{data}}$ from real data

Step 4. Sample a batch $\{z^{(i)}\}_{i=1}^{m} \sim p(z)$ from the uniform noise distribution

Step 5. $g_w \leftarrow \nabla_w \left[-\dfrac{1}{m} \sum_{i=1}^{m} D_w\left(x^{(i)}\right) + \dfrac{1}{m} \sum_{i=1}^{m} D_w\left(\mathcal{G}_\theta\left(z^{(i)}\right)\right) \right]$,

calculate discriminator gradients

Step 6. $w \leftarrow w - \alpha \times \text{RMSProp}(w,\ g_w)$, upgrade discriminator parameters

Step 7. $w \leftarrow \text{clip}(w, -c, c)$, clip discriminator weights

Step 8. end for

Step 9. Sample a batch $\left\{z^{(i)}\right\}_{i=1}^{m} \sim p(z)$ from the uniform noise distribution

Step 10. $g_\theta \leftarrow -\nabla_\theta \dfrac{1}{m} \sum_{i=1}^{m} D_w\left(\mathcal{G}_\theta\left(z^{(i)}\right)\right)$, compute generator gradients

Step 11. $\theta \leftarrow \theta - \alpha \times \text{RMSProp}(\theta, \mathcal{G}_\theta)$, update generator parameters

Step 12. end while

Figure 13.2 shows that, with the exception of the fake/real data labels and loss functions, a WGAN model is nearly identical to a DCGAN.

WGAN, like GANs, conversely trains the discriminator and generator using adversarial. In WGAN, even so, the discriminator, which is also known as the critic, trains n_{critic} iterations (steps 2–8) before training the generator for a single iteration (steps 9–11). In contrast, GANs have the same number of training iterations for both the discriminator and the generator. In other words, $n_{\text{critic}} = 1$ in GANs.

Learning the discriminator's parameters (weights and biases) is referred to as training the discriminator. After feeding the sampled data to the discriminator network, sample a batch from the real data (step 3) and a batch from the fake data (step 4) and compute the gradient of discriminator parameters (step 5). RMSProp is used to optimize the discriminator parameters (step 6).

Finally, the Lipschitz constraint is imposed in the EM distance optimization by clipping the discriminator parameters (step 7). The discriminator parameters are frozen after n_{critic} iterations of

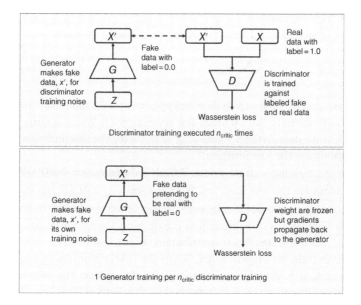

Figure 13.2 Training the WGAN discriminator requires fake data from the generator and real data from the true distribution (top). Training the WGAN generator requires fake data from the generator pretending to be real (bottom).

discriminator training. The generator training begins with a sample of fictitious data (step 9). In order to fool the discriminator network, the sampled data is labeled as real. Step 10 computes the generator gradients, which are then optimized through the RMSProp in step 11.

The discriminator parameters are unfrozen after training the generator, and another n_{critic} discriminator training iteration begins. It should be noted that because the generator is only involved in data fabrication, there is no need to freeze the generator parameters during discriminator training. The discriminator, like GANs, can be trained as a separate network. However, because the loss is computed from the output of the generator network, training the generator always necessitates the participation of the discriminator via the adversarial network. In contrast to GANs, real data in a WGAN is labeled as one, while fake data is labeled zero as a workaround in computing the gradient in step 5. Each term in steps 5 and 10 is represented as follows:

$$L = -y_{label} \frac{1}{m} \sum_{i=1}^{m} y_{pred} \tag{26}$$

where $y_{label} = 1.0$ for truth data and $y_{label} = -1.0$ for false data. To simplify formula, we excluded the superscript (i) When training with truth data, WGAN raises $y_{pred} = D_w(x)$ for the discriminator to minimize the loss function.

When training with false data, WGAN reduces $y_{pred} = D_w(\mathcal{G}(z))$ to minimize the loss function. WGAN rises $y_{pred} = D_w(\mathcal{G}(z))$ for the generator in order to minimize the loss function when the fake data is labeled as true throughout the training. Except for its sign, y_{label} makes no significant contributions to the loss function. It is hard to train the original GAN. When the GAN optimizes its loss function, it is actually optimizing the JS divergence, D_{JS}. When there is little to no overlap between two distribution functions, it is hard to optimize D_{JS}.

The EMD or Wasserstein 1 loss function, which has a smooth differentiable function even when there is little or no overlap between the two distributions, was proposed by WGAN as a solution to the problem. WGAN, on the other hand, is unconcerned about the quality of the generated image. Aside from stability issues, the generated images of the original GAN still have room for improvement in terms of perceptual quality. According to LSGAN, the twin problems can be solved concurrently. In the following section, we will look at LSGAN.

13.3 Least-Squares GAN (LSGAN)

The least squares loss is proposed by LSGAN as a solution to the problem of having poor data quality when using a sigmoid cross-entropy loss in GANs. The fake sample distribution should preferably be as near to the actual sample distribution as feasible. Even so, once the false samples are on the right side of the decision boundary, the gradients vanish for GANs.

This reduces the generator's encouragement to enhance the quality of the generated fake data. False samples that are far from the decision boundary will no longer try to move closer to the actual sample distribution. The gradients do not vanish when using the least squares loss function as long as the fake sample distribution is far from the real sample distribution. Even if the fake samples are already on the correct side of the decision boundary, the generator will attempt to enhance its forecast of the actual density distribution. Table 13.2 compare loss functions LSGAN with those of GAN, and WGAN.

The MSE between true data classification and the truth label "one" should be near to zero if the discriminator loss function is minimized. Furthermore, the MSE between the false data classification and the truth label "zero" should be near to "zero."

The LSGAN discriminator, like other GANs, is trained to distinguish between true and false data samples.

When compared to DCGAN, the outcome images have higher perceptual quality.

We addressed another enhancement to the loss function in this section. We discussed the dual problems of training the stability and perceptual quality of the GANs using MSE or L2. Some other advancements are introduced in the following section, this time in relation to CGAN.

Table 13.2 Comparison between the loss functions of GAN, WGAN, and LSGAN.

Network	Loss functions
GAN	$L^{(D)} = -\mathbb{E}_{x \sim p_{\text{data}}} \log[D(x)] - \mathbb{E}_z \log[1 - D(\mathcal{G}(z))]$ $L^{(G)} = -\mathbb{E}_z \log[D(\mathcal{G}(z))]$
WGAN	$L^{(D)} = -\mathbb{E}_{x \sim p_{\text{data}}}[D_w(x)] - \mathbb{E}_z[D_w(\mathcal{G}(z))]$ $L^{(G)} = -\mathbb{E}_z[D_w(\mathcal{G}(z))]$ $w \leftarrow \text{clip}(w, -0.01, 0.01)$
LSGAN	$L^{(D)} = \mathbb{E}_{x \sim p_{\text{data}}}(D(x) - 1)^2 + \mathbb{E}_z D(\mathcal{G}(z))^2$ $L^{(G)} = \mathbb{E}_z(D(\mathcal{G}(z)) - 1)^2$

13.4 Auxiliary Classifier GAN (ACGAN)

ACGAN is conceptually equivalent to the conditional GAN (CGAN). Both CGAN and ACGAN will be compared. The generator inputs for both CGAN and ACGAN are noise and its label. The outcome is a false photo of the input class label. The discriminator in CGAN is fed a photo (false or true) and its label. The result is the likelihood that the photo is actual. The discriminator's input for ACGAN is a photo, while the outcome is the probability that the photo is actual, and its class is a label. Throughout generator training, Figure 13.3 shows the distinction between CGAN and ACGAN. Primarily, in CGAN, we nourish side information to the network "label." Through the use of an auxiliary class decoder network, we try to rebuild the side information in ACGAN. According to ACGAN theory, trying to force the network to accomplish new responsibilities has been shown to enhance the performance of the existing task. The extra task in this case is image classification. The original task is to create false images.

Table 13.3 compares the loss functions of ACGAN and CGAN.

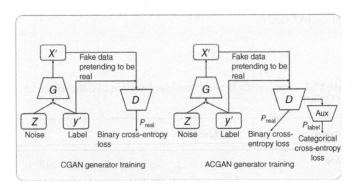

Figure 13.3 CGAN versus ACGAN generator training. The main difference is the input and output of the discriminator.

Table 13.3 A comparison between the loss functions of CGAN and ACGAN.

Network	Loss functions
CGAN	$L^{(D)} = -\mathbb{E}_{x \sim p_{data}} \log[D(x \mid y)] - \mathbb{E}_z \log[1 - D(\mathcal{G}(z \mid y))]$ $L^{(G)} = -\mathbb{E}_z \log[D(\mathcal{G}(z \mid y))]$
ACGAN	$L^{(D)} = -\mathbb{E}_{x \sim p_{data}} \log[D(x)] - \mathbb{E}_z \log[1 - D(\mathcal{G}(z \mid y))]$ $\quad - \mathbb{E}_{x \sim p_{data}} \log[\mathcal{P}(c \mid x)] - \mathbb{E}_z \log[\mathcal{P}(c \mid \mathcal{G}(z \mid y))]$ $L^{(G)} = -\mathbb{E}_z \log[D(\mathcal{G}(z \mid y))] - \mathbb{E}_z \log[\mathcal{P}(c \mid \mathcal{G}(z \mid y))]$

13.5 Supplementary Materials

https://github.com/DEEPOLOGY-AI/DL-Book-Wiley-2022/tree/main/Ch13

References

1 Goodfellow, I. J., Pouget-Abadie, J., Mirza, M. et al. (2014). Generative adversarial nets. *Adv. Neural Inf. Proces. Syst.* 11, 2672–2680. https://doi.org/10.3156/jsoft.29.5_177_2.
2 Arjovsky, M., Soumith, C., and Léon, B. (2017). Wasserstein generative adversarial networks. *International Conference on Machine Learning*, 214–223. PMLR
3 Mao, X., Li, Q., Xie, H. et al. (2017). Least squares generative adversarial networks. https://doi.org/10.1109/ICCV.2017.304.
4 Odena, A., Olah, C., and Shlens, J. (2017). Conditional image synthesis with auxiliary classifier gans. *International Conference on Machine Learning*, 2642–2651. PMLR.

14

Disentangled Representation GANs

14.1 Introduction

In previous chapters, we have studied and investigated that generative adversarial networks (GANs) are capable of generating profound outputs based on learning the data distribution. However, there has been, even so, no control over the features of the generated outcomes. Several GAN variants, such as conditional GAN (CGAN) and auxiliary classifier GAN (ACGAN), can train a generator to synthesize specific outcomes. Both CGAN and ACGAN can cause the generator to generate a particular class of image. This is accomplished using a 100-dim noise vector as well as the respective one-hot label as inputs. Even so, aside from the one-hot label, there are no other methods for controlling the characteristics of generated outcomes.

In this chapter, we will look at advanced variants, generative adversarial nets (GANs) that allow us to change the generator outcomes. Aside from determining which data instance to generate in the perspective of the underlying data, we may discover that we need the to manage the way of writing. This could include the wanted image feature. In those other sentences, GANs can learn disentangled latent codes or representations that can be used to change the features of the generator outcomes. A disentangled code or representation is a tensor that can alter one feature or attribute of the output data without impacting the others.

Deep Learning Approaches for Security Threats in IoT Environments,
First Edition. Mohamed Abdel-Basset, Nour Moustafa, and Hossam Hawash.
© 2023 The Institute of Electrical and Electronics Engineers, Inc.
Published 2023 by John Wiley & Sons, Inc.

This chapter starts by discussing the concepts of a disentangled representation in the context of generative modeling. A disentangled representation is a tensor that could update one characteristic or attribute of output data without impacting the others. In doing so, GANs show a great ability to learn disentangled latent representations that can be exploited to vary the attributes of the generator outputs.

Followingly, the chapter covers a variety of GANs that enable modifying the generator outputs according to terms of different features or attributes. As a popular example of this, we dive into the details of InfoGAN, which is an interpretable representation of learning by information maximizing in GAN [1], a GAN extension. InfoGAN learns disentangled representations unsupervised by maximizing mutual information between input and output observations.

Going ahead, we will explore stacked generative adversarial networks, or StackedGAN [2], which are an extension of GANs. StackedGAN employs a pretrained encoder or classifier to assist in deciphering the latent codes. StackedGAN is being thought of as a model's stack, with each model consisting of an encoder and a GAN. Each GAN is adversarially trained by using the corresponding encoder's input and output data. By the end of this part, we explore the process of multi-phase training of the StackedGAN and the configuration of different stages.

14.2 Disentangled Representations

The existing GAN was capable of producing meaningful outcomes, but its attributes were uncontrollable. For example, if we trained a GAN to recognize the distribution of celebrity faces, the generator would generate new pictures of celebrities. However, there is no way of influencing the generator in terms of the specific features of the face that we desire. Like, we are unable to request a face of a female celebrity with long black hair, a fair complexion, brown eyes, and a smile from the generator. The main factor for this is that the 100-dim noise code we use entangles all of the main features of the generator outcomes.

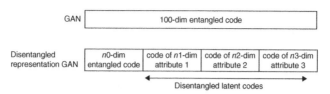

Figure 14.1 Illustration of the GAN with the entangled code and its variation with both entangled and disentangled codes.

We would indeed be ready to inform the generator what to synthesize if we could change the existing GAN so that the representation is split into entangled and disentangled interpretable latent code vectors.

Figure 14.1 depicts an entangled GAN and its variant with a combination of entangled and disentangled representations. From the perspective of the hypothetical celebrity face generation, we can specify the image attribute we want to generate using the disentangled codes such as attribute1 = "gender," attribute2 = "hairstyle," etc. The n-dim entangled code is still designed to reflect all of the remaining facial attributes that we have not disentangled, such as face shape, facial hair, and eyeglasses, to name a few. The concatenation of entangled and disentangled code vectors is used as the generator's new input. The total dimension of the concatenated code does not have to be 100.

According to the previous figure, GANs with disentangled representations can be optimized in the same way that a vanilla GAN can. This is since the generator outcome can be expressed as follows:

$$\mathcal{G}(z, c) = \mathcal{G}(z) \tag{1}$$

The code $z = (z, c)$ is made up of two parts: z denoting the noise vector-like immiscible entangled noise code of the GAN. The interpretable disentangled codes of the data distribution are represented by latent codes, $c_1, c_2, ..., c_L$. All latent codes are expressed jointly by c. For the sake of clarity, all latent representation is considered autonomous:

$$p(c_1, c_2, ..., c_L) = \prod_{i=1}^{L} p(c_i) \tag{2}$$

Both the immiscible noise vector and the latent representation are available for the generator function $x = \mathcal{G}(z, c) = \mathcal{G}(z)$. Optimizing $z = (z, c)$ is the same as optimizing z from the generator's perspective. When generating a solution, the generator network will completely disregard the constraint forced by the disentangled codes. The generator learns the distribution $p_g(x|c) = p_g(x)$. This effectively defeats the goal of disentangled depictions.

The main concept behind InfoGAN is to push the GAN to not ignore the latent code c. This is accomplished by maximizing the mutual information between c and $\mathcal{G}(z, c)$. In the following section, we will define InfoGAN's loss function.

14.3 InfoGAN

InfoGAN introduced a regularizer to the existing loss function that maximizes the mutual information between the latent codes c and $\mathcal{G}(z, c)$ to start enforcing code disentanglement:

$$I(c; \mathcal{G}(z, c)) = I(c; \mathcal{G}(z)) \qquad (3)$$

When the generator produces a function to synthesize the false photos, the regularizer compels it to take into account the latent codes. Mutual information between latent codes c and $\mathcal{G}(z, c)$ is identified in information theory as follows:

$$I(c; \mathcal{G}(z, c)) = H(C) - H(c|\mathcal{G}(z, c)) \qquad (4)$$

in which $H(c)$ is the entropy of latent representation, c, and $H(c|\mathcal{G}(z, c))$ is the conditional entropy of c upon perceiving the generator's outcome, $\mathcal{G}(z, c)$. Entropy is a measure of the uncertainty associated with a random variable or an event. Like the sun rising in the east has low entropy, whereas winning the lottery jackpot has higher entropy.

Trying to maximize mutual information in the previous equation means minimizing $H(c|\mathcal{G}(z, c))$ or reducing the uncertainty in the latent code after perceiving the generated outcome.

However, estimating $H(c|\mathcal{G}(z, c))$ is difficult as it involves the understanding of the posterior $P(c|\mathcal{G}(z, c)) = P(c|x)$. To keep things simple, we will just use the character x to demonstrate the data distribution.

The workable solution is to approximate the lower bound of mutual information using an auxiliary distribution $Q(c|x)$ to estimate the posterior. InfoGAN calculates the lower bound of mutual information as follows:

$$I(c; \mathcal{G}(z, c)) \geq L_1(\mathcal{G}, Q) = E_{c \sim p(c), x \sim \mathcal{G}(z,c)}[\log Q(c|x)] + H(c)$$

(5)

$H(c)$ is supposed to become a constant as well in InfoGAN. As a result, maximizing mutual information is synonymous with maximizing expectation. The generator must be convinced that it has produced an outcome with the desirable features. It is important to keep in mind that the highest value of this expectation is zero. As a result, the maximum of the mutual information's lower bound is $H(c)$. SoftMax nonlinearity can be used to represent $Q(c|x)$ for discrete latent codes in InfoGAN.

The expectation for continuous codes of a single dimension is a double integral over c and x. This is because samples from both disentangled code distribution and generator distribution are expected. One method for approximating the expectation is to consider the samples to be a better measure of continuous data. As a result, the loss is calculated as $c \log Q(c|x)$. We need deployment of $Q(c|x)$ to accomplish the InfoGAN network. To keep things simple, network Q is an auxiliary network connected to the discriminator's second till the last layer. As a result, this has little effect on the existing GAN's training. The structure design of the InfoGAN is illustrated in Figure 14.2. To understand the loss calculation in InfoGAN, you can refer to Table 14.1 in which we compare the loss functions of InfoGAN and GAN.

InfoGAN loss functions vary from GAN loss functions through an adjusting entry, $-\lambda I(c; \mathcal{G}(z, c))$, where λ is a slight positive constant. Reducing an InfoGAN's loss function equates to minimizing the original GAN's loss and maximizing mutual $I(c; \mathcal{G}(z, c))$. When trying to apply the InfoGAN on MNIST data, it could learn the disentangled discrete and continuous codes, allowing it to adjust the generator outcome attributes. Like the discrete code in the shape of

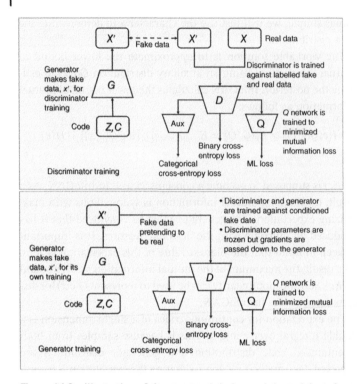

Figure 14.2 Illustration of the structural design and the training of discriminator and generator of InfoGAN.

Table 14.1 Comparison between the loss functions of GAN and InfoGAN.

Network	Loss functions
GAN	$L^{(D)} = - \mathbb{E}_{x \sim p_{\text{data}}} \log [D(x)] - \mathbb{E}_z \log [1 - D(\mathcal{G}(z))]$ $L^{(G)} = - \mathbb{E}_z \log [D(\mathcal{G}(z))]$
InfoGAN	$L^{(D)} = - \mathbb{E}_{x \sim p_{\text{data}}} [D_w(x)] - \mathbb{E}_{z,c}[\log (1 - D(\mathcal{G}(z)))] - \lambda I(c; \mathcal{G}(z,c))$ $L^{(G)} = - \mathbb{E}_{z,c}[\log (D(\mathcal{G}(z,c)))] - \lambda I(c; \mathcal{G}(z,c))$ For continuous codes, InfoGAN recommends a value of $\lambda < 1$. In our example, we set $\lambda = 0.5$. For discrete codes, InfoGAN recommends $\lambda = 1$.

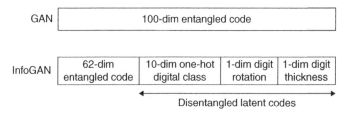

GAN	100-dim entangled code			

InfoGAN	62-dim entangled code	10-dim one-hot digital class	1-dim digit rotation	1-dim digit thickness

Disentangled latent codes

Figure 14.3 The disentangled representation for both GAN and InfoGAN in the context of the MNIST data.

a 10-dim one-hot label will be utilized to clarify the image to produce, as in CGAN and ACGAN. However, we could indeed append two continuous codes: one to control the angle of the writing style and another to adjust the stroke width.

This step is similar to the previous step, but it give a greater emphasis on the second continuous code. The second continuous code, as shown in Figure 14.3, controls the rotation angle (tilt) of the writing style.

14.4 StackedGAN

StackedGAN, like InfoGAN, presents an approach for disentangling latent representations for conditioning generator outcomes. StackedGAN, on the other hand, suggests a unique approach to this issue. StackedGAN deconstructs a GAN into a stack of GANs rather than learning how to condition the noise to achieve targeted sample generation Each GAN is trained independently using its own latent code in the traditional discriminator-adversarial fashion. Figure 14.1 illustrates the structural design of SackedGAN.

The encoder network is made up of a stack of simple encoders, E_i, where $i = 0 \dots h - 1$ represents the number of features. Each encoder extracts a different set of image features. E_0, for example, could be the encoder for texture features, h_1. All the simple encoders work together to ensure that the overall encoder makes correct predictions.

StackedGAN proposes that if we want to build a GAN that generates some fake image, we simply invert the encoder. StackedGAN is made up of a series of simpler generator G_i, *where* $i = 0 \dots h - 1$ corresponds to h features. Each G_i learns to reverse the process of the encoder it corresponds to, E_i. G_0, for example, generates fake images from fake texture feature h_1, which is the opposite of the encoder E_0 process.

Each generator G_i employs a latent code, z_i, to condition the output of its generator. The latent code, z_0, for example, can change the hairstyle from curly to wavy. The stack of GANs can also function as one to synthesize fake celebrity faces, completing the encoder's inverse process. The latent code of each G_i, z_i, can be used to change specific characteristics of phony celebrity faces.

Stacked generative adversarial networks (StackedGAN) consist of two main building blocks, namely:

- **Encoder** $y = E(x)$ where x is the image and y is its label, and
- **Decoder** $x = G(y, z)$ where z is the noise (Figure 14.4).

The decoder acts as the generator as with the vanilla GAN model. As the term "stacked" implies, the decoder and the encoder module structures in the form of a stack.

For the sake of simplicity, we concentrate on a structural design with just one level (Figure 14.5). The input image x is passed to the encoder $E1$ that seeks to map this input to a label y. This predicted label is followingly passed to the generator $G1$ that receives a noise vector z_1 to generate a fake image. After that, the $E1$ encoder takes, as input, the generated fake image to estimate the label once more.

At this point, the model has one generated image and two estimated class labels, one corresponds to the fake image and the other corresponds to the real image.

Before going into details, we modify the labels in the diagram. In a multiple-level stack, h and $\hat{h}$ are the extracted and generated features from the encoder and the generator separately. In this way, the loss function adopted to optimize the generator $G1$ consists of three constituting terms, namely adversary loss, conditional loss,

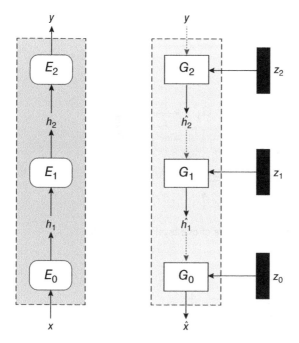

Figure 14.4 Stack of encoders and generators in the StackedGAN.

and entropy loss (Figure 14.6). This can be mathematically described as follows:

$$L_i^{(G)} = \lambda_1 L_i^{(G)\text{adv}} + \lambda_2 L_i^{(G)\text{cond}} + \lambda_2 L_i^{(G)\text{ent}} \tag{6}$$

where $\lambda 1$, $\lambda 2$, and $\lambda 3$ are weights and i represents the level on the stack.

For each generator G_i, a discriminator D_i is introduced to distinguish the generated representations $\hat{h}_i$ from the real representation h_i (Figure 14.7). Particularly, the discriminator D_i is trained with the following loss function:

$$
\begin{aligned}
L_i^{(D)} = &- \mathbb{E}_{h_i \sim p_{\text{data}}}[\log D(h_i)] \\
&- \mathbb{E}_{h_{i+1} \sim p_{\text{data}}, z_i}[\log(1 - D(\mathcal{G}(h_{i+1}, z_i)))]
\end{aligned}
\tag{7}
$$

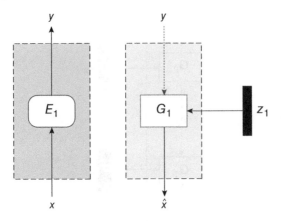

Figure 14.5 Simple structure of one level of StackedGAN.

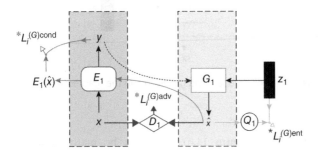

Figure 14.6 Generator loss calculation in StackedGAN.

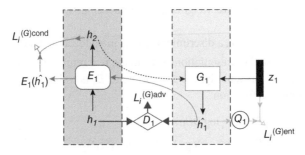

Figure 14.7 Single level of Stack GAN with hidden features.

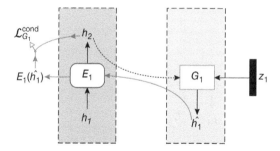

Figure 14.8 Conditional loss calculation in StackedGAN.

While G_i is trained to deceive the discriminator D_i, with an adversarial loss that is calculated in the same way as GAN and is calculated as follows:

$$L_i^{(G)\text{adv}} = - \mathbb{E}_{h_{i+1} \sim p_{\text{data}}, z_i} [\log(D(\mathcal{G}(h_{i+1}, z_i)))] \tag{8}$$

To calculate the conditional loss (Figure 14.8), the model compares the features encoded by the encoder using the real image and the generated images by calculating the distance between them using a distance function f, such as a Euclidean distance. This can be formulated as follows:

$$L_i^{(G)\text{cond}} = - \mathbb{E}_{h_{i+1} \sim p_{\text{data}}, z_i} [f((E_i(\mathcal{G}(h_{i+1}, z_i)), h_{i+1})] \tag{9}$$

The aforementioned conditional loss disintegrates the image variety. The conditional loss encourages G_i to generate images using $G_i(h_{i+1}, z_i)$ rather than $G_i(h_{i+1})$. In this way, the generator G_i will seek to overlook the noise z_i, and calculate $\hat{h}_i$ deterministically from h_i, which, in turn, negatively affects the conditional loss. To combat this, another network Q_i is created to share all the layers with D_i except for the last output dense layer to estimate $P\left(z_i | \hat{h}_i\right)$, where P represents the opportunity of examining z_i, given the feature $\hat{h}_i$. As shown in Figure 14.9, here is the entropy loss we add to train the generator:

$$L_i^{(G)\text{ent}} = - \mathbb{E}_{z_i \sim p_{z_i}} \left[\mathbb{E}_{h_i \sim G_i(\hat{h}_i | z_i)} \left[\log \mathcal{Q}_i \left(z_i | \hat{h}_i \right) \right] \right] \tag{10}$$

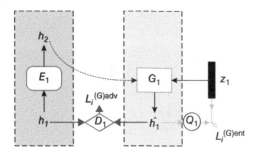

Figure 14.9 Entropy loss calculation in StackedGAN.

The training process of SGAN consists of two stages. First, training specific levels of the stack. Second, the joint training. In particular, each individual level is trained individually and in an independent fashion, and then all the levels of the model are trained jointly. To make things simpler, consider the three-level StackedGAN in Figure 14.10. The training will encounter three

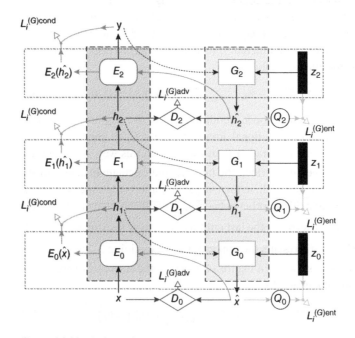

Figure 14.10 Independent training of StackedGAN.

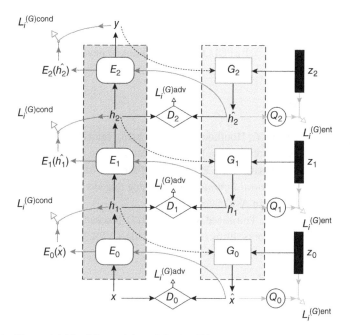

Figure 14.11 Joint training of StackedGAN.

independent and separate training beginning from the bottom to the top. It first trains the layer E_0 and G_0. As soon as it is completed, E_1 and G_1 start the training. In the end, it trains E_2 and G_2.

By the completion of independent training, the network moves to the joint training using all layers as shown in Figure 14.11. In the independent training phase, each generator accepts conditional input from encoders, while in the joint training phase, it accepts conditional input from the upper generators. In other words, $\hat{h}_i = G_i(h_{i+1}, z_i)$ through the independent training and $\hat{h}_i = G_i\left(\hat{h}_{i+1}, z_i\right)$ during joint training. The loss formula mentioned here is for separate training phase but can be easily adapted to joint training by substituting h_{i+1} with $\hat{h}_{i+1}$.

The main concept behind disentangling codes is to restrict loss functions so that only certain attributes are impacted by a code. Structure-wise, InfoGAN is simpler to deploy than StackedGAN. InfoGAN can also be trained more quickly.

14.5   Supplementary Materials

https://github.com/DEEPOLOGY-AI/DL-Book-Wiley-2022/tree/main/Ch14

References

1 Chen, X., Duan, Y., Houthooft, R. et al. (2016). InfoGAN: interpretable representation learning by information maximizing generative adversarial nets. *Proceedings of the 30th International Conference on Neural Information Processing Systems (NIPS'16)*, 2180–2188. Curran Associates Inc.

2 Huang, X., Li, Y., Poursaeed, O. et al. (2017). Stacked generative adversarial networks. https://doi.org/10.1109/CVPR.2017.202.

15

Introducing Federated Learning for Internet of Things (IoT)

15.1 Introduction

The rapid improvements of Internet of Things (IoT) technologies have been leading to their tremendous proliferation in a broad range of daily life applications generating huge amounts of data on daily basis. In this regard, the International Data Corporation (IDC) [1] reported that 79 ZB of data is expected to be generated by billions of IoT devices that, by 2025, would force companies, enterprises, and governments to reconsider their data storage, retention, and governance policies. The storage and analysis of such large quantities of data have long been performed on the cloud because of the huge number of benefits supported by the cloud-computing paradigms, such as reduced costs, unrestricted storage, and powerful computing capabilities. The incredible explosion of data volumes and the advantages of cloud computing bring in great opportunities for artificial intelligence (AI) solutions, especially deep learning, to learn and make insightful decisions from these data. This way, one could develop centralized deep-learning models to build a variety of intelligent IoT applications.

While centralized learning seems to be a comparatively straightforward, traditional approach, it has some shortcomings – specifically when applied to contemporary IoT infrastructures, with new data continually generated at the edge of IoT networks. The most

Deep Learning Approaches for Security Threats in IoT Environments,
First Edition. Mohamed Abdel-Basset, Nour Moustafa, and Hossam Hawash.
© 2023 The Institute of Electrical and Electronics Engineers, Inc.
Published 2023 by John Wiley & Sons, Inc.

important contemporary challenges associated with centralized learning are as follows:

- *Network latency concerns:* The model must be able to react very instantly in real-time apps. Data transfer may be delayed if it is run on the server.

- *Connectivity concerns:* It is necessary to have a steady Internet connection in order to facilitate the smooth transfer of data between various devices and the central server.

- *Data privacy concerns:* Images and text messages, for example, may be beneficial for creating intelligent apps, but they include private information and so cannot be shared freely with the public or other apps.

To address the above challenge of huge data distributed over IoT network, distributed learning arises to distribute the training workload across many geographically distributed IoT devices. So, they could perform collaborative training of machine/deep learning models in a synchronous or asynchronous manner. Distributed learning makes it possible to achieve high-performance computation by parallelly and collaboratively training a certain deep learning model.

Distributed learning can be accomplished in two ways: model-parallel methods and data parallel methods. In the former methods, the same dataset is stored on all machines to train distinctive parts of a deep learning model. Thus, *model parallelism* can be defined as a way of partitioning the deep learning model into parts and then distributing these parts over multiple machines to learn from the same data. For example, forward and backward propagation can be used for communication between machines wherein a single machine, a single layer from the network is saved and provides the outcome. However, this may perhaps not be appropriate for some applications for the reason that some deep learning models could not be partitioned into multiple components. Also, the synchronization between the different partitions is a time-consuming operation that can limit the whole model parallelism. In the later methods, the complete dataset is circulated among a group of geographically distributed machines that use an identical model for training. Thus, *data parallelism* can be defined as a simple way of splitting the high dimension and large-size training data into a number of partitions where these partitions can be distributed over multiple machines or devices so that the deep learning model can achieve a quicker training and computation of the data. Debating the conventional way, where the training process generates one gradient for every mini-batch, by applying data parallelism, the process can generate a number of gradients equal to the number of machines. Then, these gradients of the machines are combined using distributed stochastic gradient descent (SGD).

Even though distributed learning affords parallel as well as collaborative computation of models at geographically distributed machines, it encounters many functional challenges caused by system heterogeneity as well as statistical heterogeneity. Here, system heterogeneity denotes the differences in storage capacity, computing power, and communication protocols of IoT devices, whereas statistical heterogeneity refers to the nonindependent and identical distribution (non-IID) of data. Moreover, conventionally distributed learning solutions that depend on either data parallelism or data parallelism do not actually address the privacy concerns of data owners.

15.2 Federated Learning in the Internet of Things

Federated learning (FL) refers to a distributed learning method that enables a number of IoT devices to perform collaborative training of a particular machine learning model using their own local data. This concept was first introduced in [2] as a distributed training model that is implemented by a group of IoT devices that share local parameter updates with a server responsible for aggregating these updates to build a global machine learning model.

With its distributed and privacy-preserving nature, FL enabled revolutionizing numerous intelligent IoT applications since its launch in 2016. The evolution of such distributed learning offers a great opportunity to bring many advantages to advance the existing IoT applications. As a result of the recent breakthroughs in edge computing and the ever-increased privacy concerns, FL is a predominantly interesting option for developing distributed IoT systems, by offloading the functionality of training deep learning to the edge of IoT networks at which the data capture and reside. This way, the local data of users are certainly not communicated explicitly with the third party while enabling the collaborative training of the deep learning model, which enables saving network resources as well as users' privacy.

An FL system consists of two main components. First, data owners, which are the IoT devices that host the users' data. They are usually referred to as *clients* or *participants*. Second, the model owner, which is the server or computing node that owns the machine learning model, is trained. The model on the server side is referred to as the *global model*. Before federated training begins, each client receives the current global state of the global model in terms of model parameters. The data residing on the client side is referred to as the *local data*, while the model in called the *local model*.

By receipt of the global parameters, each client exploits its own resources to locally train the local model using its own local data depending on the received global parameters. This process is called local update. After that, all clients send the parameters learned from the local training to the parameter server. A central server receives local updates from all clients to compute the new global parameters, and this process is referred to as the *federated aggregation*, *global update*, *or global aggregation*. This server is known as the *parameter* server or *aggregation* server. A variety of aggregation algorithms can be leveraged to perform *federated aggregation* as discussed in a later section. The general structure of federated learning is illustrated in Figure 15.1.

Step 1: *System initialization*. As the name implies, the coordinator node initializes the learning hyperparameters and the training configurations for the intended deep learning model such as the number of communication rounds, learning rates, initial weights, etc. Then, the coordinator node selects the number of IoT devices to contribute to the federated training according to predefined selection aspects such as the quality of local

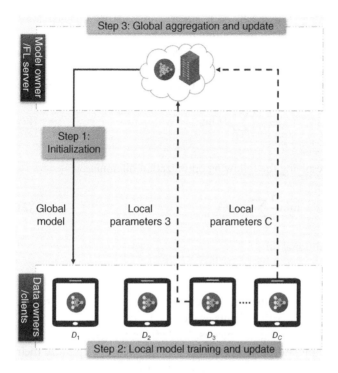

Figure 15.1 Illustration of the main steps of training federated learning in IoT network.

updates, the channel state, etc. By the end of this step, the coordinator node initializes a new global model with parameter w_G^{init}.

Step 2: *Local training*. Once the global model is initialized, the coordinator node broadcasts the initial parameter w_G^{init} to all the selected clients participating in the distributed training. Then, each client c uses its own data D_c to train a local model and calculates an update w_c by optimizing particular loss function $F(w_k)$:

$$w_c = \arg\min F(w_c), c \in C \tag{1}$$

At this point, the loss function can be defined according to the type of the problem address by the FL system. Once the local training is updated, each client c uploads its updated local parameter w_c to the coordinator node.

Step 3: *Parameter aggregation.* Once local updates from all clients are updated, the coordinator node aggregates them and computes a new variant of global model parameters as follows:

$$w_G = \frac{1}{\sum_{c\in C}|D_c|}\sum_{c=1}^{C}|D_c|w_c \tag{2}$$

By resolving the following optimization dilemma,

$$P_1: \min_{w_c} \frac{1}{C}\sum_{c=1}^{C}F(w_c) \tag{3}$$

Conditional on

$$(C1): w_1 = w_2 = ... = w_c = w_G$$

Here, the condition $(C1)$ guarantees that in each training round, all the participating clients as well as the coordinator node share the same learning parameters. By deriving the global update w_G, the coordinator node broadcasts it to all clients to optimize their local models in the following learning round. Steps 2 and 3 continue to repeat till the convergence of the global loss function.

15.3 Taxonomic View of Federated Learning

15.3.1 Network Structure

According to the network topology, the FL solutions can be categorized into three classes of systems, namely centralized FL, decentralized FL, and hierarchical FL as illustrated in Figure 15.1.

15.3.1.1 Centralized Federated Learning

Centralized FL is a prevailing FL architecture that shows wide acceptance in the IoT environment. The design of a centralized FL system consists of two key components: a group of clients that

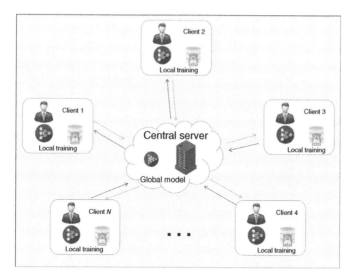

Figure 15.2 Illustration of the centralized federated learning.

participate in training the FL model. The other component is a central server (Figure 15.2). For each training round, all clients concurrently contribute to training a deep learning model in utilizing their locally hosted datasets. Next, the clients upload the updated parameters to a central server that takes the responsibility of aggregating them via an aggregation algorithm, i.e. federated averaging (FedAvg). Once the server completes the aggregation task, the new parameters of the global model are calculated and then broadcasted back to all clients to continue training in the following round. By the completion of the training procedure, each client reaches an identical global model together with its individualized model. In centralized FL settings, the server is considered the main system component as it is mainly responsible for the coordination of the aggregation as well as distribution of the model updates to the clients during the training, while keeping these data secure and private. Therefore, the server is commonly referred to as the *coordinator node*.

15.3.1.2 Decentralized Federated Learning
Different from centralized FL, a decentralized FL system is constructed as a network topology that did not contain any centralized

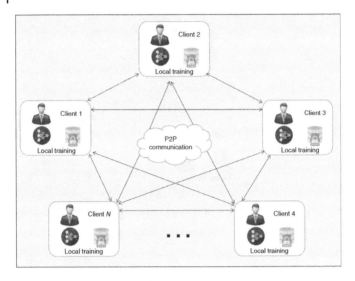

Figure 15.3 Illustration of the decentralized federated learning.

server for coordinating the training operations, but, it connects all clients together in a peer-to-peer (P2P) method to train the deep learning model, as illustrated in Figure 15.3. Like so, in each communication round, the local dataset is used to train the local model in each client. Followingly, each client aggregates the updates of model parameters from neighboring clients over the P2P communication to make a consensus on the update of global parameters. DFL is intended to completely or somewhat substitute the centralized FL under scenarios of serverless communication and/or scalable network topology. Thanks to the contemporary characteristics, there are a number of ways in which decentralized FL systems can be built using P2P technologies, e.g. blockchain such that clients in decentralized FL settings can connect with one another over blockchain ledgers, whereas the model updates being offloaded to the blockchain to ensure the security of model during aggregation as well as transmission.

15.3.1.3 Hierarchical Federated Learning

Hierarchical FL is a special case of the vanilla FL system in which two levels of aggregation take place, namely local aggregation as well as global aggregation. In the hierarchical FL system, a large number of clients are grouped into clusters $K \in \{1, ..., \mathbb{K}\}$ according to some predefined similarity measures (such as location, resources, etc.), which contain a set of clients $c \in K$. Local learning parameters of the clients residing in the same cluster are aggregated on an intermediary aggregation node, and then the computed parameters at these intermediate nodes are uploaded global server to perform global aggregation as with centralized FL. This way, each cluster has its own set of aggregated parameters w_K that can be calculated as follows:

$$w_K = \frac{1}{\sum_{c \in K} |D_c|} \sum_{c=1}^{K} |D_c| w_c \tag{4}$$

Accordingly, the global parameters can be reformulated as a federated aggregation of clusters' parameters. Typically, global aggregation takes place at a remote cloud server, while local aggregation likely takes place on an edge computing server or fog computing server. Hierarchical FL could be leveraged to improve the communication efficiency of federated training by reducing the required communication between clients and remote cloud. End-devices can communicate with intermediary aggregation nodes by the reusage of communication resources previously occupied by other cellular operators. This way, hierarchical FL can enable the scaling up of the IoT networks to span a large number of clients without incurring high communication overheads (in terms of latency, network bandwidth, and energy consumption), making it a productive solution for resource-constrained environments. Nevertheless, one should carefully take into account some design contemplations, for example, the frequency of local aggregations, data heterogeneity, and the frequency of global aggregation. For example, an increasing number of local aggregations are likely to improve the learning performance for non-IID data.

15.3.2 Data Partition

From a data-partitioning perspective, the categorization of FL is performed according to the training data distributed according to the feature or sample spaces. In view of this, the FL can be taxonomized into three groups of methods, namely horizontal FL (HFL),

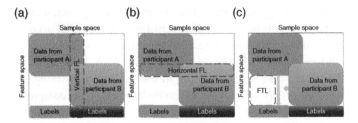

Figure 15.4 Illustration of categorization of federated learning based on the adopted data partitioning: (a) vertical federated learning; (b) horizontal federated learning; (c) federated transfer learning.

vertical FL (VFL), and federated transfer learning (FTL) as illustrated in Figure 15.4.

15.3.3 Horizontal Federated Learning

HFL refers to an FL system in which all the local datasets hosted by the clients, which are used to collaboratively train a global deep learning model, share the same feature space but vary in the sample space, as illustrated in Figure 15.5. Given that all clients own

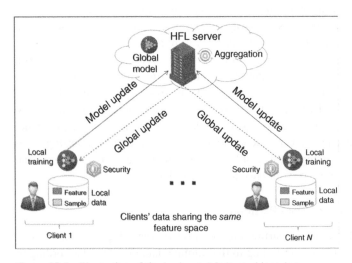

Figure 15.5 Illustration of the horizontal federated learning.

the same features of data, they could use the same deep learning model to be locally trained. For improving the security and privacy of the model, one could apply masking to the local updates with an encryption or differential privacy technique. Later, the aggregation node (either centralized or decentralized) aggregates the local parameter updates from clients and updates the global parameters with no need for explicit access to local data. Following the global updates are transmitted to all clients to continue the training for the subsequent round. The aforementioned operations iterate till the convergence of loss function or targeted performance is reached.

15.3.4 Vertical Federated Learning

Unlike the HFL scenario, VFL refers to an FL system in which all the local datasets are hosted by the clients, which are used to collaboratively train a global deep learning model, and share the sample space but varies in the feature space, as illustrated in Figure 15.6. In the VFL scenario, the overlapped data samples are accumulated from the clients using an entity alignment

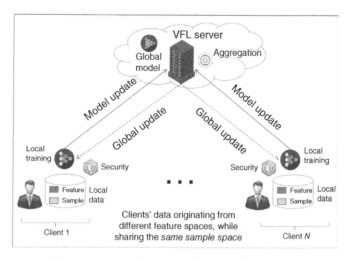

Figure 15.6 Illustration of the vertical federated learning.

method. Then, the collected samples are combined to train a common deep learning model utilizing encryption methods.

As a use case of VFL in smart cities, banking institutions and e-commerce enterprises that provide services to the citizens (same sample space) can subscribe to a VFL system to collaboratively train a particular deep learning model to make use of their local datasets (e.g. transaction data) with often different sets of features. This way, the trained model under the VFL setting can, for example, approximate the ideal personalized loans for all customers according to their shopping activities.

15.3.5 Federated Transfer Learning

As illustrated in Figure 15.7, the FTL [11] seeks to expand the sample space from the VFL system with additional learning clients whose datasets come from diverse feature space as well as different sample spaces. FTL transmits features from a variety of feature spaces to the shared representation space adopted to train the model from the data aggregated from all learning clients. Again, some security and privacy preservation methods can be applied to protect the parameters during the training rounds. The

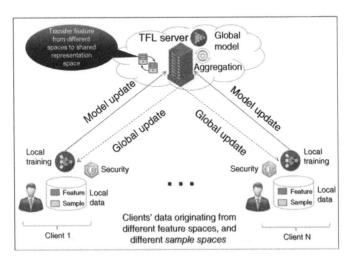

Figure 15.7 Illustration of the federated transfer learning.

aggregation node (either centralized or decentralized) exploits the updates combined from the learning clients to start model learning to search for the global update by optimizing certain loss functions [12]. The use cases of FTL in IoT are numerous and span different applications, for example, in smart healthcare, FTL can provide for disease screening under cooperation between different hospitals from different countries. Each of these hospitals comes with a distinct group of patients (sample space) as well as distinct medication protocols (feature space), which can be used to enrich the training of the model in FTL settings, thereby improving the disease-screening performance.

FTL methods can be categorized into three classes depending on the categories of transfer learning. These classes include example-aligned, feature-aligned, and parameter-aligned approaches.

In example-aligned FTL, a key assumption is that it is possible to reweight and recycle some samples from the source domain to train a model in the destination domain. When it comes to HFL, various participants' datasets might belong to a variety of distributions, which could lead to deep models trained on these datasets performing less accurately. One remedy to that is to reweight some of the carefully chosen data examples and then recycle them for model training in order to alleviate the distribution disparity. Various clients' goals may necessitate different identity alignments, which might have a detrimental impact on the FTL (negative transfer) for VFLs. One way to alleviate a negative transfer is to employ importance sampling.

On the other hand, in feature-aligned FTL, the system makes use of features to reduce domain variance and develop a "good" representation of features in the destination domain, and, therefore, successfully translate the transformation experience from one domain to another. This can be done for HFL by minimizing maximum mean discrepancies between datasets from different clients. With respect to VFL, it is possible to minimize the distance between aligned features in distinct datasets to produce the feature representation.

At its core, parameter-based FTL seeks to encapsulate transformation information by exploiting mutual parameters or hyperparameters of previous distribution across the source and destination domain models. Using datasets from several clients, a common global model is initially developed for the HFL. It is then possible to fine-tune each client's model using the global model trained on its local dataset. For the VFL, predictive models trained on supported examples can first be used to infer missing features or labels for unaligned data examples of the clients. The larger the data size, the more accurate the model can be.

15.4 Open-Source Frameworks

When it comes to the practical implementation of FL, there are a number of frameworks and software available. However, for proofs of concept and experimentations, open-source frameworks are often enough. The correct choice is extremely reliant on the objective and nature of the underlying use case. Some important considerations should be considered to develop an FL solution including the number of times you want to apply it, the standardization requirements, security requirements, and the support and maintenance. In this section, a general overview is provided of the state-of-the-art open-source frameworks for FL.

Hint: *The descriptions provided in this section are based on the recent achievements at the time of writing this book. Open-source tools are likely to encounter many changes and updates in the future.*

15.4.1 TensorFlow Federated

TensorFlow Federated (TFF) is an open-source library, which was proposed by Google, to develop and train deep intelligence solutions collaboratively on decentralized data [3]. TFF has been developed to simplify experimenting and performing public research in which training is federated. TFF contains two major API interfaces, namely Federated Core, which is a programming environment for executing distributed calculations, and the FL layer that enable integrating current deep learning algorithm into TFF without addressing the methodology of FL algorithms.

15.4.2 PySyft and PyGrid

PySyft [4, 5] is a python open-source framework for developing FL systems that can be secured with encrypted computation (like multiparty computation [MPC] and homomorphic encryption [HE]) as well as differential privacy methods. It was created by the OpenMined community and functions principally with deep learning models implemented with PyTorch and/or TensorFlow. PySyft offers three kinds of operating systems for installation: OSX, Linux, and Windows. PySyft supports a couple of modes of computations, the first one is dynamic mode over unseen data, and the other one is static computations, which build a graph of calculations that can be performed later on in various computing environments. For simulating federated training, PySyft establishes end-devices as virtual workers. Then, the data is distributed over virtual workers, whereas a PointerTensor is developed to keep the configuration of data like ownership information and storage location. This way, PySyft declare objects and models in simulation mode. Hence, it is likely to conclude that PySyft is not willing to be applied in industrial products that involve communication across networks. This could necessitate another library, known as PyGrid. PyGrid is a peer-to-peer network of data providers who could cooperatively train AI models on the web, mobile, edge devices, and different types of terminals using PySyft. It also could be defined as central server for executing data-centric and model-centric FL. PyGrid composed of three distinct elements. First, the domain, where a Flask application was employed to securely store models as well as training data. Second, the worker which is a momentary compute instance controlled by domain modules to process and handle data. Third, the network, which is a Flask application to screen and control various domain modules.

15.4.3 FedML

FedML [6] is a benchmark framework and open research library that accelerates the development of FL solutions. It establishes three computing paradigms, namely mobile on-device training, distributed training, and standalone simulation, to enable different parties to perform experimentations in any environment. FedML provide implementations of the state-of-the-art aggregation algorithms (FedAvg, FedOpt, FedNova, FedRobust, FedNAS, etc.) for each of the above-mentioned paradigms. More information about the above algorithms can be provided in the supplementary materials of this chapter. It supports diverse algorithmic research with elastic and general API design and reference implementations while affording a curated and inclusive benchmark dataset for the non-I.I.D. setting to be used for a fair comparison. Intelligible MLOps platform to facilitate cooperation and real-world deployment. Driven by the implementation of FedML Core, it supports four different deep learning tasks: Federated Natural Language Processing (FedNLP), Federated Computer Vision (FedCV), Federated Graph Neural Networks (FedGraphNN), and FedIoT. PyTorch implementation is supported in FedML. Another distinct feature of FedML is it has a Topology Manager supporting a wide range of network topologies, which makes it easy to customize for different federated settings.

15.4.4 LEAF

LEAF [7] is an open-source benchmarking framework to learn under federated configurations supporting a variety of intelligent applications involving multitask learning, FL, on-device learning and meta-learning. It is composed of constituting components, namely open-source datasets, reference implementations (i.e. minibatch SGD and FedAvg), and statistical metrics. The design of LEAF follows the modular design to make it easier to use and customize for different experimental settings.

15.4.5 PaddleFL

PaddleFL is an open-source FL framework based on PaddlePaddle which enables distributed training and flexible arrangement of training jobs on Kubernetes. It supports two primary FL schemes, namely VFL and HFL. There are generally dual elements in PaddleFL, namely FL with multiparty computation (PFMPC) and data parallel. In data parallel, distributed data owners can collaboratively participate federated training using federated algorithms, such as FedAvg, differentially private SGD (DPSGD), and SecAgg. PFMPC was adopted to implement secure training and prediction based on different protocols such as PrivC and Mixed Protocol (called ABY3), which are high competent multiparty computing (MPC) algorithms.

15.4.6   Federated AI Technology Enabler (FATE)

FATE [8] is declared as the first open-source industrial-grade FL framework, hosted by Linux Foundation, to empower the organizations to collaboratively learn from data whilst keeping it secure and private. Secure computation protocols are supported by implementing different encryption and multiparty computation (MPC) techniques such as SecretShare MPC protocol (SPDZ), RSA, Paillier encryption, Affine homomorphic encryption, RSA encryption, fake encryption, and others. FATE enables learning under horizontal and vertical data partitioning. FATE offers two deployment modes, namely standalone for single host deployment, and cluster for deployment on multiple nodes. It recommends the deployment of ML/DL solutions via Docker Compose and Kubernetes. As declared, the FATE cannot be declared as framework agnostic as it just supports specific backends, i.e. TensorFlow and PyTorch.

15.4.7   OpenFL

OpenFL [2] is an open-source python framework developed by Intel Labs and Intel IoT Group. It supports framework-agnostic to train statistical deep learning models such as TensorFlow or PyTorch. It supports different aggregation mechanisms FedAvg, FedProx, FedOpt, and FedCurv. It currently supports offers two methods to develop federated experimentation namely the Director-dependent workflow and aggregator-based workflow.

15.4.8   IBM Federated Learning

IBM FL is an open-source Python framework to build FL solutions using any ML/DL frameworks (like Keras, PyTorch, and Tensorflow) while supporting a variety of learning topologies such as supervised learning and unsupervised learning, and reinforcement learning (e.g., DQN, DDPG, PPO, etc.). It establishes many advanced aggregation algorithms (i.e. Iterative Averaging, FedAvg, Gradient Averaging, Coordinate-wise median, Fed+, FedProx, Shuffle Iterative Averaging, etc.) to accumulate the local updates coming from various IoT parties. Adjustments in these algorithms could accelerate the convergence, decrease training time or enhance model security, and so on. It supports some fairness methods (such as Local Reweighing, Global Reweighing, Federated Prejudice Removal) that improve to alleviate bias in FL.

15.4.9 NVIDIA Federated Learning Application Runtime Environment (NVIDIA FLARE)

NVIDIA FLARE is an open-source domain-agnostic, extensible software development kit that allows researchers and practitioners to extend the prevailing ML/DL solutions (such as TensorFlow, Nemo, RAPIDS, PyTorch, etc.) to a develop a federated system and supports platform developers to develop a secure, privacy preserved, and distributed multiparty cooperation. NVIDIA FLARE is developed on a componentized architecture, which permits researchers to adapt workflows to their needs and experiment with various designs rapidly. NVIDIA FLARE supports the implementation of Differential privacy and Homomorphic encryption to preserve the privacy of a federated system. FedAvg, FedProx, and FedOpt aggregation are supported in NVIDIA FLARE. It comes up with two training workflows, namely Scatter and Gather (SAG) and cyclic workflow.

15.4.10 Flower

Flower [9] is an open-source framework for developing FL solutions, which is designed to satisfy the following characteristics. First, customizable such that it can allow for a broad range of federated settings according to the needs of each use case. Second, extendable, such that it was built by taking the AI research into consideration. So, the diversity of modules can be extended and overridden to build new advanced systems. Third, framework-agnostic, such that it could be used with any ML framework, for instance, TensorFlow, TFLite, PyTorch, MXNet, Hugging Face Transformers, JAX, Scikit-learn, PyTorch Lightning, or even raw

NumPy for users who enjoy computing gradients by hand. Fourth, plausible, such that it was written with maintainability in mind. Fifth, interoperable such that work on various operating systems and heterogeneous edge devices.

15.4.11 Sherpa.ai

The Sherpa.ai [10] was released and proposed as an open-source framework for secure federated computing and differential privacy that executes secure computing protocols to offer regulation-acquiescent data partnership, simplifies experimentations and research, and delivers a modular method to improve scalability by means of federated methods, tools, and models. Like previous frameworks, it enables collaborative training of models from decentralized training data, communicating the local updates of the models to securely aggregate the final model. Sherpa.ai is not devoted to only one kind of model or tool, but instead includes the whole spectrum of the machine and deep learning models that are applicable for any data. It also provides the facility to integrate FL with different kinds of differential privacy to guarantee to pre-serve the privacy of local data during the training. These techniques can help the developers prevent malicious agents from interfering in the communication of local parameters. So, it cannot track down the information back to the original data. Furthermore, Sherpa.ai provides subsampling methods, adaptive differential privacy, sensitivity sampler, and federated attack simulations.

15.5 Supplementary Materials

https://github.com/DEEPOLOGY-AI/DL-Book-Wiley-2022/tree/main/Ch15

References

1 International Data Corporation (2019). *The Growth in Connected IoT Devices Is Expected to Generate 79.4ZB of Data in 2025*. International Data Corporation. https://www.businesswire.com/news/home/20190618005012/en/The-Growth-in-Connected-IoT-Devices-is-

Expected-to-Generate-79.4ZB-of-Data-in-2025-According-to-a-New-IDC-Forecast.

2 Reina, G.A., Gruzdev, A., Foley, P. et al. (2021). OpenFL: an open-source framework for federated learning, May 2021 [Online]. http://arxiv.org/abs/2105.06413.

3 Li, Q., Wwen, Z., Wu, Z. et al. (2021). A survey on federated learning systems: vision, hype and reality for data privacy and protection. *IEEE Trans. Knowl. Data Eng.* https://doi.org/10.1109/TKDE.2021.3124599.

4 Ziller, A., Trask, A., Lopardo, A. et al. (2021). PySyft: a library for easy federated learning. In: *Studies in Computational Intelligence*, vol. 965 (ed. A. Trask, A. Lopardo, et al.), 111–139.

5 Ryffel, T., Andrew, T., Morten, D. et al. (2018). A generic framework for privacy preserving deep learning. *arXiv preprint arXiv:1811.04017*.

6 He, C., Li, S., So, J. et al. (2020). FedML a research library and benchmark for federated machine learning, July 2020 [Online]. http://arxiv.org/abs/2007.13518 (accessed 21 August 2022).

7 Caldas, S., Wu, P., Li, T. et al. LEAF: a benchmark for federated settings, December 2018 [Online]. http://arxiv.org/abs/1812.01097 (accessed 21 August 2022).

8 Kholod, I., Yanaki, E., Fomichev, D. et al. (2021). Open-source federated learning frameworks for IoT: a comparative review and analysis. *Sensors (Switzerland).* https://doi.org/10.3390/s21010167.

9 Beutel, D.J., Topal, T., Mathur, A. et al. (2020). Flower: a friendly federated learning research framework, July 2020. https://doi.org/10.48550/arXiv.2007.14390 (accessed 21 August 2022).

10 Rodríguez-Barroso, N., Stipcich, G., Jiménez-López, D. et al. (2020). Federated learning and differential privacy: software tools analysis, the Sherpa.ai FL framework and methodological guidelines for preserving data privacy. *Inf. Fusion* 64: 270–292. https://doi.org/10.1016/j.inffus.2020.07.009.

11 Nguyen, D.C., Ding, M., Pathirana, P.N. et al. (2021). Federated learning for internet of things: a comprehensive survey. *IEEE Commun. Surv. Tutor.* 23 (3): 1622–1658 (thirdquarter). https://doi.org/10.1109/COMST.2021.3075439.

12 Khan, L.U., Saad, W., Han, Z. et al. (2021). Federated learning for internet of things: recent advances, taxonomy, and open challenges. *IEEE Commun. Surv. Tutor.* 23 (3): 1759–1799 (thirdquarter). https://doi.org/10.1109/COMST.2021.3090430.

16

Privacy-Preserved Federated Learning

16.1 Introduction

In the previous chapter, we have learned about the concept of federated learning (FL) as a promising form of distributed learning that has shown great achievements in realizing distributed intelligence in a broad range of applications. The success of FL is attributed to the fact that it can train deep learning models while keeping the client's data on their machines. Though FL seems secure and privacy–privacy-preserving from the first look, it still suffers from many security vulnerabilities and privacy concerns.

This chapter dives into the main challenges that might be encountered when it comes to applying FL to the Internet of Things (IoT) infrastructures. Understanding these challenges is essential for specifying and improving the design considerations to be considered to develop any federated solution. The existing challenges are broadly grouped under three main categories including statistical challenges, security challenges, and privacy challenges. It is worth noting that these challenges are equally important from either conceptual or technical perspectives.

Going ahead, we dive into the details of each of these challenges and the corresponding sub-challenges, and the possible solutions and design considerations that can be used to address them in the IoT infrastructure.

Deep Learning Approaches for Security Threats in IoT Environments,
First Edition. Mohamed Abdel-Basset, Nour Moustafa, and Hossam Hawash.
© 2023 The Institute of Electrical and Electronics Engineers, Inc.
Published 2023 by John Wiley & Sons, Inc.

16.2 Statistical Challenges in Federated Learning

When dealing with FL's statistical obstacles, it is helpful to break them down into four distinct subproblems, each of which is addressed with a different set of statistical methodologies. More than half of the techniques for tackling statistical difficulties focus on non-IID data issues.

16.2.1 Nonindependent and Identically Distributed (Non-IID) Data

The challenge of non-IID data stems from the inherent variability in the local data generated by clients on their IoT devices. There are wide differences in sizes, features, and class distributions of data among devices because of the individuality of the user's actions. In practice, this means that a single client's local data is not an accurate representation of the total data spread. Size imbalance, distribution imbalance, and class imbalance are all common forms of non-IID data challenges in FL. This section explains each scenario in-depth, presents a taxonomy of the methods to address each form, and explores in detail the possible options proposed under each method [1].

16.2.1.1 Class Imbalance

This refers to the case in which the overall number of cases identified as belonging to a specific target class (e.g. legitimate traffic flows) is significantly greater than the count of samples belonging to a different class (e.g. malicious traffic flows). It is a problem that arises frequently in machine learning, but it is made worse by the geographical dispersion of the users when dealing with huge, single-centered datasets in FL. With the FL framework, for example, you can use it to anticipate emojis on mobile keyboards by analyzing data from a huge number of mobile users dispersed throughout the globe. It is possible that some emojis could be prohibited or restricted in certain regions in the event of this. Active learning and data augmentation are the primary methods employed to address the issue of class imbalance.

Active Learning Its special form follows the idea that a model could do well when it is able to select the information it wishes to understand. This is called active learning. A model could energetically query the human specialist to label a particular part of data with the required outputs aiming to improve the performance of the underlying task. Conventionally, passive learning approaches have relied on collecting a significant amount of data that is unintentionally picked from a given distribution and utilized for prediction. To be honest, this job takes a long time, specifically in gathering properly labeled data. To better understand this concept, imagine you have been tasked with forecasting the fatality rate of COVID-19 cases among millions of deaths across the world. This seems impossible due to the shortage of examination services and staff. Hence, rather than picking patients at random, you might look for people who meet certain criteria, such as having a chronic illness and being over 50 years old. It is possible to dynamically determine such criteria. Using age as a criterion, for instance, would be appropriate if you see that the model does well in forecasting death rates for persons over 60 but fails to do so for those between 45 and 60. Figure 16.1 depicts the process of selecting examples depending on a set of criteria, which is known as active learning. As an example, federated training uses active learning, which allows the algorithm to prioritize clients that have data that is linked with minority groups. The ultimate goal is to provide a more equitable distribution of data across the chosen clients.

Data Augmentation The primary goal of this strategy is to improve the worldwide distribution of data across the various target classes by supplementing local data of training participants with strategically prepared supplementary data. In this regard, four common data augmentations come into sight, namely over-sampling, data warping, geometric transformations, and generative adversarial networks (GANs).

Data warping is all about creating modeling character deformations that seem like irregularities in the original data. The classification bias is reduced by using warped individual data to balance the number of class samples. When it comes to a class imbalance in real IoT data, over-sampling is primarily used to remedy the issue

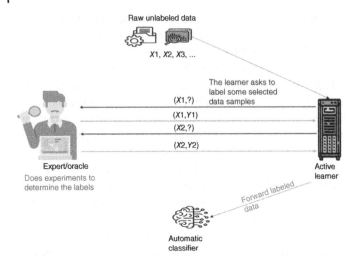

Figure 16.1 Illustration of the concept of active learning in which the algorithm is able to energetically ask an expert to learn the appropriate modeling for a certain task.

of under-sampling. As a result, an arbitrary set of actual minority class examples are used to generate artificial examples in the feature space. Improved representation quality could be attained by increasing the comparative volume of probable instances within the representation space, restricting the amount of unwanted data instances. To achieve that, extrapolation, interpolation, and noise infusion is some of the straightforward adjustments that could be performed on the feature space to synthesize new data instance. Like *data warping, over-sampling* approaches depend on updating the actual data instances to augment the training data. however, a point of distinction is that the *over-sampling* is task-unbiased as it generates the artificial data instances in the modeled representation. Moreover, Augmenting data via geometric transformations encompasses rotations, flipping and brightness. Clipping, cropping and channel adjustments also fall under this category. Only picture datasets can be used for these forms of augmentation, which produces data that are merely alterations of the originals. As discussed in an earlier chapter, GAN has a *generator* and a *discriminator* subnetwork. As part of the training process, a random noise vector is fed into the generator to help it produce more convincingly fake data. The goal is to fool the discriminator into thinking the data are real. It uses both genuine and artificial training examples so that it can distinguish between real and produced data samples. You'll get a probability value from it that indicates how likely it is that a particular sample came from a specific data source. Zero-sum training means that the generator and discriminator models are trained jointly so that increases in one model are offset by decreases in the other's capabilities [2].

16.2.1.2 Distribution Imbalance

An unbalanced feature distribution is one that differs dramatically among different participants. This indicates that the features accessible in the local data of participants differ significantly from the local data of other participants, which is the case with FL. Given the task of federated estimation of the loveliness of human expressions utilizing data from multiple participants, individuals may have differing opinions on the beauty of specific profiles, such as bald guys. in this case, one model could not possibly anticipate the attractiveness of bald males to all clients at once. Because FL relies on the SGD approach, which is the most often used approach for optimizing deep models, an imbalance in distribution is an issue. When it comes to FL scenarios, a stochastic gradient is basically the whole gradient that can be computed from a client's data because the data is so little. This violates the premise that the distribution of gradients is the same for all clients, making it impossible to perform the data shuffling and aggregation operations that are intended to avoid local minima in the gradient distribution. In this regard, to deal with the problem of distribution imbalance, four major strategies are employed: multitask learning, transfer learning, clustering the participants, and parameter tuning.

Multitask Learning   An optimization issue for a single metric is the goal of standard ML. Training and fine-tuning a particular to achieve a steady performance is necessary. Though this has seen positive results from using this strategy in a variety of disciplines, the model may be missing crucial information that could help it improve the original metric if it sticks to just one task per time. The ML model can better generalize on its original job if it is trained on a variety of related tasks and shares representations between them. Multitask learning (MTL) is the name given to this approach. For instance, to educate somebody to be a successful scholar, universities teach technical research methods, language, communication, and presentation skills. Though these seem irrelevant tasks, they work out to supply the scholar with important skills that could improve the performance of the primary job, i.e. learning to be a researcher. Realistic MTL could be achieved by applying either hard or soft sharing of parameters. The former method is commonly used to minimize overfitting, whereby overall tasks share the hidden layers, while each task has its own output layers dedicated to it as shown in Figure 16.2a. Soft parameter sharing, in contrast, lets each task keep its own model and set of parameters as needed. The multiple models' parameters are then brought closer together using $L2$ regularization methods as shown in Figure 16.2b. In the context of FL, MTL based on soft sharing of parameters has been extensively applied to handle the challenge of non-IID data through allocating various task models to various clients. Federal MTL is built on the premise that there is some kind of pattern shared between the task models of the clients with non-IID data,

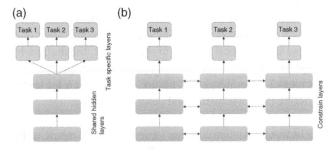

Figure 16.2 Illustration of the concept of soft and hard multitask learning: (a) hard sharing multitask learning; (b) soft sharing multitask learning method.

thereby FL could exploit the similarity among the various tasks to extract interrelationships among the non-IID data [3].

Transfer Learning (TL) This kind of ML allows for the training process to begin from previously learned representation rather than beginning from scratch. For instance, a basic learner trained to predict if a picture has a table might then be used to identify couches because of the intelligence gathered during training. In supervised learning, TL solves the issue of decreased performance in the case of changing the problem domain without having sufficient labeled data for the other domain. As an example, think about a learning model trained to recognize creatures in photographs collected during the daytime. Daytime is regarded as the domain of the current task. To train another model to identify creatures in night-time photos requires millions of night-time images that have been categorized. Due to its inability to adapt to various environments, the performance of a model trained on daytime data would deteriorate seriously if it is used on night-time images. This can be attributed to the inability of the model to perform generalization on a newly encountered domain. Pretrained models that have been learnt with big volumes of data can be used to meet the goal of TL, which is to use a pretrained model that has been trained to solve a comparable problem. To begin, a basic source network is built using a foundational dataset and a foundational task. In order to train a second network on a different dataset and job, we must repurpose (or transfer) the learned features. In essence, we apply the model's weights from "task A" to "task B." As long as the characteristics are general enough to be applicable to both the base and target jobs, this procedure is effective. Because the low-level representations in deep networks are extremely transferable, transfer learning can profit from this phenomenon. This is due to the fact that these features concentrate on teaching the most common and basic aspects. As a result, the source model's parameters could be shifted to the targeted domain in order to learn the model's unique traits. In Figure 16.3, the general concept of TL is illustrated.

FL could make use of TL to address the problem of FL only being applicable to data that is vertically or horizontally partitioned. The

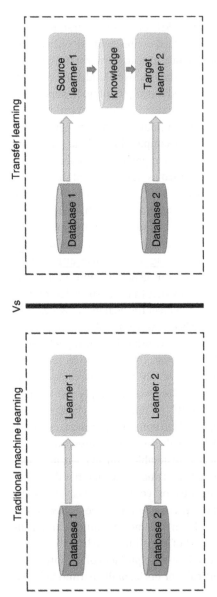

Figure 16.3 Illustration of the concept of transfer learning.

FL framework would be unable to make full use of most available data since they share only a few familiar representations and contain a large proportion of nonoverlapping information. TL is a possible answer to this problem because it does not put any restrictions on the distribution of the data and so provides findings for the full population and feature space.

Clustering the Participants In this method, the participants are grouped into groups based on shared features using the client clustering method. MTL adoption in an FL system can be made easier with this strategy. Each client is assigned a model that best suits their local data distribution in federated MTL. Nevertheless, this runs counter to the FL concept, which holds that all clients should be represented fairly and that only one global learning model should be used. The participants' clustering techniques aim to fill this gap by grouping participants into distinct clusters, where each of them is assigned a one-job model. The local updates are clustered based on their similarity to one other. In general, it makes sense to assume that participants with analogous gradients will also share analogous distribution of data. This means that the participants in the same cluster can work together to train one model as part of the federated MTL as a whole.

Parameter Tuning The goal of parameter tuning is to improve the ability of the federated model to converge rapidly when trained with non-IID data. This is achieved by altering the SGD algorithm to accelerate global convergence. As a result of this, two basic approaches can be employed in this regard, one for momentum correction and another for parameter correction. For the momentum strategy, the primary goal is to direct all of the gradient vectors in the correct direction. When a sequence of data is denoised by shifting the average of this data closer to the original function, a method called momentum is used (e.g. linear, exponential, etc.). In FL, SGD with momentum is used for averaging the gradients accepted from participants across various rounds to aid in deriving the gradient information in the appropriate direction. On the other hand, the parameter correction approach seeks to update various parameters to meet specified goals.

16.2.1.3 Size Imbalance

Because participants are anticipated to have varying amounts of training data, this form of inequity is prevalent in FL systems. Many variables influence how much training data an individual customer has. These include where they live, their gender identity, and how often and how long they exercise. Women's mobile phones are more likely to contain a high number of images than men's mobile phones when it comes to image recognition. Due to the size disparity, data augmentation and adaptable client contribution are promising methods being employed to address the problem. Adaptable client contribution approaches seek to make it as simple as possible for customers to participate in federated training by reducing the barriers that currently prevent them from doing so. The goal is to increase the number of customers who have data that is comparable to the data held by customers who have smaller volumes of data.

16.2.2 Model Heterogeneity

One way to think about model heterogeneity is that each client creates its own training model autonomously. Owing to worries over their own privacy and the protection of their property rights, clients in this scenario may be reluctant to provide model specifics. As in supply chain and health care, this scenario is suitable for small-scale FL environments where a limited number of players wish to create a distinctive model in order to meet specific unique requirements. The problem here is to adjust the FL system to a situation in which each participant trains a variety of models that are invisible to the remaining participants. This problem is addressed using the notion of knowledge distillation (KD).

16.2.2.1 Extracting the Essence of a Subject

Deep learning models that are capable of difficult tasks are plentiful, but the challenge remains in deploying these models on small devices, such as smartphones, for immediate usage.

Small-scale deep learning models can benefit from KD, which addresses this issue. It seeks to answer the next query: "How to build a small network that can really run on devices with limited resources?" Training a huge complicated deep network to extract significant elements from data and generate correct estimates is the basic goal of KD. After that, the large model is used to train a smaller network, which can then reproduce or at least provide results comparable to those of the larger network. Small, distilled models are taught to emulate the output of complex models using hierarchical abstractions of deep network characteristics instead of training directly on raw data. The complicated network and small network are respectively viewed as teacher and student networks, respectively. For the sake of brevity, "soft targets" are used in the transmission of generalization ability from the former network to the later one. Hard targets are the final outputs of the classifier, whereas soft targets represent the probability of each class provided by the final softmax function of the source training model. The soft target can be used to restore the variation within a class and the distance between classes by providing more detailed information for model training. To train the small model, a much smaller amount of data is needed, but the learning rate is significantly higher than that of the large model. KD and TL appear to be similar concepts, but they serve quite different objectives. It is possible to use transfer learning to transfer weights from a pretrained network to an untrained network with an identical topology. In other words, the new network must be as complex as the pretrained one. While weights are transferred in KD, generalizations are transferred to a much smaller model. Figure 16.4 illustrates the general concept of KD.

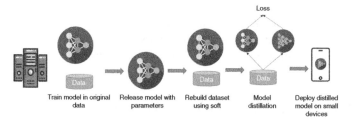

Train model in original data   Release model with parameters   Rebuild dataset using soft   Model distillation   Deploy distilled model on small devices

Figure 16.4 Illustration of the concept of active learning knowledge distillation.

16.2.3 Block Cycles

To maintain accuracy, the SGD approach relies on randomly selected data samples. There are times when certain data points are combined in an order that is not random enough to be considered cycling. Using a video as an example, a sequence of closely comparable frames is an instance of this condition. Centralized data, which are stored on a single system, could have this problem, but distributed, FL systems make things much more difficult. In FL, just those charging, unused, and connected machines are the ones that the server selects to take part in federated training. As a result, device availability varies greatly throughout the day and night, with some devices only being available at certain times of the day. For example, it is more likely that the devices held by Arabic speakers in the middle east and those held by Arabic speakers in Canada will be available at varying times throughout the day, thereby increasing the likelihood of seeing cyclic patterns in the data [4].

In FL, the method of plurality is commonly used to combat block cycles. As with ensemble learning, the FL could be established on either a consensus methodology or a *pluralistic* one. The goal of a consensus strategy is to come up with a conclusion that is in the best interest of all parties concerned and, more precisely, to create a single predictor from all the local models. An alternative to this is a pluralistic approach, which accepts diversity and encourages people to develop their own models. A model may be learned for each block of data in a data set with a block-cyclic structure, making this method helpful. If each client is assigned a specific training time, this can be accomplished, for example. Given the data distribution related to a certain block, an averaging operation could be calculated for the training steps that belong to that block, rather than calculating the average of all iterations to arrive at the final prediction, the same as in agreement-founded approaches.

16.3 Security Challenge in Federated Learning

With the wide acceptance of FL in IoT environments, it turned to target a broad range of cyberattacks that seek to illegally control the cooperative learning system. These attacks could be separated into two types: targeted attacks and nontargeted attacks. As the name implies, untargeted assaults are those that have no specific focus on the target system, but instead, try to degrade model performance or create a failure of the overall training process. Targeted attacks, on the other hand, have specific goals and deploy sophisticated means to achieve them. In the next sections, we examine each of these types of attacks and describe the known countermeasures for each one [5].

16.3.1 Untargeted Attacks

Untargeted attacks are the most prevalent and ubiquitous type of intentional threat. These attacks are motivated by the desire to harm people's software, but there is no specific individual or institution which is being targeted. Malware, worms, and viruses are the most common types, and they are typically distributed via the Internet. So, if you accidentally hit on an ad that subsequently installs something to your system, there's a good possibility you're being exposed to an untargeted cyber threat.

For two major factors, untargeted attacks are significantly more common than targeted attacks. First and foremost, it is simpler to carry out. Rather than figuring out how to break into a specific system, hackers just send a general email containing illegal content, such as an attachment or a link. They'll then send it to all of the email addresses they have access to. This could result in ransomware extortion, the installation of keyloggers to track user passwords, the deployment of spyware, or the compromise of company and/or private details, depending on the type of malware employed in the email. Because they don't have a specific target audience in mind, the email's content is intentionally ambiguous so that it can be applied to anybody. It could, for example, be a bogus tracking link for a recent "buy."

16.3.2 Targeted Attacks

Attackers who use targeted methods, as opposed to Byzantine methods, have particular goals in mind and use more advanced methods to achieve them, as opposed to the former. They are attempting to alter the training model's behavior on a specific set of data while maintaining the model's overall performance unaffected by this change. There are two forms of targeted assaults on FL including model poisoning and data poisoning attacks. The goal of data poisoning adversaries is to tamper with the training data prior to the start of the training process. A data poisoning assault isn't expected to affect the training operations. Because an attacker only has access to the data on his or her own device in the FL system, data poisoning attacks have had little success and, as a result, have gotten little attention from the security community.

In contrast, the adversary, in model poisoning settings, seek for illegally modification in the deep network rather than stealing data. Attackers specifically aim to make the cooperatively trained federated model incorrectly classify a set of selected inputs with great certainty, while guaranteeing a rapid convergence of that model in the inference stage to evade detection. in technical terms, these kinds of attackers calculate the local updates by optimizing for a malevolent purpose that seeks to cause targeted misclassification, whilst attempting to neutralize the cumulative impact of the truthful updates provided by the innocent participants. Security analysis and statistics are the two key areas under which several strategies were presented in the academia and industry to combat data and model poisoning attacks.

16.4 Privacy Challenges in Federated Learning

FL has as one of its primary goals the protection of participants' privacy by requiring them to contribute only model parameters rather than their own personal data. Recent studies, on the other hand, reveal that hostile FL participants or FL servers can raise privacy and security issues. To put it another way, this is counterproductive to FL because the global model could be distorted or participants' privacy exposed during model training, which undermines the aim of FL. In this context, a malevolent participant can nevertheless infer sensitive information from other participants according to their shared models even if FL does not need the transmission of training data for cooperative training. Two categories are explored to address these privacy issues, namely secure aggregation, and perturbation methods. Here follows a detailed breakdown of the current approaches based on how they are employed to handle each of these challenges.

16.4.1 Secure Aggregation

As the name suggests, it denotes the dilemma of calculating a summation of elements from different parties while maintaining the value of each party in-revealed. The same concept applies to FL, in which the secure aggregation denotes the dilemma of averaging the gradient updates from training participants with no exposure of the donation of any participant. In this regard, Secure Multiparty Computation (SMPC), Homomorphic Encryption, and Blockchain are regarded as the primary methods for realizing secure aggregation in FL.

16.4.1.1 Homomorphic Encryption (HE)

It is possible to execute computations on encrypted data using Homomorphic Encryption (HE), a type of encryption that has an extra evaluation capacity. Federated computation operations could be immediately run-on encrypted data and produce the same effect as if they were conducted on the plaintext. An example of this would be a hospital that wants to calculate some explanatory analysis on a samples of COVID-19 infected cases at one of the branches that belong to it. Due to Insurance Portability and Accountability Act (HIPAA) privacy restrictions, the medical organizations, in general, are unpermitted to share the confidential information of patients to other parties. Encrypting the health-records before transmitting them to the research institution can help the hospital overcome this difficulty. Private and protected health information can be maintained in this manner. The encrypted data is subsequently analyzed by the research organization, which takes the ciphertext and decrypts it to the original form of data. From a technological standpoint, HE uses a global key to encode data, then the parties that own the corresponding private key are the only ones to retrieve original data, similar to the other encryption modes. When compared to other encryption systems, HE utilizes an algebraic structure to allow computations on encrypted data. Full HE, partial HE, and somewhat HE is all types of HEs, and each has its own advantages and disadvantages. HIPAA-compliant encryption is utilized for messages transferred between servers and clients in FL environments, preventing curious users from obtaining confidential material from the local data of their peers.

16.4.1.2 Secure Multiparty Computation

SMPC is a branch of cryptography concerned with devising ways for parties to simultaneously calculate a functionality over given inputs whilst maintaining the privacy of these inputs. Unlike standard cryptographic methods that seek to guarantee the truthfulness and security of the storage and networking in circumstances in which the attacker is not a member of this network. SMPC strives to preserve the privacy of participating parties from each other. In FL, SMPC is leveraged to enable a server to securely aggregate local updates uploaded by a huge number of participating devices without the need to expose the confidential contribution of each participant.

16.4.1.3 Blockchain

Rather than being controlled by a single body, a distributed network of computers maintains a chain of irreversible data blocks called a blockchain. To protect and bind these chunks of data (blocks), cryptographic concepts (i.e. chains) are used. Due to the lack of a centralized authority, the blockchain is considered a decentralized system. When it comes to the technical details, the blockchain is a basic yet effective means of securely and automatically transmitting data between two parties. Once a transaction has been initiated, one side creates a block, which is then validated by a huge number of computers dispersed across the globe (intended to be as vast as possible). Adding the validated block to the chain creates an entirely new record with its own distinct past. It would be nearly impossible to fake the entire chain in this infrastructure if a one record were to be tampered with. Decentralizing the process of global aggregation in the context of FL is achieved by allowing the blockchain to interchange updates from local models while validating them (Figure 16.5). Blockchain is a great tool for both protecting and verifying the integrity of local model modifications [6].

16.4.2 Perturbation Method

An important principle in perturbation is to add random noise to a data set, resulting in data that is barely non-discernable from the original data. Additive perturbation, differential privacy (DP), and multiplicative perturbation are all common perturbation methods. DP methods rely on statistical theories to determine the extent to which individual instances in a dataset have their confidential information disclosed. For the most part, DP methods could be classified into two categories, namely the global DP and local DP. The goal of the global DP strategy is to prevent the query results from being utilized to discover further information about any examples in the training data if the consequence of replacing a random sample in the data is modest enough. Compared to local DP strategies, this method is more accurate because it does not need to introduce a lot of noise to the dataset. Using a local DP approach, the need for a central authority to be trusted is eliminated. Compared with global DP techniques, the local DP does not necessitate an external source of trust. Compared to a global DP solution, the overall amount of noise is substantially greater.

Combining arbitrary noise from a particular distribution (e.g. a Gaussian/uniform distribution) to the original data is the goal of additive perturbation, which is a straightforward method that keeps the statistical properties intact. The data's usefulness will be reduced and may be susceptible to noise lessening. Multiplex perturbation seeks to multiply a source dataset by an appropriate distribution of random noise. Multiplicative perturbation, as opposed to simply adding noise, attempts to map the raw data instances to a specific location in space. The multiplicative perturbation is further successful than the additive perturbation because it is more difficult to recreate the source data from the disturbed counterpart from multiplicative perturbation.

To sum up, perturbation methods are quick and do not necessitate an understanding of the underlying distribution. It is, however,

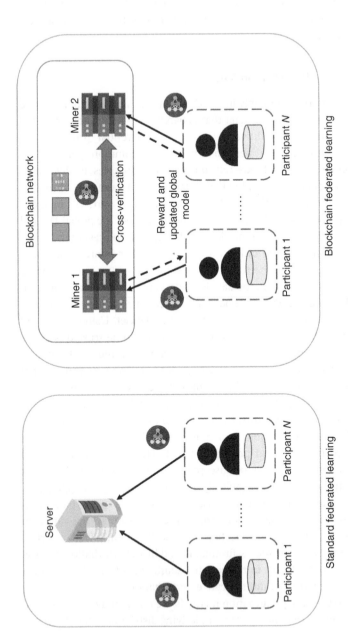

Figure 16.5 Illustration of the concept of blockchain FL vs. standard FL.

difficult to decrease the danger of probabilistic assaults on perturbed data without lowering the data's utility.

16.5 Supplementary Materials

https://github.com/DEEPOLOGY-AI/DL-Book-Wiley-2022/tree/main/Ch16

References

1 Lim, W.Y.B., Luong, L.N., Hoang, D. et al. (2020). Federated learning in mobile edge networks: a comprehensive survey. *IEEE Commun. Surv. Tutor.* https://doi.org/10.1109/COMST.2020.2986024.

2 Wahab, O.A., Mourad, A., Otrok, H., and Taleb, T. (2021). Federated machine learning: survey, multi-level classification, desirable criteria and future directions in communication and networking systems. *IEEE Commun. Surv. Tutor.* https://doi.org/10.1109/COMST.2021.3058573.

3 Nguyen, D.C., Ding, M., Pathirana, P.N. et al. (2021). Federated learning for internet of things: a comprehensive survey. *IEEE Commun. Surv. Tutor.* https://doi.org/10.1109/COMST.2021.3075439.

4 Yin, X., Zhu, Y., and Hu, J. (2021). A comprehensive survey of privacy-preserving federated learning: a taxonomy, review, and future directions. *ACM Comput. Surv.* https://doi.org/10.1145/3460427.

5 Khan, L.U., Saad, W., Han, Z. et al. (2021). Federated learning for internet of things: recent advances, taxonomy, and open challenges. *IEEE Commun. Surv. Tutor.* https://doi.org/10.1109/COMST.2021.3090430.

6 Li, C., Yuan, Y., and Wang, F.Y. (2021). Blockchain-enabled federated learning: A survey. *ACM Comput. Surv.* https://doi.org/10.1109/DTPI52967.2021.9540163.

Index

Deep Learning Approaches for Security Threats in IoT Environments,
First Edition. Mohamed Abdel-Basset, Nour Moustafa, and Hossam Hawash.
© 2023 The Institute of Electrical and Electronics Engineers, Inc.
Published 2023 by John Wiley & Sons, Inc.

Printed and bound by CPI Group (UK) Ltd, Croydon, CR0 4YY

27/10/2024

14580125-0001